The Iron Cage

Also by Rashid Khalidi

British Policy towards Syria and Palestine, 1906–1914

Palestine and the Gulf (coeditor)

Under Siege: PLO Decision-Making during the 1982 War

The Origins of Arab Nationalism (coeditor)

Palestinian Identity: The Construction of Modern National Consciousness

Resurrecting Empire: Western Footprints and America's Perilous Path in the Middle East

The Iron Cage

The Story of the
Palestinian Struggle
for Statehood

Rashid Khalidi

Beacon Press, Boston

BEACON PRESS
25 Beacon Street
Boston, Massachusetts 02108–2892
www.beacon.org

Beacon Press books
are published under the auspices of
the Unitarian Universalist Association of Congregations.

09 08 07 06   8 7 6 5 4 3 2 1

This book is printed on acid-free paper that meets the uncoated paper
ANSI/NISO specifications for permanence as revised in 1992.

Arabic words have been transliterated in keeping with a modified version of the
system used by the *International Journal of Middle East Studies* (the only diacritics
represented being the 'ain and the hamza), with exceptions for common nouns,
individual names where there is a common spelling, and words within quotations.
All translations from Arabic and French are the author's own.

Composition by Wilsted & Taylor Publishing Services

Library of Congress Cataloging-in-Publication Data
Khalidi, Rashid.
    The iron cage : the story of the Palestinian struggle for statehood /
Rashid Khalidi. — 1st ed.
        p. cm.
    Includes bibliographical references (p.   ) and index.
    ISBN-13: 978-0-8070-0308-4 (hardcover : alk. paper)
    ISBN-10: 0-8070-0308-5 (hardcover : alk. paper) 1. Palestinian Arabs—
Politics and government—20th century. 2. National liberation movements—
Palestine. 3. Arab-Israeli conflict. 4. Fath (Organization) 5. Munazzamat
al-Tahrir al-Filastiniyah. 6. Palestinian National Authority. I. Title.

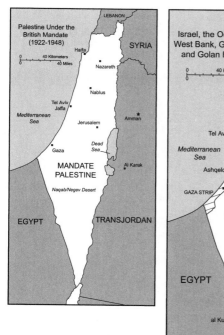

Palestine Under the
British Mandate
(1922-1948)

0   40 Kilometers
0   40 Miles

LEBANON

SYRIA

Haifa

Nazareth

Nablus

Tel Aviv
Jaffa

Mediterranean
Sea

Jerusalem

Dead
Sea

Amman ★

Gaza

Al Karak

MANDATE
PALESTINE

Naqab/Negev Desert

EGYPT

TRANSJORDAN

Israel, the Occupied
West Bank, Gaza Strip
and Golan Heights

0   40 Kilometers
0   40 Miles

Tyre

LEBANON

Al Qunaytira

GOLAN
HEIGHTS

Haifa

Tiberias

SYRIA

Nazareth

Jenin

Netanya

Tulkarm

Nablus

Jarash

Tel Aviv-Yafo

WEST BANK

Mediterranean
Sea

Ramallah

Jericho

Jerusalem

Amman ★

Ashqelon

Bethlehem

GAZA STRIP

Gaza

Hebron

Dead
Sea

Beersheba

al Karak

ISRAEL

Mizpe
Ramon

EGYPT

JORDAN

al Kuntilla

Taba

Elat

Contents

Introduction

Writing Middle Eastern History
in a Time of Historical Amnesia

This book examines the failure of the Palestinians to establish an independent state before 1948, the year of Israel's founding and of the dissolution of Arab Palestine, and the impact of that failure in the years thereafter. Such a topic provokes a sequence of questions that relate to the present as much as to the past: What purpose is served by such a study when, nearly six decades after 1948, an independent Palestinian state—in any real sense of the word "independent"—still does not exist, and when its establishment continues to face formidable obstacles?

The obstacles to independent Palestinian statehood only appeared to grow as violence escalated in the Gaza Strip and Lebanon during the summer of 2006. As these lines are written, in late July, Lebanon is the scene of hundreds of civilian deaths, enormous destruction, and fierce ground combat. Almost forgotten as a result of the carnage visited on Lebanon by Israel, and of Hizballah's repeated rocket barrages against northern Israeli cities and towns, has been the suffering in Gaza caused by months of Israeli siege and bombardment. It is also forgotten that all of this started with Palestinian efforts to create a democratic structure of governance while still under Israeli occupation.

Specifically, this latest escalation began with response by Israel and the United States to the elections for the Legislative Council of the Palestinian Authority (PA) in January 2006, which brought to power a Hamas-led government. Their campaign quickly moved from a crippling financial siege of the PA, with the aim of bringing down that government, to an escalation of Israeli assassinations of Palestinian militants, and to artillery and air attacks in Gaza that killed and wounded scores of civilians. Hamas had for eighteen months observed a cease-fire in the face of these and earlier provocations (other factions were not so restrained, firing rockets into Israel). However, after a major spike in Palestinian civilian deaths and the particularly provocative Israeli assassination of militant leader Jamal Abu Samhadana, whom the PA government had just named to a security post, Hamas finally took the bait and responded with the capture of one Israeli soldier and the killing of others. The predictably ferocious Israeli response—even more killings of civilians, more assassinations, and ground incursions in Gaza—finally provoked Hizballah (or perhaps gave Hizballah and its allies, Iran and Syria, the preemptive opportunity they had been searching for). The rest of this tragic scenario then unfolded with the grim, bloody, unthinking precision we have seen so many times before in the conflict between Israel and the Arabs.

This book is not about that conflict but about its Palestinian component, specifically the effort of the Palestinians to achieve independence in their homeland. The ongoing war in Gaza and Lebanon illustrates once again how intimately this effort is intertwined with regional and international factors. It illustrates also the crucial importance of a careful reading of recent Palestinian history to attain an understanding of the Middle East conflict. The one-dimensional and ahistorical approach to the conflict through the prism of terrorism that is prevalent in the United States obscures thoroughly the specificity of Palestine, Israel, Lebanon, and other regional actors, like Syria and Iran, and how these relate to one another. The Palestinian quest for independence is only one of many elements that must be grasped in order to understand the causes of conflict in the Middle East. But because for nearly a century this quest has been so central to events there, willfully ignoring it leads to the kind of reductive, partial, and misguided American official thinking that has helped produce the profound problems that afflict the region. This book raises other questions as well: Is a historical study of why something occurred—or in this case did not occur—justified because it sheds light on apparent similarities with events that are currently taking place? Or are these two failures in state building—one in the past and the other ongoing—completely unrelated, and is any attempt to examine them in relation to one another an historical error, not to say an abuse of history?[1]

It might be asked why I describe this failure to achieve independent statehood as a *Palestinian* failure. Specifically, why should the focus be on the role of the Palestinians in their past defeats, when they were the weakest of all the parties engaged in the prolonged struggle to determine the fate of Palestine, which culminated in 1948? These parties include the British Empire, until World War II the greatest power of its day, which actively opposed Palestinian aspirations for statehood and independence, and other major states, among them the United States, the Soviet Union, and France, all of which supported Zionism and the partition of Palestine into an Arab and a Jewish state, but did nothing to prevent the abortion of the embryonic Arab state of Palestine in 1947–48. They include as well the Zionist movement, composed of a worldwide network of institutions capable of mobilizing extensive diplomatic, propaganda, and financial resources, and the highly motivated and well-organized *yishuv* (the pre-state Jewish community in Palestine). Both Britain and the Zionist movement always treated the prospect of an independent Arab state in Palestine as a grave threat. The Zionist movement saw such a prospect as a particular challenge to the Jews' aspirations to exclusive sovereignty over what they considered Eretz Israel (the land of Israel). Finally, there were the seven newly independent Arab states, all of them relatively weak and heavily influenced by the Western powers; these states acted in ways that frequently excluded the interests of the Palestinians, and sometimes contradicted them.

To rephrase the question in light of these facts, why concentrate on the failures or incapacities of the Palestinians to achieve independence before 1948, when the constellation of forces arrayed against them was so powerful, and in the end proved overwhelming?

Why not focus on the external forces that played a predominant role in preventing the Palestinians from achieving self-determination? Others have countered that the Palestinians, or their leaders, should bear responsibility for their own failures, some going so far as to blame the victim entirely for the tragic history of the Palestinian people in the twentieth century and after.[2] The benefits of blaming the victim, in light of the heavy responsibilities of various other parties in this story, are obvious, explaining the continuing vitality of this school of thought, although most of its core claims have long since been discredited. Others have argued that even if the Palestinians cannot be fully blamed for their own misfortunes, and even if the overwhelming balance of forces ranged against them must be taken into account, they nonetheless are accountable for their actions and decisions. Similar arguments can be heard today regarding Palestinian responsibility for the dire situation faced by the Palestinians after the collapse of the Oslo peace process of 1991–2000, the full reoccupation of the West Bank by Israel in 2001–6, and the election in January 2006 of a Palestinian Authority (PA) government headed by the radical Hamas movement.

Needless to say, all of these questions will be colored by the recognition that to this day the Palestinians remain considerably less powerful by any measure than the forces that stand in the way of their achieving independent statehood. It seems clear that in the decades since 1948 the Palestinians have been plagued by some of the same problems that afflicted them before that date. It is an open question whether examining past failures might help to prevent future ones, on the theory that there is a link between those structures and forces, internal and external, that operated in the past to hinder Palestinian self-determination, and those at work today. Either way —whether external forces or internal Palestinian weaknesses (or a combination of both) have prevented the establishment of an independent Palestinian state—a final question remains: Is statehood the destined outcome for a people who, since the early part of the twentieth century had a clearly defined national identity but who have been unable to develop lasting, viable structural forms for it, or to control a national territory in which it can be exercised? Is it not possible that the Palestinian people will continue to exist indefinitely into the future, as they have since Ottoman hegemony ended in 1918, in a stateless limbo? Are we perhaps too obsessed with the very idea of the state, demonstrating the bias in favor of the state that Hegel found in historical discourse, in our attempts to place the state at the center of the historical narrative?[3]

These are questions that perplexed me for several years after I finished an examination of Palestinian identity published in 1997.[4] I had planned to devote a sabbatical leave beginning in September 2001 to completing my research and writing about why the Palestinians had not achieved statehood. After the attacks of September 11, 2001, however, a different set of questions diverted my attention from this task. With the United States at war in Afghanistan and about to invade Iraq, there seemed to be more pressing inquiries concerning the Middle East than the issue of Palestinian statelessness. Moreover, the spectacular events of September 11 and its aftermath had rendered every aspect of the Middle East once again a subject of intense interest, a subject that was difficult to deal with objectively, in view of the powerful emotions these events had unleashed.

At the time, given the background of the assailants of September 11, given the reverberations of the U.S. invasion of Afghanistan and of a war with Iraq that already appeared inevitable in 2001–2, it seemed to me that Middle East experts had a responsibility to illuminate the fraught history of the region's relations with Western powers, against which any intervention in Iraq would necessarily be judged. Admittedly, even in the best of times, it is difficult to engage Americans in an objective discussion of Middle Eastern history; Americans often come to such discussions with a dearth of knowledge about the region (and the world), and they are often oblivious to their country's massive impact on, and complex role in, the world generally, and the Middle East in particular. However, this was the worst of times.

Partly in response to these concerns, in 2002–3 I therefore stopped working on the topic of Palestinian statelessness, and instead wrote *Resurrecting Empire: Western Footprints and America's Perilous Path in the Middle East.*[5] In so doing I was trying to elucidate for Americans who would have to live with the consequences of their government's actions some of the key historical issues that were obscured, largely deliberately, as the United States rushed into an invasion of Iraq that, even before its inception, promised to be disastrous to those acquainted with the region's history.

Having completed that book, I realized that I had largely failed to address an issue generally ignored in American public discourse about the Middle East. This is the long, involved, and often close relationship of the U.S. government with some of the villains of the tragedy of 9/11, a relationship far more complex than Americans have generally been led to believe. Delineating these ties would of course in no way mitigate the full and terrible responsibility of those who had planned and perpetrated the atrocious murders of thousands of innocent Americans. Nevertheless, it would show that these individuals did not materialize out of a vacuum, and that they were not in fact as utterly alien as they appeared to be, or were made to appear by the government, the media, and assorted self-proclaimed experts. To show this, it would be necessary to explain how for many decades the United States fostered or allied itself with some of the reactionary, obscurantist, and illiberal Islamic tendencies that, metastasizing over many years, engendered the individuals and groups who carried out the attacks of September 11. It would also be necessary to explain to Americans—many of whom hold the belief that their country acts only for good in the world—that various actions of their government over several decades have had disastrous consequences in Iraq, Afghanistan, Palestine, and elsewhere in the Arab and Islamic worlds.

In the wake of September 11, some commentators have argued that to refer even obliquely to such matters was tantamount to acting as an apologist for the assailants, and for terrorism generally. Irrespective of the sometimes sordid reality of American involvement in the Middle East for well over a half century, those who made such references were described as "blame America firsters." Here is a clear case of how a traumatic atrocity can be cynically exploited to suppress historical truths. The result was a rejection of any attempt to explain the historical context for the events of 9/11 and other gratuitous acts of terrorism against Americans, and the preponderance of grotesque and thoroughly ignorant caricatures as conveyed in such statements as, "They hate our freedom," "They resent our culture," and "Their religion preaches hatred."

This avoidance of the hard realities of the Middle East in some quarters in the United States is not a new phenomenon. In particular, there has been a traditional aversion on the part of many Americans to hearing any serious analysis, let alone criticism, of their country's Middle East policies, or of those of U.S. allies in the region. This is true even though the veil that had generally been maintained in public discourse over the undemocratic domestic policies of the Saudi Arabian and Egyptian regimes has slipped considerably since September 11, 2001. In consequence, both governments are now subject to more congressional and media criticism, especially Saudi Arabia.[6] Beyond this, Israeli excesses have occasionally forced the media to show some measure of objectivity. This happened in 1982 during the ten-week siege and bombardment of Beirut and the subsequent Sabra and Shatila massacres,[7] and at times during the first Palestinian intifada, from 1987–91. In recent years, however, especially since the second intifada began in late 2000, the resistance in the United States to any criticism of Israel's policies has increased, even as a military occupation over millions of Palestinians that in June 2006 began its fortieth year grows ever more suffocating.[8]

In consequence of all these factors, there has been little coverage of certain types of Middle Eastern news in the United States. This virtual blackout has largely been a function of American media self-censorship. Especially on television, where most Americans get their news, there has been little detailed reportage on conditions in the Israeli-occupied territories (indeed of the very fact that there is an Israeli occupation, maintained by violence), and there has been little coverage of routine domestic repression, violations of human rights, and restrictions on democracy and freedom of expression in America's Arab allies and client states. Such reports are common in the media of Europe and the rest of the world, and even in Israel. Only since the unrealistic war aims of the Bush administration in Iraq have produced chaos in that country has a willingness to critique some aspects of U.S. Middle East policy crept into American public discourse.

Nevertheless, it is an undeniable fact that many of those who planned and carried out the attacks of September 11, or those who guided, led, taught, and supported them, were not so very long ago the welcome allies of the United States and various Middle Eastern regimes to which it is closely linked. This is true whether these individuals belonged to one of the radical offshoots of the Muslim Brotherhood, an Egyptian Islamist political party founded in 1928, or adhered to some extremist version of the Wahhabi doctrine, which represents religious orthodoxy in Saudi Arabia, or aided the Afghan mujahideen during the war against the Soviet occupation during the 1980s. Specifically, the masterminds of 9/11, and their intellectual forebears and spiritual guides,[9] were frequently the ardent and devoted foot-soldiers of the United States and its allies in the murky covert struggles against the Soviet Union and other opponents in the Middle East from the mid-1950s until the early 1990s. American and allied policymakers supported them against such identified enemy forces as Arab nationalism, Pan-Arabism, local communist parties, radical regimes, Palestinian nationalism, and later the Soviets in Afghanistan.[10]

All of this exceedingly germane history, some of it quite recent, has been obliterated or forgotten. Over the past few years, the intellectual progeny of these U.S. clients, their successors, and in a few cases the very same individuals (figures such as Shaykh 'Umar 'Abd al-Rahman, convicted in connection with the 1993 World Trade Center bombing,[11] the late Shaykh Ahmad Yasin, founder of Hamas, Salman al-'Awda and Safar al-Hawla, both Saudi clerics,[12] and the two top leaders of al-Qa'ida, Ayman al-Zawahiri and Usama Bin Laden) who once were allies, fellow travelers, or salaried agents of the United States and the Middle Eastern governments it supports, came to regard the United States and its allies in the region as their enemies. Another example would be the transformation of the Palestinian branch of the Muslim Brotherhood and its offspring, Hamas, from the protégés of the Israeli occupation into Israel's fierce enemy.[13] One hears little about this history in the United States today, perhaps out of deference to the individuals and institutions that directed and executed American policy during the Cold War.[14]

Uncomfortably for both American policymakers and for their critics, these Islamic radicals, beyond their reactionary social and cultural stances, which generally have had a narrow appeal in the Arab and Islamic worlds, also espoused other causes that have been broadly popular throughout the region. These causes included several related positions: opposing Israeli occupation and supporting Palestinian self-determination; condemning the sanctions regime imposed on Iraq after the Gulf War of 1991 and the 2003 invasion of that country; demanding the removal of unpopular American bases from Saudi Arabia, Iraq, and other Arab countries; and resisting the undemocratic, oligarchic, and often corrupt regimes like those of Saudi Arabia and Egypt—most of them shored up by the United States and other Western powers—that dominate the Middle East.

This situation is deeply problematic for American policymakers, especially those in the Bush administration, who claim that the United States always acts in the name of freedom and democracy. Yet if most people in Middle Eastern countries could freely express their opinion, they would likely be opposed to U.S. policy on all of these issues, from Palestine and Iraq to the presence of U.S. military bases, and including the propping up of unpopular autocracies. On the other hand, long-standing domestic opponents of American Middle East policies find it discomforting to hear Usama Bin Laden or other such radical figures attack these policies. The last thing they want, after years of being virtually ostracized for criticizing America's actions in the Middle East, is to be identified in any way, even indirectly, with the people who killed thousands of innocent Americans on September 11, 2001. The task of policy critic thereafter became even harder as media self-censorship intensified, and as an especially problematic form of political correctness took hold in some quarters, one that implied that any critique of past policies amounted to treason in the "global war on terror."

In reflecting on these considerations, I realized that there is a link between these pressing current issues of terrorism, war in Iraq, United States policy, and the seemingly unconnected question of the Palestinians' failure to achieve independence. It lies in a striking continuity of Western policies in Palestine and elsewhere in the Middle East—most especially a carryover from the policies of the once-dominant power, Great Britain, to those of the current hegemon, the United States. Both have tended to favor outcomes that fit distorted accounts of the situation in Palestine (notably, the Zionist vision of Palestine as "a land without a people for a people without a land"). Both have favored outcomes that were politically convenient domestically, over what was in keeping with the actual realities of the situation on the ground and with the principles of self-determination and international law. Long before there was an American position on the Palestine question, driven primarily by domestic political concerns, there was a British position, similarly driven by concerns almost entirely external to Palestine. For reasons of self-interest, strategy, ideology, and domestic politics, both powers consistently privileged the interests of the country's Jewish population over those of its Arab residents (and, after about half of them were made into refugees, former residents). And facing both was a weak and ineffective Palestinian leadership that seemed to grasp only dimly, if at all, the strategic challenge facing their people, the actual balance of forces in the field, the exact nature of the relationship between the great power of the day and its local Zionist allies, the way politics functioned in London and Washington, and how best to use the meager resources at their disposal to overcome these long odds.

A second link to current issues in the Middle East is the fact that over time, Palestine has proven to be the Achilles' heel for both past British and current American policies in the Middle East. While each power has had to deal with various local sources of dissatisfaction with its Middle East policies, their respective handling of the Palestine question has rendered them unpopular in a broad range of Arab, Middle Eastern, and Islamic countries. This has become most apparent in times of crisis. Thus on the eve of World War II, at the height of the 1936–39 Palestinian Arab revolt against colonial control, British policymakers realized that their policy of forcibly repressing Palestine's Arab population in the interest of the Zionist movement threatened to be a major strategic liability throughout a region that promised to be, and in the end was, a major arena of conflict with the Axis powers. They thus reversed some of their core policies in Palestine via issuance of the 1939 White Paper, in which they made apparent concessions to the Palestinians and placed restrictions on Jewish immigration. Similarly, on the eve of the invasion of Iraq, Bush administration officials apparently felt obliged to shore up the United States' sagging image in the region by an endorsement of a Palestinian state. However, there were deep structural factors of support for Zionism in Britain and for Israel in the United States that remained unchanged in spite of these measures, and that in the end prevented either of them from having any significant effect. An examination of how Britain's handling of the Palestine issue helped to make it highly unpopular in the Middle East might shed light on a similar process that appears to be unfolding with regard to the United States.

There are several aspects of continuity between the British Empire and the new post–World War II age of American hegemony insofar as Palestine is concerned. When Britain and the international community, whose will was then expressed by the League of Nations, solemnly committed themselves to self-determination and the establishment of a national home for the Jewish people in the Mandate for Palestine in 1922, at a time when the Jewish population of the country was less than 10 percent of the total, most Jews had probably not become political Zionists. This fact is easily forgotten today, now that there are over 5 million Jewish citizens of Israel,[15] and that political Zionism—the idea of the Jewish people as a national entity—has become the prevalent ideology among Jewish communities everywhere. Nevertheless, despite the fact that in the first part of the twentieth century Jews were a tiny minority of the population of Palestine, and the Zionist movement was as yet probably unrepresentative of mainstream Jewish opinion, Britain and the dominant institution of the international community, the League of Nations, were broadly faithful to that commitment. The reasons for this stand had primarily to do with the utility of Zionism to British imperial purposes, the sympathy of a major sector of the British elite for Zionism, and the skill of the Zionist leadership in cultivating those who might be of use to them.

There was, however, no similar British or international commitment to the self-determination of the Palestinian people, in spite of the Palestinians' insistence on the justice of their claim, and on Britain's obligation to make good on its World War I promises of independence to the Arabs. Both the Covenant of the League of Nations—which defined the former Arab provinces of the Ottoman Empire, Palestine among them, as Class A mandates, regions that had achieved a level of development that made them "provisionally independent states"—and the text of the various British and allied pledges to Arabs, supported the Palestinian claims. Nevertheless, only after three years of a bloody Palestinian revolt that started in 1936, and with the shadow of another world war looming in 1939, did the British grudgingly, indirectly, and conditionally grant the principle of independence for Palestine with majority rule (to be implemented after ten years, and only if the Jewish minority was in agreement, a condition that was presumably intended to be impossible to fulfill). Soon thereafter, World War II and the Holocaust changed circumstances so drastically as to render this promise effectively meaningless. In fact, the British government of the day always intended to subvert even this highly conditional projected extension of independence to the Palestinians. This is clear from the minutes of a British cabinet meeting of February 23, 1939, detailing the British approach that resulted in the White Paper of 1939, in which this promise was embodied. There it appears that the British colonial secretary, Malcolm MacDonald, and his cabinet colleagues meant to prevent Palestinian representative government and self-determination, even while appearing to grant the "independence" of Palestine.[16]

Similarly, the United States, the first country to recognize the independence of the Jewish state in May 1948, has yet to support in deed (as opposed to word) the independence of Arab Palestine. This remained the case in 2006, although with war looming in Iraq in 2002, President George W. Bush stated that an independent Palestine had "always" been an American policy goal (in fact, this was the first time that such an objective was ever enunciated by an American president). On the contrary, in practice the United States is, and for over sixty years has been, one of the most determined opponents of Palestinian self-determination and independence. It has aligned itself closely with the Israeli position: thus, only when the position of Israel on this matter changed in 1992–95, under the government of Yizhaq Rabin, did U.S. policy change.

Another area where there are profound continuities between the British Mandate period and today is in the interrelation between indigenous Palestinian leaderships and outside forces. One constant has been the frequent incapacity and weakness of these leaderships vis-à-vis the great imperial powers of the day. Another less visible continuity lies in the way in which this interrelation contributed to the genesis of political Islam in the interwar period and again in recent decades. The British Mandate government from the outset assiduously fostered the creation and development of ostensibly "traditional," but in fact newly created, "Islamic" institutions such as the post of "Grand Mufti of Palestine" and the Supreme Muslim Council. At the same time, the British authorities assiduously denied legitimacy to Palestinian national bodies and prevented the establishment of Palestinian representative institutions.[17] The British gave these Islamic institutions—"invented traditions" in every sense of this term[18]—full control of extensive public revenues (those of the public religious foundations, or *awqaf 'amma*) and broad patronage powers. For nearly two decades, until the spontaneously initiated popular revolt of 1936, this policy served its intended purpose of dividing the traditional leadership and providing a counterweight to the Palestinian national movement. By giving a crucial portion of the Palestinian elite both some control over resources and a measure of prestige, but no access to real state power, these institutions successfully distracted many Palestinians from a unified focus on anticolonial national objectives, including the control of the mandatory state, and building an effective nationalist para-state body to rival that state.

There is a parallel between this policy and the decades-long U.S. fostering of the Muslim Brotherhood and other Islamically oriented groups throughout the Middle East as counterweights to what were perceived as radical, nationalist, anti-American forces. Conservative Arab regimes allied with the United States, like those of Jordan and Saudi Arabia, followed a similar policy. For well over two decades after the occupation of the West Bank and Gaza in 1967, Israel did much the same thing with the Palestinian branch of the Muslim Brotherhood and its offshoot Hamas in Gaza as a counterweight to the nationalist Palestine Liberation Organization (PLO). This reached the point where the Israeli military occupation encouraged Brotherhood thugs to intimidate PLO supporters.[19]

There are of course major differences between the Mandate-era Islamic institutions headed by the mufti, Hajj Amin al-Husayni, who ultimately became a much-hated enemy of the British and the Zionists, and the indigenous Palestinian organization Hamas, which since its foundation in late 1987 has always posed as an uncompromising foe of Israel's existence. This is still the case with Hamas, although relatively recent calls by some of its senior leaders, later assassinated by Israel, including Shaykh Ahmad Yasin and Dr. Ismail Abu Shanab, for a multi-decade "truce" with Israel probably did amount to a tacit and de facto acceptance of Israel and of a two-state solution with a Palestinian state alongside Israel. Among other contrasts, Britain itself created the institutions headed by the mufti as a bricolage of old Ottoman and Islamic structures, and imports from other parts of the British Empire, while the Muslim Brotherhood in Palestine was purely indigenous, and only obtained Israeli patronage after 1967 (although at times it had Jordanian and Egyptian patronage before that). Similarly, there are great divergences between how Britain consistently fostered and then belatedly came to oppose the mufti, and the complex, covert, and often conflictual relationships between the American, Saudi, Egyptian, and Israeli intelligence services, and the Muslim Brotherhood, Hamas, and other Islamic religious movements in several Arab and Islamic countries. Some of the offshoots of these movements that for long enjoyed the clandestine support of Western countries, their Arab allies, and Israel, ultimately produced stridently anti-Western, anti-regime, and anti-Israeli offspring such as al-Qaʻida, Hamas, the Groupe Islamique Armé (GIA), and Takfir wa Hijra, and similar groups in Afghanistan, Palestine, Algeria, Egypt, and elsewhere.

Political Islam has served as a vehicle for resistance as well as collaboration in different eras of Palestinian history, notably in the form of the grassroots combination of Islamic revival and nationalism espoused by the charismatic Shaykh 'Iz al-Din al-Qassam, whose "martyrdom" in 1935 can be said to have inspired the revolt of 1936–39.[20] The same can be said of the more recent Islamic Jihad movement, an offshoot of the Palestinian branch of the Muslim Brotherhood. Its founders were disgusted with the Brotherhood's quietism and passivity toward—and, some even alleged, collaboration with—the Israeli occupation. Their attacks on Israeli military personnel in 1986 and 1987 helped spark the first Palestinian popular uprising, or intifada, which broke out in December 1987 and helped provoke the transformation of the major part of the Muslim Brotherhood organization into Hamas. Hamas itself has played a major part in the resistance to Israel, although some of the tactics that both Hamas and Islamic Jihad have pioneered in the Palestinian arena, particularly suicide attacks on civilians inside Israel, have been both morally indefensible and disastrously counterproductive strategically.[21]

These divergences and continuities between the Mandate period and the recent past pale beside an overarching similarity: Islamic institutions, leaders, and movements, far from being invariably anticolonial, radical, anti-Western, or anti-Zionist (which of course they often were), were also at various times over the past century seen as useful allies by the Western powers, by Israel, and by conservative Arab regimes aligned with the West. As one of many examples, during the 1980s, the Muslim Brotherhood in Gaza and the West Bank for years eagerly sent radical young Palestinian Muslims off to Afghanistan to combat the Soviet Army invasion. It did so on the basis of the curious argument that the path of "true jihad" could be found not in resisting the Israeli occupation of the Gaza Strip, but rather far away in Central Asia. The covert agencies of numerous states were involved in sponsoring this "jihad," not the least of them the CIA and the Saudi and Pakistani intelligence services. Needless to say, the Israeli military occupation authorities and their attentive intelligence services regarded this development with benevolent indulgence, encouraging any movement that fostered the departure of these young radicals and that weakened the unpalatable nationalism represented by the PLO.[22]

It is yet another ironic twist in the obscure early part of this strange story that the man described by the young Usama Bin Laden as his "guide" in the early 1980s was the charismatic Palestinian Islamic militant Dr. 'Abdullah 'Azzam, who met his death in a mysterious car bombing in Peshawar in 1988.[23] 'Azzam played a key role in the flow of hundreds of young Palestinians from the refugee camps and towns and villages of Gaza and the West Bank to the madrassas and training camps of Peshawar and the battlefields beyond in Afghanistan.[24] 'Azzam had his intellectual roots in the philosophy of the Palestinian branch of the Muslim Brotherhood. He thereafter became one of the leading theoreticians and practitioners of the transmutation of the Brotherhood's ideas into a radical new version of Islam, including a militant variant of Wahhabi doctrine, which became a new kind of political tool. This tool was first employed against the Soviet Red Army and its Afghan allies, in a campaign blessed, armed, trained, and financed by the American Central Intelligence Agency (CIA), the Pakistani Inter-Services Intelligence Directorate (ISI), and the Saudi intelligence service. Usama Bin Laden seems to have been a central figure in arranging the clandestine financing of this campaign: indeed, it appears that at some point he may even have served as a senior representative of Saudi intelligence in Afghanistan.[25]

Today we all know the middle of this story, even though none of us can yet foresee the end. American troops have since late 2001 been hunting their erstwhile Afghan and Arab allies (the latter in the meantime having transmuted into al-Qa'ida) in Afghanistan and elsewhere around the world; the ISI and the Pakistani military have ostensibly switched sides and turned on the Taliban regime they had helped install in Kabul only a few years previously; and Saudi Arabia has been the scene of attacks for which al-Qa'ida has claimed responsibility. But the beginning of the story is still being kept from us. It is obscured by analyses that purport to shed light on the roots of terrorism, excoriating Saudi Arabia for its support of Usama Bin Laden and the Taliban, while passing in silence over the policies of the United States, which once encouraged, enabled, and benefited from Bin Laden and his ilk, and was complaisant toward successful Pakistani and Saudi efforts to install the Taliban regime in Afghanistan.[26]

In order to cast essential light on this murky earlier phase of American policy in the Middle East, both overt and covert, it is necessary to drop the pretense that the United States has always supported democracy and the rule of law in that region, that it was invariably evenhanded in its dealings with the Arabs and the Israelis, and that it was always scrupulously fair in implementing international law, whether in Iraq or Palestine. Rather, as I argued in *Resurrecting Empire*, the United States had entirely different agendas, rooted in Cold War imperatives, the desire to control oil-producing regions, and support for Israel's regional hegemony: all these aims were often misleadingly summed up under the rubric of "stability." The sad fact is that, alien as the attacks of September 11 may seem, they were in fact a refraction, distorted beyond recognition over the years, of policies and practices emanating from Washington, the blowback, more horrible than anyone could have imagined, of covert operations gone disastrously awry.

In a 1998 lecture, one year before his death and three years before 9/11, the distinguished Pakistani scholar Iqbal Ahmad described his own first meeting with Usama Bin Laden and warned prophetically against the danger to the United States of covert alliances with Islamic radicals:

Covert operations and low-intensity warfare . . . are the breeding grounds of terror and drugs. . . . This fellow [Bin Laden] was an ally. He remained an ally. He turns at a particular moment: in 1990, when the U.S. goes into Saudi Arabia with its forces [a reference to the basing of U.S. troops in Saudi Arabia after the Iraqi invasion of Kuwait].... For him, America had broken its word: the loyal friend has betrayed. The one to whom you swore blood loyalty has betrayed you. They're going to go for you. They're going to do a lot more. These are the chickens of the Afghanistan war coming home to roost. This is why I said to stop covert operations. There is a price attached to them that the American people cannot calculate, and that people like Kissinger do not know, that they do not have the history to know it.[27]

This prescient observation has been borne out brilliantly by the analysis of my Columbia University colleague Mahmood Mamdani in *Good Muslim, Bad Muslim: America, the Cold War and the Roots of Terror*.[28] Mamdani shows precisely how illegal covert operations, carried out without the consent and sometimes against the will of Congress, from Southeast Asia and southern Africa to Central America and Afghanistan, from the 1970s until the 1990s, have necessarily and inevitably engendered drug traffic and terrorism. None of this had much impact at home, until brutal terrorism nurtured in the bloody cauldron of the Afghanistan war suddenly and unexpectedly struck the United States, years after the U.S. government had ceased to pay serious attention to Afghanistan.

Of course, there is an indigenous, local aspect to Bin Laden and al-Qa'ida's specific variety of the terrorism engendered by illegal, covert warfare that has nothing to do with the United States or its policies: but it cannot be stressed strongly enough that this indigenous quality has little to do with Islam per se. Islam was a political force of immense power (and had built one of the greatest civilizations the world has known) centuries before western Europe had climbed out of the Dark Ages. Moreover, Wahhabism was a potent religious and political force before the American Constitution was adopted. Certainly, the specific forms that extreme Islamic radicalism took at the end of the twentieth century were shaped by aspects of the Islamic heritage, and by the narrow vision of Islam propa-

gated in the eighteenth century by Muhammad ʿAbd al-Wahhab
and by later radical Islamic revivalists like Hassan al-Banna, Sayyid
Qutb, and other leaders of the Muslim Brotherhood. It is true also
that the violent extremists of al-Qaʿida are in some measure products of their societies and of certain strands of the Islamic heritage.
But it takes an extraordinary degree of self-interested blindness to
ignore that they were also significantly shaped by the policies of
the United States and its closest allies in the Middle East and South
Asia in the last decades of the Cold War, and that the most virulent
strains of this witches' brew came into existence in the hell's kitchen
of the savage Afghan war. Indeed, the very term "al-Qaʿida," meaning "base," is short for "qaʿida maʿlumatiyya," or database, originally
a reference to the database developed by Usama Bin Laden during
the Afghan war to keep track of the various Islamist factions allied
with the United States in the Afghan "jihad."[29]

And if there is ill will toward the United States in many Middle
Eastern countries, it is a mistake to try to explain it by reference
to Islamic doctrine, to the alleged propensity of Muslims for violence, or to the supposed centrality of the concept of jihad to Islam.
One need look no further than the corrupt and autocratic regimes
propped up by the United States all over the Middle East, and at
American policies regarding Palestine, Iraq, and other issues that
are highly unpopular in the region.

For many years, the United States largely escaped the perils and
pitfalls of its unilateralism and its insensitivity to opinion in the
Middle East—the repeated bombings of U.S. embassies and military
barracks in the region notwithstanding. Again and again, top policymakers in Washington resolutely ignored the many warning signs
of a growing level of unhappiness with American policy among
Arabs and Muslims. They in turn helped to anesthetize the general
public, lulling it with bogus nostrums such as the U.S. role as a
peacemaker in the Middle East and as a supporter of democracy in
the Arab and Muslims worlds. It seems that even a shock of the mag-

nitude of September 11 was not sufficient to free most Americans of such illusions, and to force them to examine the history of their own country's deeply flawed policies for the origins of much of the violence and instability today in the Middle East and the rest of the Islamic world. Notwithstanding all the shocks produced by American misadventures in Iraq, Palestine, Afghanistan, and elsewhere in this region, we still seem to be living in an era of historical amnesia.

The Palestinians in Their Own Right

Why is this study of the failure to achieve Palestinian statehood important? It is important, first, because Palestinian history has significance in its own right. It is a hidden history, one that is obscured, at least in the West, by the riveting and tragic narrative of modern Jewish history. Where it is recognized at all, it tends to serve as an appendage or feeble counterpoint to that powerful story. Palestine is a small country—and the Palestinians even today number perhaps only 9 or 10 million people—and yet the people and the land of Palestine loom large in world affairs beyond all consideration of their size. Their drama has been a central one.

Recognizing, and making restitution for, the harm done, primarily to the Palestinian people but also to others, as a result of that drama involves a major moral challenge to the international community, and particularly to the West, which bears a grave responsibility for helping to engender this conflict. Moreover, it has become clear in recent years that this is an issue that deeply moves major elements of international opinion, even if the bulk of public opinion in the United States appears indifferent to it. However, achieving any serious understanding of this poignant conflict, which has for decades rent the Middle East and has had such a wide-reaching political and moral impact outside it, requires a broad comprehension of Palestinian history in its own terms, and in its own context, which includes but cannot be subsumed by or subordinated to Jewish and Israeli history. Just as one cannot understand the history of France without taking into account its conflicts with Germany and Britain over the past three centuries, it would be unthinkable to reduce French history to these conflicts, or treat it as an addendum to the history of its erstwhile rivals.

In a sense, this is what has happened to the history of the Palestinians, under the powerful impact of the painful and amply recounted story of the catastrophic fate of the Jews of Europe in the first half of the twentieth century (and of the less well told story of the tragic calamities that befell most of the well-established Jewish communities in the Arab world in the middle of the century). I hope that this book will remedy that situation, in however modest a way, and will explain a crucial set of issues in Palestinian history that have profound implications down to the present day.

I hope secondly in this book to ascribe agency to the Palestinians. I thereby seek to avoid seeing them either as no more than helpless victims of forces far greater then themselves, or alternatively as driven solely by self-destructive tendencies and uncontrollable dissension, as do many analyses of their actions in the years leading up to 1948. This is not to say that the Palestinians were not facing an uphill struggle from the beginning of the British Mandate: we have already seen briefly how this was the case, and the pages to come will explore these long odds further. And Palestinian society and politics were most definitely divided and faction-ridden, in ways that gave hostile forces many cleavages to exploit. But the Palestinians had many assets, were far from helpless, and often faced a range of choices, some of which were better, or at least less bad, than others. In this way, I propose to put the Palestinians at the center of a critical phase of their own story.

I hope thirdly to show that the unfortunate case of Palestine illustrates strikingly the long-term perils and pitfalls of great powers following shortsighted policies that are not based on their own professed principles, and are not consonant with international law and legitimacy. This was just as true during the many decades during which Britain dominated the Middle East, as it has been of the more than half a century since then, during which time the United States has been the preeminent power in that region. As we have seen, because of its commitment to Zionism, Great Britain constructed a mandatory regime for Palestine that was in important ways in contravention of the Covenant of the League of Nations and of its World War I pledges of independence to the Arabs. For decades, Britain twisted and turned between these two contradictory poles of respect for the principle of self-determination embodied in the Covenant, and faithfulness to its commitment to create a Jewish national home, embodied in the Balfour Declaration and reiterated in the Mandate for Palestine. There was, however, never any question that the commitment to Zionism was the stronger. In the process, Great Britain enabled the Zionists to create the springboard from which they were ultimately able to take over the entire country at the expense of its indigenous population. It thereby helped significantly to produce a conflict that only became more bitterly intractable as time went on.

Similarly, the United States voted in the General Assembly for the creation of an Arab state in Palestine alongside a Jewish one, but acquiesced in the extinction of that Arab state before its birth by the combined efforts of the new state of Israel, Britain, Jordan, and other actors. Thereafter, the United States repeatedly sponsored or supported measures in the United Nations or on its own that might have alleviated the conflict. These ranged from General Assembly Resolution 194 of December 1948, which would have allowed the return of Palestinian refugees to their homes and compensated them for their losses, to the efforts of the Palestine Conciliation Commission of 1949, established by the U.N. General Assembly through Security Council Resolution 242, which laid down a basis ultimately agreed to by all the parties for resolution of the conflict, to a variety of essentially unilateral American initiatives toward peace. In all of these cases, however, the United States never unequivocally and in practice supported the self-determination and independent, viable statehood of the Palestinians, and often acted to undermine this and other universal principles of international law and legitimacy. Without these principles, needless to say, a just and lasting resolution of this problem is impossible.

In making policy on Palestine over most of the past century, leaders in both Britain and the United States were driven primarily by powerful strategic and domestic political considerations, rather than by principle. The strategic considerations included the goals of dominating this crucial piece of territory, keeping it in friendly hands, and denying it to others.[30] The political ones included cold calculations of the considerable domestic electoral and financial advantages to be obtained from supporting Zionism, as against the negligible domestic political costs. There also existed naive sympathy for Zionism among many British and American politicians, based on a particularly Protestant immersion in the Bible. This sympathy was often combined with a laudable desire to make amends for the persecution of the Jews in different parts of Europe (often combined with a less laudable, indeed reprehensible, desire to have the victims of persecution find haven somewhere other than Great Britain or the United States). The result of such attitudes, which necessarily ignored or downplayed vital realities on the ground in Palestine, has been an enduring tragedy.

Revisiting History

This is not a "revisionist" history, along the lines of those that have emerged from Israel in recent years. Revisionist history requires as a foil an established, authoritative master narrative that is fundamentally flawed in some way. In this sense, the "revisionist" works written by a number of Israeli historians and social scientists—Avi Shlaim, Ilan Pappé, Tom Segev, Benny Morris, and others[31]—are fully within this tradition, for what they are arguing against is the nationalist mythology of the state of Israel as it has informed and shaped Israeli accounts of that country's history. That mythology is additionally the backbone of the received version of the history of the conflict as it is perceived in the West.

To revisit one of the most important of these myths about the infant state of Israel, the number of Arab armies that invaded Israel after its establishment is described in a range of standard accounts as ranging from five to seven.[32] However, there were only seven independent Arab states in 1948 (some hardly independent, and some hardly states in any meaningful sense of the word), two of which, Saudi Arabia and Yemen, did not even have regular armies and no means of getting any armed forces they might have had to Palestine. Beyond this, of the five Arab regular armies, one (that of Lebanon) never crossed the international frontier with Palestine,[33] two (those of Iraq and Transjordan) scrupulously refrained from crossing the frontiers of the Jewish state laid down in the United Nations partition plan as per secret Jordanian understandings with both Britain and the Zionist leadership and thus never "invaded" Israel,[34] and one (that of Syria) made only minor inroads across the new Israeli state's frontiers.[35] The only serious and long-lasting incursion into the territory of the Jewish state as laid down under the partition plan was that of the Egyptian army. Meanwhile, the fiercest fighting during the 1948 war took place with the Jordanian army during multiple Israeli *offensives* into areas assigned by the U.N. to the Arab state, or into the U.N.-prescribed *corpus separatum* around Jerusalem. This story of an invasion by multiple, massive Arab armies, and other legends, is not just an important element of the Israeli myth of origin: it is a nearly universal myth, and in taking it on, the Israeli revisionist scholars, or "new historians," as they are more often called in their own country, are shouldering a doubly daunting task.

By contrast, there is no established, authoritative Palestinian master narrative, against which this work can be set, although there is a Palestinian nationalist narrative that includes its share of myth. This version is in any case virtually unknown outside the Arab world (and is in some respects contested within it), drowned out as it is by the Israeli national myth-epic, which substitutes for any kind of substantive, critical history in the minds of most Westerners. Moreover, as the Israeli new historians have been showing, many elements of the standard Palestinian narrative have in fact been borne out by archival research. These include the causes for the flight of the Palestinian refugees; the collusion between Israel and Jordan, and Britain and Jordan, against the Palestinians; and the absolute superiority of the Zionist and later the Israeli armed forces against those of their adversaries in the field throughout most stages of the 1947–49 conflict.

This is not to say that there are not many myths worth debunking in the Palestinian version of events: there are indeed, particularly ideas relating to the Zionist movement and Israel and their connections with the Western powers, the relation of Zionism to the course of modern Jewish history, particularly the central place of the Holocaust in this history, and the reductionist view of Zionism as no more than a colonial enterprise. This enterprise was and is colonial in terms of its relationship to the indigenous Arab population of Palestine; Palestinians fail to understand, or refuse to recognize, however, that Zionism *also* served as the national movement of the nascent Israeli polity being constructed at their expense. There is no reason why both positions cannot be true: there are multiple examples of national movements, indeed nations, that were colonial in their origins, not least of them the United States. Deconstructing these ideas will be crucially important to an eventual reconciliation of the two peoples.

Because of the disparity in the Palestinian and Israeli archival sources, I am obliged to take an approach that prevents this from really being a revisionist history. Revisionist history, at least of the kind undertaken by the Israeli new historians, depends largely on archival revelations to upset established narratives. One major impetus for the efforts of these historians came from the opening up in the 1980s of materials in the Israel State Archives relating to the 1948 period. They were able to utilize this wealth of material, weeded and sanitized though it had been—as all archives inevitably are—to lay a documentary foundation for their effort to show the deeply flawed nature of the dominant line of thinking about the origins of the state of Israel. In so doing, they found ample support for a number of arguments about the 1947–49 fighting, such as the fact that most refugees were forced to leave their homes in 1948, that had previously been put forward by Arab historians, but that were ignored outside an extremely restricted circle. Thus a state's well-organized records were used to undermine the version of its genesis that its founders and supporters had always espoused, and that has since gained universal currency worldwide.

The archival situation could not be more different on the Palestinian side. I have already explained that the Palestinian version of events is far from being hegemonic or authoritative even in the limited confines of the Arab world, and that it embodies a number of elements that contradict the standard Israeli version of events that has wide international currency. Moreover, there is no Palestinian state to create and maintain a Palestinian state archive. Beyond this, more than half of the Arab population of Palestine fled or were driven from their homes in 1947–49, while the two cities in Palestine with the largest Arab populations, Jaffa and Haifa, were ethnically cleansed of most Arabs. As a result, there is no central repository of Palestinian records, and a vast quantity of private Palestinian archival material—a considerable portion of the patrimony of an entire people—has been either irretrievably lost or was carried off by Israel, to be deposited in the Israeli national library and national archives.[36] There is therefore no equivalent independent state archival base from which to challenge or supplement either the received Israeli version of history or that of the Palestinians themselves.

There is, however, a plethora of scattered archival and other documentary sources that can be used to piece together the Palestinian side of what happened in 1948. These include the records of the various great powers involved in the Palestine question, notably Great Britain, the United States, France, and the Soviet Union, and the archives of the League of Nations and the United Nations. A number of official Arab archives can also be tapped, particularly those of Egypt, Jordan, Iraq, and the Arab League, all of which have been utilized for this or other periods by historians, although they have been used only in a limited fashion as a source for the history of the Palestine question, and their very accessibility has been falsely cast into doubt by some.[37] Among the most important sources is the Israel State Archives, where beyond the voluminous records of the Israeli state itself, many sets of private papers of leading Palestinian figures now reside, by default rather than due to the choice of their authors. There are also a number of official or semi-official histories written primarily by Israeli insiders with privileged access to these archives before they were open to the public, and that contain considerable documentary material.[38] The collections of private papers held by the Institute for Palestine Studies in Beirut are all available for examination, as are many others in private hands, albeit sometimes with difficulty, and it is finally possible to consult profitably the newspapers and the records of radio broadcasts of the period, as well as published memoirs by participants in events in Palestine before 1948. Given the fragmentary nature of the sources and the absence of a central Palestinian archive, even a fully archivally based work could not be called revisionist history in the same sense as the writing of the Israeli new historians can, for the simple reason that in the Palestinian case one is unable to start from the same massive, central, unified documentary base, or with the same resources, as are provided by a successful, modern state like Israel, or Egypt, or any other.

This basic asymmetry with respect to archives is a reflection of the asymmetry between the two sides. While one side, operating through a modern nation-state, has used its documentary and other resources to produce a version of its history that has subtly shaped the way the world sees the conflict, a version that is now ironically being undermined from within via use of these same resources, the production of a standard "official" Palestinian narrative was never really possible on the other side. In the absence of a central Palestinian state archive, a significant proportion of those archival resources which were painstakingly amassed and organized on the Palestinian side at various research institutions, were at different times attacked, confiscated, sequestered, or destroyed by the Israeli army and security services, efforts that jeopardized the Palestinians' historical patrimony. One of the most important of these institutions, the PLO's Palestine Research Center in Beirut, was attacked by Israel with rockets and artillery on at least two separate occasions before 1982 (and its director was maimed by a package bomb), and during the Israeli occupation of Beirut of that same year its contents were seized. Another, the Arab Studies Society, was closed by order of the Israeli government for many years before 1992, and again in 2000. As of this writing, neither archive, including in particular many collections of private papers,[39] is accessible to researchers.[40] Other less important collections suffered similar treatment.

In this book I will in any case follow an approach that is not primarily dependent on archival sources. While I have utilized some primary sources, notably newspapers, private papers, and some material from diplomatic archives, I have started from the assumption that enough research has been done by others in the existing archives, such as they are, to provide the basic framework of events necessary for examining the limited set of questions I have set out to answer. And there is no way to make up for what does not exist—a Palestinian national archive or a Palestinian national library. Unlike the historians of the subaltern studies school, I do not propose to attempt to read the history of the losers in the records of the victors, useful though such an exercise would be. Sadly, some of what has been done thus far using these records, far from enabling the subalterns to speak, has only further deepened their silence. This is the case even with groundbreaking works such as Benny Morris's *The Birth of the Palestinian Refugee Problem, 1947–1949*. This book shattered many myths on this subject, but was almost entirely based on

Israeli sources, as its author disdained one of the possible supplements to these sources, the testimonies of the refugees themselves.[41]

I propose rather a rereading and rethinking of what is already known, with what I hope is the judicious addition of archival material that will help to illuminate the points I am making. I do not intend primarily to present documentary revelations, or significant new evidence, although it is undoubtedly possible to do so, and a few minor revelations have emerged from the research I have done. Rather, I hope to present new answers to rarely asked questions about why the Palestinians were as badly defeated as they were, and why they failed to create state structures. These are questions that in the past have found answers that in my view are too glib, too easy, and unfair to the actors involved. It is a tall order to explain why something did not happen, and taller still when much of the evidence has been scattered by the very events I am trying to elucidate. I nevertheless think not only that an explanation can be offered, but also that it will illuminate the history of the Palestinians before 1948 and indeed much that has happened to them and to others since then.

How to Approach a Nonevent

The narrative I propose in the following pages is neither linear nor chronological. I propose instead to focus thematically on different aspects of the problem of how the Palestinians related to the question of building an independent state before 1948. This procedure should provide illumination of the problem's contours, and at the same time suggest some answers to why it has recurred in the ensuing period. Each of these themes constitutes the core of a chapter, and each chapter, with the exception of the final two, ranges over much of the entire thirty years of British control of Palestine.

The story of how the Palestinians acted and reacted throughout three decades of British control of Palestine has been told at length. I see no purpose to adding my own full-blown version of this depressing story, which has been told in narrative histories and in a number of monographs.[42] The years since the turn of the twenty-first century have seen the appearance of a large number of new works devoted to examining the Mandate period or crucial aspects thereof.[43] None of these new books, nor the earlier monographs, focus specifically on how and why the Palestinians related to the issue of control of the apparatus of state. They therefore do not tell us why the Palestinians failed not only to take control of the mandatory state apparatus, but to create alternative state structures and structures of legitimacy of their own, and how these failures in turn made inevitable their defeat in the mid-1940s during the confrontation with the Zionist para-state and its successor, the state of Israel.

In order to provide an appropriate context in which to judge the Palestinian case, this book looks thematically at Palestine in comparison with other Arab countries that fell under League of Nations mandatory regimes, and avoids the more conventional approach of comparing the Palestinians and the Zionist movement, and thus comparing the incomparable. My argument is that rather than being compared with the yishuv, a community to which they were not in any way similar (but with which they were in deadly conflict for control of the country), Palestinian society should instead be compared with other Arab societies at an analogous stage of development. Such a comparison reveals that the Palestinians were at least as advanced by most available indices as most of their neighbors in the region. Since the Palestinians had a highly developed sense of national identity by the early 1920s,[44] the question arises of why they failed to realize their national aspirations, unlike all the neighboring peoples, including the yishuv.

The major constitutional problem created for the Palestinians by a mandatory regime that explicitly refrained from mentioning them or their achievement of self-government—and whose legal structure, it could be argued, was specifically designed to exclude any such achievement—and the Palestinian response to this challenge, already touched on briefly above, is another major theme of this book. Historians underestimate the extent of this obstacle to the realization of Palestinian aspirations, or the tenaciousness of successive British governments and their Zionist allies in rejecting both the principle and the practice of real representative government in Palestine, and any constitutional modification that would have made it possible. Yet this obstacle was something the Palestinians themselves were acutely aware of, even though they remained utterly unable to overcome it throughout thirty bitter years of British rule.

Yet another theme is the religious structures created by Great Britain from the very outset of its rule over Palestine, and the role they played in sidetracking the energies of a sizable proportion of the Palestinian elite. This was only one facet of a broader policy of co-optation of these elites, giving them the trappings and perquisites of power without any of the substance. The policy was highly successful from a British perspective, helping to keep a lid on what was often an explosive and might otherwise have been an unsustainable situation for nearly two decades, until the great revolt of 1936–39. The fact is that there were a number of alternative paths, some of them very divergent, to that taken by the central elite leadership of the Palestinian national movement. The most important division in Palestinian politics may well not have been among elite factions, which garnered most attention from observers at the time and afterward. It was rather between most of the traditional notable politicians, with their narrow, conservative view of how to deal with the challenges the Palestinians faced, and a broad range of other Palestinian individuals, political groupings, and social groups who proposed more imaginative and often more radical approaches.

The manner in which all of these strands led to Palestinian failures in the climactic circumstances of the 1936–39 revolt, the partition of 1947, and the 1947–48 fighting is the final theme of the first part of this book. My basic thesis is that the causes for the crushing defeats suffered by the Palestinians in 1948 cannot be found in the events of that fateful year. It is first necessary to examine the peculiarly disadvantageous terms for the Palestinians of the League of Nations mandate that the British crafted for themselves, the unique dilemmas that were consequently created for the Palestinians and the structural problems in Palestinian society, and in Palestinian leadership, that prevented them from better handling these dilemmas. Starting from that point, one can understand the incapacity of the Palestinian national movement to oblige Britain to change its policies, which culminated in the great revolt of 1936–39, the success of the British in repressing it, and the profound effects of this revolt and of its failure to improve the Palestinians' situation.

Thus the core problem was the failure of the Palestinians to create national structures that perhaps might have enabled them to wage a more coherent struggle before the 1936–39 revolt, to weather the repression that accompanied it, and to extract a better outcome from the 1939 negotiations in London, not what happened later. Comparisons with the more successful Indian effort in precisely the same period are of relevance here. Thus, to explain why Palestinian society fell apart with such rapidity in 1947–49, one must go back to well before the fighting of those years. Only thus can one fully explain the striking lack of organization, cohesion, and unanimity in the Palestinian polity in the years immediately preceding 1948, particularly in view of the marked contrast with the improving situation of the yishuv in the same period.

The concluding chapters of the book explore how this thirty-year-long failure to seize the levers of power of the mandatory state or to create alternative state structures may have affected the Palestinians during the many decades of statelessness that followed 1948, down to the present. They examine both the structural constraints on the Palestinians—their falling under the tutelage of several Arab states, none of which initially welcomed their efforts to reorganize their national existence—and the impact of the defeats and failures of preceding decades on their society and their national movement, when it was reconstituted in the late 1950s and 1960s. I also examine the less than successful experiences in state building of the PLO, which wielded many aspects of state power in several different places and ways from the late 1960s onward, and of the Palestinian Authority (PA), created to govern those tightly circumscribed areas of the West Bank and the Gaza Strip from which Israel withdrew its forces in the mid-1990s—temporarily as it turned out.

Both of these entities, the PLO and its offshoot, the PA, have operated in situations of great difficulty, and against overwhelming odds—by no means an unusual experience for the Palestinians historically. But their failures were not just the result of the long odds facing them, any more than were the failures of the 1920s through the 1940s, for Palestinian agency and Palestinian decisions played a major part. While the past certainly cannot tell us how the future will turn out, it definitely helps to explain a variety of trends in the present, and can be useful in avoiding otherwise unanticipated pitfalls in the future. But if the main lesson of the past is that we do not learn from it, over eight decades of Palestinian statelessness may well be prolonged even further.

The Iron Cage

1

Arab Society in Mandatory Palestine

David and Goliath in 1948

The year 1948 was to prove so decisive for the history of the Palestinians that if one seeks to understand subsequent history, one must have a clear sense of how it changed their world. At the beginning of 1948, Arabs constituted an absolute majority of the population of Palestine within its British mandatory borders between the Mediterranean Sea and the Jordan River—approximately 1.4 million out of 2 million people. They were a majority as well in fifteen of sixteen subdistricts of the country.[1] Arabs owned nearly 90 percent of the country's privately owned land.[2] However, over a period of only a few months, as war in Palestine escalated from March until October 1948, a striking transformation took place. More than half of the country's Arab majority, probably over 750,000 people, were expelled from or forced to flee the areas that became part of the state of Israel.[3] About half were obliged to depart from their homes before the formal establishment of Israel and the entry of several Arab armies into Palestine on May 15; the rest left after that date.[4]

Thereafter, 150,000 or so Palestinians remained within Israel (which now controlled 78 percent of the territory of former mandatory Palestine rather than the 55 percent allotted to the Jewish state under the 1947 partition plan). They were reduced to a small minority within the new state, while the Jewish population rapidly swelled as a result of large-scale immigration.[5] The rest of the Palestinians were either scattered as refugees in Lebanon, Syria, or farther afield, or lived in the 22 percent of Palestine controlled after the war ended by Jordan and Egypt, essentially those areas that their armies had managed to hold onto at the time of the 1949 armistices negotiated under UN auspices. However, the majority of the Palestinians, under whichever regime they now found themselves living, were dispossessed of their property, with little control over most aspects of their lives. In a period of a few months, an Arab majority that constituted over two-thirds of the population of Palestine had been decisively defeated, and most of the Palestinians turned into refugees by a Jewish minority, which proceeded to establish a state that sealed its victory over the Palestinians by vanquishing several Arab armies.

The degree of harm done to Palestinian society in 1948 is hard to convey. Over a few weeks in the spring of 1948, Jaffa and Haifa, the cities with the largest Arab populations in Palestine, which were the most dynamic centers of Arab economic and cultural life throughout the Mandate period, were conquered by Zionist militias (a few weeks later these militias became the core of the Israeli army), most of their Arab population dispersed, and their property taken over. The same thing happened to the smaller cities and towns of Lydda, Ramleh, Acre, Safad, Tiberias, Beisan and Bir Sabe' (Beersheva). All, except for Safad and Tiberias, which also had Jewish populations, were almost entirely Arab in character.[6] In 1948 the Palestinian urban population of the country amounted to over four hundred thousand people.[7] About two hundred thousand Palestinians had lived in Jaffa, Haifa, and the seven other cities and towns mentioned here, before these places were captured by the Israelis. About thirty thousand Arab inhabitants of the western part of Jerusalem were also forced to flee their homes.[8] So by the end of 1948, a majority of the Arab urban population of Palestine, the most highly educated, the wealthiest, and the most culturally active, had lost their property and become refugees.

The calamity that was visited upon the urban minority of Palestinians struck the rural majority of about 1 million with even greater force. Of the more than five hundred Arab villages in the territory of what became the state of Israel, by the end of 1948 over four hundred had been conquered by either pre-state Zionist militias (such as the Hagana, the Palmach, the Irgun, and the Lehi), or the Israeli army into which the militias were later incorporated, their populations were driven out or fled in terror, their land was confiscated, and they were forbidden to return. The Israeli government subsequently destroyed nearly all of these empty villages.[9] The 120,000 residents of one hundred Palestine villages that remained within Israel, as well as tens of thousands of Bedouins in the south of the country, were thereafter subjected to martial law for nearly two decades. These disruptions constituted massive and long-lasting changes: in the 78 percent of Palestine that became part of the state of Israel in this fashion, the end result was the creation of a sizable Jewish majority. Most of the new country's land was now owned—or at least controlled—by the Israeli state or its para-state agencies, such as the Israel Lands Authority or the Keren Kayemeth Lisrael, the Jewish National Fund. The basic demographic contours (and the property relations) created by this seismic event are extant to this day, whether inside Israel, in the Palestinian territories Israel occupied in 1967, or in the Palestinian diaspora.

What were the causes for this debacle, in which Palestinian society, urban and later rural, crumbled with a rapidity that astonished even the Zionists at the time, and that has been inscribed in Palestinian memory as *al-Nakba* (the catastrophe)?[10] The traditional Israeli narrative of these events ascribes responsibility almost entirely to the Arabs, claiming that Arab leaders told the Palestinians to flee and denying that Israel bore any responsibility for the flight of the refugees.[11] Israel's new historians, using Israeli, British, United Nations, and other archives opened since the early 1980s, have shown these claims to be groundless.[12] The work of these and other historians indicates that while in a few areas noncombatants were urged by the Palestinian leadership to evacuate their homes for their safety, and some fled before the fighting reached them, most Palestinians left because they were forced to do so either by direct

Israeli attacks on their cities and villages or due to conditions of extreme insecurity. Far from telling them to leave, by April 1948 the Palestinian leadership and the Arab governments were so horrified by the flood of refugees that both made fruitless efforts to stem the flow.[13]

Another basis for denying Israeli responsibility for the flight of the refugees is the claim that the Palestinians attacked the yishuv, the Jewish community in Palestine before 1948, first, and that the flight of the refugees was simply a by-product of a war that the Arabs had started and lost. This argument simplistically and falsely reads a desperate and unequal communal conflict between two peoples until the end of the Mandate on May 15, 1948, as Arab aggression. It also blurs the vital distinction between a first stage of civil war between Palestinians and Jews living inside Palestine before May 15, which the smaller but far better armed and organized yishuv eventually won decisively, and a second one, the war between the new Israeli army and the armies of several Arab states that entered Palestine after May 15. After a difficult early period, this second phase also ended in a decisive Israeli victory. Both segments of the war were hard-fought,[14] and both witnessed significant gains of territory for the Jewish state and concomitant expulsions of the Arab population: during each phase several hundred thousand Palestinians fled their homes.

This argument furthermore ignores the fact that in many cases Palestinians were driven out of areas where there was no fighting, where there were local truces, or where fighting had long ended, and that the vast majority were not allowed to return to their homes even after the fighting was over. Most importantly, it ignores a basic fact, which had been clear to those with any sense on both sides since the beginning of the conflict a few decades earlier. This was that if a state with a Jewish majority controlling the bulk of the land was to be created in Palestine, a country with a massive Arab majority with uncontested legal claim to the lion's share of privately owned land, the expulsion of a large part of this majority and the seizure of their land were absolutely necessary. This fact was the basis of the extraordinary discussions among mainstream Zionist leaders in the 1920s and 1930s (always in private, so as not to reveal to unfriendly ears the true intentions of the movement) concerning the "transfer" of the Arab population outside the frontiers of mandatory Palestine, meaning their removal from the country. This was a fantastic concept at best, and a sinister one at worst, since it was manifestly clear to all concerned that the Palestinians had no intention of allowing themselves to be "transferred" out of their own country, and that if they were to be made to leave, massive force would be required.[15]

The very term "transfer," still occasionally used in Israeli public discourse, is an Orwellian euphemism for the violent removal of a people from a country, in order to create new demographic, and therefore national, realities. It is what today would be called "ethnic cleansing," but that is a term that is rarely applied to what happened in 1948, most parties to the discussion inside Israel favoring "transfer" or some other sanitized and neutral designation.

Important though the work of the Israeli new historians was, their primary subject was Israeli policies and actions, and they drew their conclusions mainly from Israeli, British, and American sources. They used relatively few, if any, Arab sources,[16] none interviewed surviving Palestinian participants in the events,[17] and none utilized the contemporary Arabic-language press. There is a striking contrast with European historians of these events like Henry Laurens and Gudrun Kramer, who both used the existing Arabic sources extensively in their work.[18] Moreover, as the Israeli new historians were understandably primarily interested in writing their own country's history, they only tangentially focused on the actions and motivations of the Arab states and the Palestinians. In analyzing the effect on the Palestinians of Zionist and Israeli actions and those of the great powers, these Israeli writers tended to stress the weakness of Arab social and political cohesion. Some gave great weight to the flight of many members of the Arab upper and middle classes before the fighting in most of Palestine reached its height.[19]

Indeed many well-to-do Palestinian families, particularly those with relatives or other connections in neighboring Arab countries, did leave the country, or stayed abroad, in response to the growing insecurity in Palestine from late 1947 onward.[20]

In ascribing responsibility for the large-scale flight of ordinary Palestinians to the previous departure of many upper- and middle-class families, these authors appear to have ignored the fact that the conquered cities (as well as the neighborhoods of West Jerusalem) in which most of these families lived, and the immediately adjacent villages, were the targets of most of the initial attacks of Zionist forces in the winter and spring of 1947–48, and were overrun well before most of the four-hundred-plus villages were conquered in the more far-flung areas of Palestine. These attacks on the areas where Palestinian elites were located may or may not have been specifically intended to decapitate Arab society, but in any case the effect was disastrous for the Palestinians in rural areas, who saw much of the urban population, and the bulk of the middle and upper classes, flee their homes early on, before the tides of the conflict reached them. It was also harmful to the cohesion of these urban areas facing an armed onslaught, and undoubtedly contributed to their fall.

If these are some of the most recent Israeli interpretations of what happened in 1948, what of accounts from the other side? Most Arab explanations have tended to describe the Palestinians as simply having been overwhelmed by superior armed force and by a multiplicity of enemies. The stress in these analyses is on the greater strength, better equipment, and superior organization of the Zionist forces, the complicity with the Zionists of the withdrawing British army, and the support for them of the United States and the USSR.[21] Other accounts stress the complicity between Israel and Transjordan (later the Hashemite Kingdom of Jordan), whose army, the British-led Arab Legion, was by far the most powerful Arab army in the field in Palestine after May 15, 1948.[22] This thesis was grounded in the experiences of many of the Legion's Arab officers (all the top commanders of the Arab Legion were British), recorded a few years afterward in the memoirs of one of the most senior of them, Col. 'Abdullah al-Tal,[23] and since then confirmed by Avi Shlaim's pioneering research on the topic in the Israeli and British archives.[24] Also stressed were the military weakness of the Arab states and the debilitating internecine divisions among them.[25] Yet other Arab writers underscore the willingness of Zionist factions to resort to ruthless terrorist attacks on civilians, notably at Deir Yasin,[26] and their bombardment of heavily populated urban areas, especially Jaffa and Haifa.

Even if we ignore the proximate causes of these climactic events, if we leave aside the imbalance of power in favor of the Zionists and the plethora of opponents faced by the Palestinians, we are left with the question of why Palestinian society crumbled so rapidly in 1948, why there was not more concerted resistance to the process of dispossession, and why 750,000 people fled their homes in a few months. With the exception of a small number of Palestinian and Arab historians who have touched on the reasons for the Palestinians' own failures and weaknesses in this period,[27] such questions have tended to get relatively little attention in Arab historiography, which has generally focused on the external causes for defeat, rather than examining the internal dynamics of Palestinian society. And while it may be that the better part of the explanation resides in these external causes (the power of the Zionist movement, the wall-to-wall international support that it enjoyed after the revelations of the Holocaust, the weaknesses of the Arab states), combined with factors common to armed conflicts (such as that in dangerous wartime situations, many civilians on the losing side leave their homes, whether in northern France in 1940, in Palestine in 1948, or in South Korea in 1950), there nevertheless remains a need to explore the causes internal to Palestinian society for what happened and why.

There is little question that Palestinian society suffered from deep internal divisions in the decades before 1948, and that these divisions contributed to the debacle of that year, although the most important cleavages may not have been those that were most apparent to external observers, and the obvious ones may not have been as serious as appeared. Regarding the rivalry between the dominant faction led by the Husaynis and that led by the Nashashibis, both powerful Jerusalem families, for example, a well-informed French diplomat in Jerusalem in the early 1930s commented that key figures in the Nashashibi faction were subsidized by the Zionists, and that the "opposition" posed by the Nashashibis to the man who was to become the paramount Palestinian leader empowered by the British, the Grand Mufti of Palestine, Hajj Amin al-Husayni, "thus has no financial power, no moral values and has no Islamic significance whatsoever."[28] He added soon afterward that whatever personal differences separated their leaders, members of the two factions "have the same national goals, and are animated by the same hatred of the Jewish newcomer."[29] Thus Palestinian society was divided, but the differences among the elite on which most observers focused may have been less important and less debilitating than others, between generations, between the urban and rural populations, between classes, and between the educated and the illiterate.

In any case, it is futile to try to explain the collapse of Palestinian society in 1948 by means of a simplistic analysis comparing it with the highly cohesive and unified yishuv, relating, through a process of circular reasoning, Palestinian political and military failures to the lack of unity and relative social backwardness of Palestinian society. Such an exercise can and indeed does lead to the denigration of the Palestinians, their society, and their national movement, as backward, inferior, or even nonexistent, all persistent underlying themes in a broad range of popular and "scholarly" writing on the subject.[30] These themes are sadly still all too present in much Western, and especially American, public discourse about the Palestinians.

Comparing the Incomparable

Examinations of the troubled history of Palestine before 1948 frequently compare Palestinian Arab society with the burgeoning Jewish community in Palestine, the yishuv. This is especially the case where the events leading up to the 1948 war are concerned, but these comparisons are common for the entire period before 1948, and more infrequently, thereafter. Among the indices commonly compared are the two societies' respective levels of economic development, the growth of their political and cultural institutions, their ideological cohesion, and their military capabilities. These comparisons can be found in the social scientific literature and in historical accounts, as well as in popular treatments of both societies and of the conflict between them.[31] The rationale for making such comparisons between the two communities is obvious: until 1948, they uneasily shared the country and were in increasingly fierce competition with one another. In that year, they finally and formally became two distinct entities, as one of them, after May 15, organized as the nascent state of Israel, decisively bested the other, the Palestinian people, establishing demographic dominance in Palestine, control over most of its land, and a sovereign, independent state. In so doing, Israel succeeded in instituting effective hegemony over Palestine that has lasted until the present day, and that has so far been instrumental in preventing the creation of a Palestinian state.

Engaging in some sort of comparison of the two communities before 1948 is therefore both necessary and worthwhile, if one is careful not to ignore crucial external factors, especially foreign political, military, and economic support. This is a particularly important consideration where a quintessentially transnational movement such as Zionism is concerned. Both communities in confrontation in Palestine had important links with communities outside the country. However, only one, the yishuv, and the Zionist movement that represented it, in consequence received powerful external support, both from many of its coreligionists elsewhere and from the greatest imperial power of the day, as well as from the League of Nations.

By contrast, the Palestinians were largely bereft of significant, practical external support. This was true although they enjoyed the increasingly strong sympathy of public opinion in the surrounding Arab countries: indeed, that popular sympathy in 1936–39 and 1947–48 produced numerous volunteers willing to fight alongside the Palestinians. This was mildly ironic, since manpower was not one of the Palestinians' pressing needs, and it translated into little in the way of arms, funds, or effective international diplomatic support.[32] The lack of such practical outside assistance was not surprising, since until well after 1948 most Arab countries were still under colonial rule. Most of those that were nominally independent in 1948 remained subject to neocolonial forms of control and foreign military occupation: British troops remained in Egypt, Iraq, and Jordan until the 1950s, and French troops were in Syria and Lebanon until 1946. The other two, Saudi Arabia and Yemen, were hardly organized as modern states. All other parts of the Arab world, from Morocco, Algeria, and Tunisia to Libya and the Sudan, as well as South Yemen, Oman, and the other four countries of the Gulf, were still fully subject to direct or indirect colonial rule.

Needless to say, the colonial powers, in particular Great Britain and France, did their best to prevent the Arab peoples under their control from supporting the Palestinians. Thus, the French archives for the interwar period are replete with cases in which the Foreign Ministry in Paris or officials in Morocco, Algeria, or Tunisia prevented the sending of funds from North African Muslims to Palestine, or the sending of emissaries from the Maghribi community (of North African origins) in Palestine to North Africa to request aid, for example after the 1929 Wailing Wall disturbances. In contrast, the French authorities allowed considerable sums to be raised for the yishuv among the large Jewish communities of North Africa, and themselves often transferred the funds immediately to Palestine, while Zionist representatives from Palestine were permitted to travel to French North Africa with little hindrance for these and other purposes.[33]

The two sides were thus in very different positions as far as external support was concerned. If one avoids the pitfalls of glib comparisons, however, careful examination of the similarities and differences between the two societies can be particularly revealing in understanding what happened and why during the crucial period beginning in the 1930s, which witnessed a growing disparity in power between them and a decisive shift in favor of the yishuv. At the outset of the fateful decade of the 1930s—during which Palestine was effectively lost to its indigenous population, although the final denouement came only in the late 1940s—the Jewish population of Palestine amounted to only 17.8 percent of the total. Indeed, this proportion had been declining slightly for several years, in spite of unstinting external financial support. For several years at the end of the 1920s and early 1930s, annual Jewish immigration to Palestine came to only a few thousand, an insignificant figure in a total population of over 1 million, especially given that the Arab birth rate was much higher than that of the Jewish community.[34] By the end of the 1930s, however, after the rise to power of Hitler spurred the annual arrival of many tens of thousands of refugees fleeing persecution in Germany and elsewhere in Europe, Palestine's Jewish population rose to more than 30 percent of the total. The year 1935 alone, the high point of Jewish immigration before 1948, witnessed over sixty thousand Jewish immigrants, as many as the country's entire Jewish population in 1919.

The Palestinian Arabs and the yishuv were acutely aware that the outcome of the struggle between them depended largely on which one would win the "demographic battle." This led both to pay extraordinary attention to questions related to immigration. Without massive immigration the Zionist movement could not hope to claim majority status, dominate the Palestinians demographically, and build a Jewish national home in Palestine. Farsighted Zionist leaders such as David Ben-Gurion realized that the massive wave of immigration to Palestine sparked by the Nazis' rise to power in the early 1930s finally provided the critical demographic mass that would soon make it possible for the Zionist movement to achieve absolute Jewish hegemony and sovereignty over the entire country. He stated at the time that he could understand Arab fears: "immigration at the rate of 60,000 a year means a Jewish state in all Palestine."[35] Dr. Wolfgang von Weisl, a representative of the Zionist Revisionist movement, the leading rivals to Ben-Gurion's Zionist Labour Party, Mapai, said much the same thing to a senior French official in 1935: after only a few more years of immigration at the current rate of sixty thousand per year, a Jewish state in all of Palestine and Jordan would be possible, it could not be seriously harmed by the Arabs, and would be "strong enough to defend itself all by itself."[36]

Such an outcome was impossible to foresee when the Jewish population of Palestine as a proportion of the total population actually declined in the late 1920s and early 1930s.[37] Economic difficulties in Palestine, followed by the Great Depression of 1929, together with other factors, led to a decrease in immigration rates and the emigration of many Jews from Palestine during this period. The resulting wave of pessimism affected even some of the most stalwart Zionist leaders.[38] But when the immigration wave of the mid-1930s, which was accompanied by a major inflow of capital brought by German Jewish refugees fleeing Nazi Germany, reached Palestine, the situation changed dramatically. Thereafter, the possibility that they could be outnumbered in their own country came to be a growing concern for the Palestinians, even as that same outcome promised security, victory, and absolute sovereignty to the Zionists. Equally important, during the 1930s the Jewish sector of Palestine's economy came to have the larger share of the country's national income: by 1933 the part of the economy controlled by the considerably smaller Jewish community had already grown bigger than that belonging to the Arabs, although the disparity between them did not widen much further until 1948.[39]

Comparisons between the two communities before 1948 are useful beyond comprehending the course of the conflict between them, including understanding some aspects of each side's political, economic, and social development.[40] However, these comparisons are far less useful in other ways, and indeed they can be quite misleading, for reasons that are often ignored, such as the incommensurability of many things being compared. Five main factors of incommensurability seem particularly important in understanding the two societies' subsequent trajectories.

The first and perhaps most marked difference between Arabs and Jews in Palestine before 1948 was economic. It can best be understood in terms of capital investment, and in particular in terms of capital inflow per capita. According to the Israeli scholar Zeev Sternhell, during the entire decade of the 1920s, "the annual inflow of Jewish capital was on average 41.5% larger than the Jewish net domestic product (NDP). . . . Its ratio to NDP did not fall below 33% in any of the pre–World War II years and was kept at about 15% in all but one year since 1941."[41] By another calculation, the contributions of American Jews alone to the Zionist project until 1948 totaled well over $375 million,[42] a considerable sum when one considers that in the 1930s the average national income of the Jewish sector of the economy was $75 million. For a Jewish population that was less than two hundred thousand in 1930, and that by 1948 had barely reached six hundred thousand, these were phenomenal absolute, relative, and per capita rates of capital inflow.

In consequence of this massive inflow of capital, and the concomitant arrival of skilled immigrants, the Jewish sector of the Palestinian economy grew extraordinarily rapidly. During the quarter century between 1922 and 1947, it maintained an *annual* growth rate of 13.2 percent. By contrast, the Arab sector of the economy grew at less than half that rate during the same period: by the much less spectacular (but still respectable) figure of 6.5 percent annually.[43] This translated into an annual growth rate in real income per capita over these twenty-five years—including the Great Depression—of 3.6 percent for the Arabs and 4.8 percent for the Jews.[44] This meant that during the Mandate, while the Arab economy of Palestine had a vigorous average growth rate, the Jewish economy had one of the highest sustained growth rates in the world. Put in other terms, and considering the respective assets and starting points of the two economies, the result of these considerable capital and skilled-labor inflows and related disparities was that in relative terms one society was well off and the other remained comparatively poor. Thus in 1936, per capita national income in the Jewish sector was LP (Palestinian pounds) 44; in the Arab sector it was LP 17.[45] Thereafter the broad disparity in per capita income stayed about the same, with individuals in the Jewish sector enjoying on average 2.6 times as much income as those in the Arab sector.[46]

Beyond these major economic inequalities, there was a second related set of perhaps even more extreme disparities between the Arab and Jewish sectors: these lay in the sphere of what might be termed human capital. This was notably the case in terms of literacy, education, and technical and professional training, in all of which the Arab sector suffered from serious deficiencies by comparison with the Jewish community, especially when one considers that the latter came to be dominated by relatively well-educated new Jewish immigrants from Europe, who became the overwhelming majority of the population of the yishuv during the Mandate period. According to the 1931 census, the last such complete enumeration before the end of the Mandate, only about 22 percent of Palestinian Arabs were literate, as against 86 percent of the country's Jewish population.[47] Even though Arab literacy rates rose markedly over the following decade and a half, the gap in this regard between the two communities remained wide. By the end of the Mandate, according to the best existing figures, while 77 percent of the Jewish school-age population (ages five to nineteen) received schooling,[48] 44.5 percent of school-age Arab children were in school.[49] The latter figure in fact represented a relatively high proportion for a Middle Eastern country like Palestine at this time. As one of the most astute students of the subject, the respected Israeli economist Jacob Metzer, has noted: "Arab school enrollment... though low, was not 'too low.'... Compared with other countries in the same income range, including... Egypt and Turkey, the Arabs of Palestine did rather well."[50] This relatively creditable performance paled, however, by comparison with the extraordinarily high level of education among Jews in Palestine.

The disparity in education in particular, and in human capital in general, was not simply a function of the fact that as time went on, immigration during the Mandate had the effect of swelling the yishuv with a growing literate population. Beyond this, a high proportion of these newcomers were young and active, with a generally high level of education, and a relatively high and widespread level of technical aptitude, as was to be expected given the central and eastern European countries from which most of them came, and the traditionally high regard for education among Jews. This can be seen from a number of other indicators, such as the number of physicians per ten thousand people. The ratio among the Jewish population of Palestine in 1940 of 40 doctors per 10,000 people was the highest recorded in the world at the time (Switzerland, the next highest, had only 17 per 10,000), whereas by contrast, the ratio among the Arabs of 2.4 per 10,000 was much lower, although it was higher than the most advanced countries in the region: Egypt (2.2), Iraq (1.7), and Turkey (0.9).[51]

The disparity in doctors was a product of profound deficiencies in education in the Middle East as a whole by comparison with Europe, where most immigrants originated. While there had been extensive progress in education in the late Ottoman period, and that progress continued during the Mandate, the development of a modern Palestinian educational system started from a very low base.[52] Arab society in Palestine thus suffered from severe inherited educational disadvantages. Beyond this, it was primarily rural and therefore had not been extensively exposed to modern technology. In terms of the United Nations Development Program's "Human Development Index," which is meant to be a "comprehensive, comparative measure of a society's all-inclusive state of development," around 1939 Palestine's Jews placed fifteenth out of thirty-six countries measured, behind Belgium and Finland and ahead of Czechoslovakia and Italy, while the Palestinian Arabs placed thirtieth, falling behind Brazil and Peru, but ahead of Egypt (thirty-third) and Turkey (thirty-fifth).[53] In light of the advantages that the yishuv enjoyed in the realm of human capital, it can be imagined what a benefit its phenomenally high ratio of capital investment per capita gave it by comparison with Palestinian Arab society, a benefit reflected in the exceedingly high growth rate of the Jewish economy already mentioned.

A third factor of incommensurability between these two communities is that while before 1948, Palestinian society was predominantly rural, the yishuv was always overwhelmingly urban. This was the case notwithstanding the enormous emphasis that Zionist ideology and propaganda placed on rural settlement, and on an almost mystical connection with the land; relatively few Jews lived in rural areas during the Mandate period, before, or since. The highest proportion reached by the rural sector of the total Jewish population of Palestine before 1948 was under 27 percent.[54] Notwithstanding this lopsided imbalance in favor of the urban population, there was clearly an important ideological purpose to the attachment of the Zionist movement to a "return to the soil" and to control of the land. Beyond this, the Zionist fixation on the land also had a crucial strategic motivation, for the establishment of heavily fortified rural settlements along several major geographic axes was instrumental in enabling the Zionist movement to take control of most of Palestine during the fighting of 1947–49. In the words of Kenneth Stein, by 1939 these settlements already provided "a geographic nucleus for a Jewish state... in Palestine."[55]

Ideology and strategy aside, the Jewish population of Palestine during the Mandate (and afterward) was principally concentrated in the urban and semi-urban regions of coastal Jaffa/Tel Aviv and Haifa, and Jerusalem. It constituted a majority in each of these three urban centers, which (to revert briefly to strategy) ultimately helped give it military control of the country's three largest cities and of both its main ports. By contrast, Palestinian society was, and had always been, overwhelmingly rural. The events of 1948 were to change that reality drastically, turning most Palestinians into refugees, and ultimately city dwellers—or rather refugee camp dwellers, which in practice for most of them meant residence in some of the poorest quarters of the cities of Palestine and the rest of the Levant (the eastern Mediterranean coast). In the event, the strategic advantages that might have accrued to the Palestinians from their being spread out over so much of the country were never realized, as we shall see in Chapter 4.

Even at the end of the Mandate, by which time a significant shift of the Arab population from country to city had taken place, Palestinian society was still predominantly rural: only 32.7 percent of the country's Arab population lived in cities and large towns, by contrast with the Jewish population, which was 76.2 percent urban.[56] The related disparities in terms of occupation were also great: while only 13 percent of the Jewish population was dependent on agriculture (indicating incidentally that a large portion of the nonurban Jewish population was engaged in services and industry rather than agriculture), about half of the Arab population was involved in agricultural pursuits.[57] In terms of communications, military mobilization and indoctrination, and many other factors, this concentration of the Jewish population in urban areas proved to be a great advantage, as it was strategically during the fighting of 1948, when the small yishuv benefited from being concentrated on interior lines, fighting first against the Palestinians and later against the more formidable Arab armies.

The fourth factor of incommensurability is the wide disparities between the politics of the two communities. All observers have agreed on the essentially European nature of Zionist ideology and of the major political currents within the yishuv. This contrasted strikingly with the diverse range of local, Arab, Islamic, European, and other sources influencing the political trends found within Palestinian Arab society, which in this respect was very similar to other societies in the Middle East. As Zeev Sternhell and others have convincingly shown, in the development of national identity and of "ethnic, religious and cultural particularity," Israel was "not dissimilar to other states in Central and Eastern Europe."[58]

Moreover, the great majority of the population of the yishuv in effect constituted a self-selecting sample, united by the Zionist ideology that had brought most of them to Palestine. An overwhelming majority of the Jews leaving eastern Europe in the late nineteenth and early twentieth centuries were non-Zionist, and had made the conscious choice to avoid Palestine, with most of them preferring the United States as a destination. Thus, of the 3.3 million Jews estimated to have emigrated from Europe between 1881 and 1939, 2.6 million went to the United States, while less than a sixth of that number, 420,000, went to Palestine (and many of those later left). The bulk of this latter group came to Palestine only after the Immigration Act of 1924 effectively closed America's doors to further large-scale immigration from countries other than those of northern Europe.[59] Nevertheless, most Jews who came to Palestine, at least before the horrors of the Nazi persecutions left many hundreds of thousands with no choice, had done so because they wanted to, and because they shared the Zionist ideology and aspirations of the yishuv. This self-regulating winnowing-out process made for a Jewish society in Palestine that was remarkably homogeneous at this early stage, at least in ideological terms.

By contrast, as I have argued at length elsewhere, the sense of Palestinian identity that emerged during approximately the same period as did modern Zionism included elements of Ottoman, Arab, Islamic and Christian, local Palestinian, and European ideologies and thought.[60] While a certain synthesis of these elements eventually emerged to constitute modern Palestinian nationalist political consciousness, Palestinian politics nevertheless remained considerably less homogeneous ideologically than politics within the yishuv. The differences between the kinds of influences on Zionism and Palestinian nationalism could not be more obvious than in the realm of ideology, although both were ostensibly national movements. These disparities could be seen along the entire spectrum of the politics of the era, whether with regard to the divergent impact of communism, fascism, or any other ideology on the two communities, or in terms of phenomena that were unique to either polity. Thus, eastern and central European ideas about nationalism and socialism had a major impact on the yishuv; the impact of nationalism was less widespread among Palestinians, but those affected by it tended to be influenced by western European models. Communism had quite a different impact on both societies, although it was relatively minor in both cases.[61] The political influence of Islam was naturally felt only among Palestinians.

Along with these ideological and political differences, and the profound social and economic dissimilarities in which they were rooted, came great disparities in types of political formations and organizational capabilities. Put simply, Palestinian society during the Mandate period was completely different from the entirely new society being constructed out of a mainly European immigrant population on an ideological basis by the Zionist movement, and the political trends in the two societies reflected that enormous difference.

This brings us to the fifth and last factor of incommensurability between the two societies, illustrating why comparison between them should only be undertaken with great care, and with due regard for the specificities of each. Perhaps the most striking of these specificities to contemporary observers were the profound social differences, notably the divergent class structures and social formations of each society. On the one hand, the yishuv was for the most part an entirely new, largely secular society (there existed as well an "old yishuv" composed of Oriental Jews—originally from different parts of the Muslim world—and religious Ashkenazim—European Jews—both of which groups had long been in Palestine, some of them with family roots going back many centuries). This new society was drawn primarily from the secular elements of the Jewish communities of Europe, albeit with some Oriental Jewish and religious admixtures. It was composed of a relatively developed capitalist class, powerful para-state institutions dominated by the Zionist movement, and strong unions, cooperative movements, and socialist-oriented (albeit heavily subsidized) agricultural settlements, with the whole relatively free of strong social tensions.[62]

On the other hand, Palestinian society was generally quite similar in most respects to those of the surrounding Arab countries. It was dominated by a sizable landholding class, which was largely made up of traditional notable families that had held high religious offices and served as intermediaries between the Ottoman authorities and the population,[63] but increasingly also included new merchant entrepreneurs who had purchased land with their newfound wealth. It also included small but growing industrialist and merchant groups and professional elites, a small and rapidly expanding urban working class, and, by far the largest group, a mass of peasants, most of whom owned some land. These socioeconomic differences in turn produced greater income disparities on the Arab side by comparison with the relatively egalitarian yishuv, although the egalitarian rhetoric of Zionism was not always reflected in practice.[64]

Another major difference between the two societies was the contrast between their starkly different ethnic makeups. On the one hand, there was the highly diverse yishuv, which during the Mandate period came to be constituted mainly of immigrants from dozens of countries (most of whom came to share a single vernacular language and culture only after they arrived in Palestine), and on the other there was the generally quite homogeneous ethnic, cultural, and linguistic composition of Palestinian society. Thus, ironically, Palestinian society, which was divided internally by political and social differences and included both Muslims and Christians, was highly homogeneous in ethnic, cultural, and linguistic terms, while the more ideologically and politically unified Jewish society was much more diverse in terms of the places of origin and original languages and cultures of most of its members.

That Palestinian Arab society was radically different from, and had not developed to the same degree or in the same ways as, the growing Jewish society with which it uneasily shared the country should be obvious. The consequence of this disparity in terms of the capacity of the two polities for social, political, and, ultimately, military mobilization should be equally obvious. All the gauges of the economic, social, and political advancement of the yishuv—the massive import of capital, the inflow of highly skilled human capital, the community's predominantly urban nature, its high degree of ideological homogeneity, its unique social makeup and governing structures—when taken together, indicate its capacity for generating considerable state power. This capacity was fully realized in 1948 and afterward, right up to the present day. Small though the Jewish population of Palestine was, and recent though the inception of the modern yishuv had been, by early 1948 it already contained within it many of the institutions characteristic of a fully developed modern society, headed by a highly developed state structure.

As a result of the untiring efforts of the yishuv, the international Zionist movement, and Great Britain, which for at least two decades faithfully carried out its mandatory responsibilities to build up the Jewish national home, these institutions included, notably, a completely formed government bureaucracy and representative institutions, together with the core of a modern European-style regular army. By 1948, all had grown far beyond the embryonic stage, and indeed were fully ready to be born into independent statehood. As was clear from the one-sided outcome of the conflict between the two peoples in 1948, Palestinian society had not developed in a similar fashion. In fact it generated neither a state structure, nor representative institutions, nor an army to match those of the yishuv, with disastrous consequences for its capabilities when the crisis of 1948 broke.

This discussion makes clear why the competing Arab and Jewish communities in Palestine during the Mandate period should be compared only with great care. There is another context in which to place the Palestinians, however, that yields a less problematic comparison. This context might further our understanding of why the Palestinians performed as they did in the face of the challenge from the yishuv and the British mandatory power, and allow us to accurately assess their performance.

The Palestinians and the Arab World

For a clearer understanding of Palestinian Arab society during this period, fruitful comparisons can in fact be made between it and the societies of neighboring Arab countries like Lebanon, Syria, and Jordan, and even with much larger and more distant ones like Egypt and Iraq. Comparisons with non-Arab Turkey and Iran are occasionally useful as well. Here again, the reasons should be obvious. Over at least the past few centuries, Palestine had always been intimately linked economically, administratively, and in social terms to the surrounding regions, and in particular to the other parts of *bilad al-sham* (Greater Syria), what is today Syria, Lebanon, Jordan, Israel, and the occupied Palestinian territories. Like them, for four centuries it had been part of the Ottoman Empire, a powerful state that strongly influenced many aspects of the history and social makeup of the region. In spite of the myriad differences among Middle Eastern countries, Palestine's level of economic development, its social structure and patterns of land tenure, and the political and ideological trends that affected it were all broadly similar to those in neighboring Arab countries, particularly those immediately adjacent to it to the north and east. It was similar as well in some respects to other Middle Eastern states. In developing a meaningful comparative context for Palestine, these are manifestly the countries to examine.

One reason that comparisons with neighboring Arab societies are particularly useful is that it is often claimed that Palestinian society before 1948 was incomplete or distinctively flawed in some fashion, and that this largely explained its rapid collapse in 1948 during the decisive phase of its conflict with Zionism. The unspoken implication of this allegation—sometimes explicitly expressed —is that the Palestinians did not have the preconditions for a successful national effort and were therefore doomed to lose in a conflict with a Jewish society that, events have amply proven, did have these preconditions. Leaving aside for the moment the question of precisely why the Palestinians were so overmatched in 1948, it is worth looking at the degree to which Palestinian society had developed before 1948 in comparison with its Arab neighbors.

Most of the Arab countries immediately surrounding Palestine received their independence only a few years before Israel did, and by 1948 already possessed relatively complex governmental structures with many of the features characteristic of an independent state, including ministries dealing with a range of internal matters, some representative institutions, and military forces. All of them had developed these structures well before they won their nominal freedom from their French and British colonial masters in the years leading up to 1948. In the case of Egypt, these institutions had been in place since even before the British occupation of 1882. Although Palestine was in this important respect highly dissimilar to these newly independent Arab countries, it can still be fruitfully compared with them in the social, economic, and cultural spheres, as well as in terms of the institutions of what is today fashionably called civil society. Such a comparison can help us understand why Palestinian society was less successful than other, otherwise similar, Arab societies in meeting the challenges of the mandatory period, although the Palestinians obviously faced challenges of a completely different order than those facing their Arab neighbors.

Any serious attempt to compare Palestinian and other Arab societies in the interwar period comes up against a complicating factor: the economic and social data available for Palestine is considerably more extensive and detailed than that which exists for most other Arab countries, partly because the Palestinian Arabs were the majority population of a country dominated by a colonial power practicing direct rule. More data was thus collected in Palestine than in other nearby Arab countries, where British and French control was more indirect.[65] It is nevertheless possible to make illuminating comparisons between Palestine and its Middle Eastern neighbors in a number of areas, if one takes careful account of the imprecision of some of the data. One such area is literacy. Here Palestine was clearly in advance of some other countries of the region. Thus the literacy of Muslim males over the age of seven in Palestine, Egypt, and Turkey was 25.1 percent, 20.3 percent, and 17.4 percent, respectively, at about the same time in the middle of the Mandate period.[66] Given the existence in both Palestine and Egypt of a large number of Christians, who as a general rule had higher literacy rates due to superior education thanks in part to the spread of missionary schools, the overall literacy rates of these two countries, including both Muslims and Christians, compared even more favorably with those in Turkey, whose population was overwhelmingly Muslim, than these figures would indicate. The abysmally low rates of female literacy in all three countries (only 3.3 percent of Muslim females in Palestine were literate in 1931) brought down the overall totals. As late as 1947, in spite of massive efforts to expand and improve education in the interim, only 22.8 percent of all Egyptian adults were literate,[67] a figure matched by Palestinian adults sixteen years earlier, in 1931.[68] In Syria and Lebanon, male literacy rates were higher than in other countries of the region: in 1932 Syria's was 32 percent and that of Lebanon a very high 53 percent.[69]

Another area where comparison is useful is education. We have seen that in Palestine by 1947 nearly half the Arab school-age population was enrolled in schools. In that year, 147,000 of an estimated

Arab school-age population of 330,000 (or 44.5 percent) were being educated in government and private schools, with 103,000 in the former and the rest in the latter.[70] While these figures may seem modest by recent standards in many countries of universal or near-universal schooling, they represent a significant improvement in little over two decades: just over 20 percent of Arab school-age children were in school in 1922–23. And in the towns in 1945–46, 85 percent of boys and 65 percent of girls were in school. The problem was in the countryside, where, as we have seen, the large majority of the Arab population lived, and where only 65 percent of boys and 10 percent of girls were in school. These very low numbers were in large part a function of the fact that only 432 of about 800 Arab villages had schools.[71] It is nevertheless striking that by the end of the Palestine Mandate a majority of Arab boys in both city and countryside, and of Arab girls in the cities, was in school.

In Egypt there was a major expansion of the educational system in the same period, during which time education became a national issue, in view of the reluctance of the British authorities since the time of Lord Cromer, who effectively ruled Egypt from 1883 until 1907, to allow significant expenditure on education. School enrollment went from 324,000 in 1913 to 942,000 in 1932, but even with further expansion by education-minded national governments in the late 1930s, by the end of World War II Egypt's schools were able to accommodate only well under half of the school-age population.[72] The situation of public education in Syria compared even more unfavorably with that in Palestine. In 1938 there were 58,867 students in 472 state schools in Syria, while in Palestine 402 state schools had 49,400 Arab pupils.[73] The Syrian numbers compare very poorly with those in Palestine, given that the Arab population of Palestine was less than half that of Syria. Moreover, these figures do not reflect the proportionately larger number of Palestinians than Syrians in foreign and missionary schools.

With respect to the press, a realm related to and dependent on literacy and education, Palestine also compared favorably with some of its neighbors. Although there are no fully reliable circulation figures for any Middle Eastern country for this period, the press obviously grew and expanded in direct relation to the expansion of literacy and education. In spite of its relatively small population, Palestine supported a remarkable number of newspapers and other periodicals. Many were ephemeral or had a restricted number of readers, although the audience for a newspaper was often larger than might be imagined, and often considerably higher than the number of subscribers, because newspapers were commonly read out loud in homes, coffee shops, and other private and public gathering places, and were passed from hand to hand. In an age before the invention of the Internet and television, and in a part of the world where radios were still not to be found in every home, and where literacy was less common, newspapers were a far more important source of news, information, and entertainment, and were certainly considered more important, than they are today.[74]

The number of newspapers and periodicals established in Palestine from World War I to the end of the Mandate was striking: it totaled 200, with 48 founded by 1929, 85 in the 1930s, and 67 between 1940 and 1948.[75] By way of contrast, in Syria's two main cities, Damascus, and Aleppo, during the same years of the Mandate, only a total of 123 titles appeared.[76] The number of papers published in both Egypt and Lebanon was certainly greater than the total for Palestine, and the quality was often higher, due to the large market of the former and the sophisticated level of the journalism in both Cairo and Beirut. Even before 1914, Beirut and Cairo had become the preeminent centers for Arabic-language journalism. In Beirut and other parts of what was to become Lebanon, 143 periodicals had been founded by 1914,[77] and no less than 263 in Beirut alone in the interwar period.[78] Nevertheless, the Palestinian press generally compared quite favorably with that in most other Arab countries in this period, as any reader of leading papers like *Filastin* (Palestine) and *al-Karmil* (Mount Carmel) could attest.[79]

One last set of figures can be provided: these are economic

statistics. Unfortunately, it is difficult to make good comparisons here, since the nature of the existing figures is so different, and often incommensurate, where data exists at all. For Egypt, where the best statistics exist outside of Palestine, estimates of national income for the late 1930s range from LE (Egyptian pounds) 168 to 200 million,[80] while we have seen that the national income of Palestine for 1936 was LP 33 million, of which the Arab sector produced LP 16 million (both the Egyptian and Palestinian pound were at parity with sterling, so the figures are comparable). This amounted to a national income per capita for the Arabs of Palestine of about LP 17.4, as against a range of LE 10.5–12.5 per capita for Egypt in 1937, at a time when Egypt's population was 13.8 million.

Although reliable national income estimates for other Arab countries are hard to come by, there is one other set of figures that perhaps provides a yardstick for comparison: government revenue and expenditure. The only trick here is to estimate what share of the revenue and expenditure of the British mandatory government in Palestine should be allocated to each community. This was a vexed issue during the Mandate, with the relatively wealthy yishuv claiming that they provided a disproportionate share of revenue, while the Arabs (who did not enjoy either the para-state services of the quasi-governmental Jewish Agency established under the terms of the Mandate or the yishuv's lavish capital inflows) benefited from a disproportionate share of expenditures. These numbers are nevertheless of some comparative utility.

Government revenue in Palestine grew from LP 2.45 million in 1930–31 to LP 4.64 million in 1936–37, and to LP 8.9 million in 1942–43.[81] Expenditure in the same years totaled LP 2.56, 6.07, and 10.25 million. Even if one assumes that more than half of both revenue and expenditure should be allocated to the Jewish sector of the population, the contrast is striking with countries like Iraq, Syria, and Lebanon, whose populations were respectively triple, double, and the same size as that of Arab Palestine. Iraq's revenues were ID (Iraqi dinar) 3.84, 6.02, and 12.00 million and its expenditures ID

3.83, 7.15, and 11.23 million in the same three years (like the Egyptian and Palestinian pounds, the Iraqi dinar was at parity with sterling during this period). Syrian government revenues and expenditures were much smaller: converted into sterling, the former amounted to L 1.24, 1.13, and 2.49 million, with the latter in similar ranges. Lebanon's government was even smaller: its revenue and expenditure were about half those of Syria.

These numbers relate to a period of just over a decade, when overall the Arab sector of the economy produced about half of Palestine's national income (although its share was much larger than that of the Jewish sector at the beginning and somewhat smaller at the end). During that time, the Palestinian government raised far more money per capita from, and spent far more money per capita on, its Arab population than did that of Iraq. Moreover, in absolute terms it raised and spent more than those of Syria and Lebanon by multiples ranging from two to ten over these eleven years, from 1930–31 until 1942–43. By another set of calculations for the year 1935, government spending per capita in Palestine was more than double that in Syria and Iraq.[82]

The size of government may be less likely to be considered an index of progress today than it once was, and it is certainly no measure of the growth of what is usually understood by the term "civil society." In the Palestinian case this is particularly true, given that from 22 percent to 33 percent of expenditure during these years was on "security."[83] The higher overall per capita expenditure of the Palestinian mandatory government with respect to that of the governments in Syria and Iraq was matched by its relatively higher per capita spending on "public security," even in the relatively calm year of 1935.[84] Throughout the Mandate, but in the late 1930s during the Arab revolt in particular, "security" generally meant the forcible suppression of the aspirations of the Arab majority in the interest of the aims of the Jewish minority.[85] While it could be argued that public security in all three countries reflected colonial interests more than those of the peoples involved, this was most blatantly the case for the Arabs of Palestine, most of whom received little or no benefit from this expenditure on British-controlled security forces, while often suffering great harm from them.[86] By contrast, at least some spending on security in Iraq and Syria involved the establishment of law and order and the creation of national military, police, and judiciary institutions that were maintained after independence, and may be seen as having served to further some Iraqi or Syrian "national" interest.

Nevertheless, when these figures on the money raised and spent by government are taken together with the figures cited earlier on national income, the press, and education and literacy, a clear picture emerges. This is of a Palestinian Arab society and economy that were certainly as fully developed as those of any neighboring Arab country in the same era, and more developed than some. By some indices Palestine was indeed better off: thus in 1935 it exported more than either Syria or Iraq, and while slightly more than half of these exports were produced by the Jewish sector of the economy, it should be remembered that in that year the Arab population of Palestine was less than 1 million, while both Syria and Iraq had more than 4 million people.[87] A myriad of subjective observations about the relative general prosperity of Palestinian Arab society, or the high standard of Palestinian journalism, or the excellent quality of the Palestinian educational system, as visitors from other Arab countries perceived them, support such quantitatively derived conclusions, for all the flaws and the many gaps that exist in the data.[88]

None of this in any way explains what happened to Palestinian society in 1948. It should, however, help to dispose of the canard that this was in some measure a less than complete society, or the suggestion that it was a society irremediably mired in social backwardness. Palestinian society was certainly overmatched by the European standards of the yishuv in a variety of economic, social, and organizational realms. It definitely could not match the yishuv's truly exceptional levels of capital investments per capita and human capital inflow, which were among the highest in the world at that time. Nonetheless, it was manifestly as advanced as any other society in the region, and considerably more so than several. As I have tried to show elsewhere, by the early years of the Mandate the Palestinians had already developed a modern national consciousness, which had taken hold among important segments of the population. Nevertheless, as the climactic decade of the 1930s went on, in spite of the remarkable national effort embodied in their abortive revolt of 1936–39, the Palestinians certainly fell short of the high standards of political cohesion and advanced political organization exhibited by the Zionist movement.

During this critical decade, the yishuv managed to surmount the grave challenges posed by the flood into Palestine of Jewish immigrants fleeing the Nazis, the Palestinian revolt of 1936–39, and the shock of Great Britain's 1939 White Paper, which for the first time placed a significant limit on British support for Zionism.[89] For reasons I will explore later, the Palestinians did not succeed in surmounting the related and graver challenges they faced during this decade from Britain, Zionism, and internal Palestinian and inter-Arab divisions.

These failures notwithstanding, by comparison with neighboring Arab societies, Palestinian society before 1948 was relatively coherent and reasonably developed in some respects. By the standards of its time and place, it could be seen as at least a half-full glass, even as by the far more demanding standards of comparison, competition, and conflict with the rapidly growing yishuv it may have appeared less than half empty. What the Palestinians lacked, in other words, was neither a sense of identity nor a vibrant economy and civil society. What they apparently did lack, however, was the capacity for social and political mobilization sufficient to overcome the challenges they faced, and the support for this process that a state or para-state structures would have provided.

2

The Palestinians and the British Mandate

The Mandate's Iron Cage

Comparisons of the constitutional position of the Palestinians and the Jewish community vis-à-vis the British during the Mandate period often ignore basic realities, just as do economic and social comparisons between them. Thus it is frequently simply assumed that the two sides were in much the same situation as regards the mandatory power, with each enjoying certain advantages and laboring under certain disadvantages. The British contributed mightily to this profound misperception by portraying themselves as dispassionate, evenhanded arbiters between two relatively evenly matched local groups, whose interests they attempted to balance. According to an even more myopic and partisan view, the British are seen to have favored the Arabs over the Zionists throughout most of their thirty-one years of rule over Palestine.[1] These are both completely false depictions of the actual situation. To understand why, it is necessary to look carefully at the complex and unique legal and constitutional framework through which Britain managed its occupation of Palestine. A careful examination of this framework reveals that it constituted a kind of iron cage for the Palestinians, from which they never succeeded in escaping.[2]

The Mandate for Palestine issued by the League of Nations in July 1922 was an internationally recognized document representing the consensus of the great powers of the day as to the disposition of the former Ottoman territory of Palestine. By this time, many of the Arabs of Palestine were already coming to think of themselves in national terms as a people. As I have shown elsewhere, this was only one of their overlapping senses of identity, which included being part of the larger Arab people and of Greater Syria, as well as having other religious, local, and familial identities.[3] In the wake of Great Britain's occupation of their country and the collapse of the Ottoman Empire, of which Palestine had been a part for four centuries, the Palestinians were confronted with a number of unpalatable realities. These included most importantly the fact that the League of Nations Mandate for Palestine, constituting the entire legal basis for the British regime erected in their country (and which was never modified until the demise of the League with the outbreak of World War II), explicitly refrained from mentioning either the Palestinians as a people or their national self-determination. By contrast, the Jewish minority of the population was so recognized. Indeed, it could be argued that the "constitutional" structure of the regime built in Palestine on the basis of the League of Nations Mandate was specifically designed by its British architects to exclude national self-determination for the Arab majority, even while facilitating the same end for the Jewish minority.

The Mandate for Palestine included the entire text of the Balfour Declaration, named for the British foreign secretary, Arthur James Balfour, notably its provisions relating to the establishment in Palestine of a "national home" for the Jewish people. It included six articles (2, 4, 6, 7, 11, and 22) relating to the obligations of the mandatory power to foster and support this endeavor. In both documents, the Palestinians were never once cited by name, whether as Palestinians or as Arabs, and were referred to only as "non-Jewish communities," possessing solely civil and religious rights; their national and political rights were mentioned in neither. By contrast, national rights were ascribed to the "Jewish people," and the League of Nations Mandate made it a solemn responsibility of Great Britain to help the Jews create national institutions. The mandatory power was specifically called upon to extend all possible assistance to the growth and development of this national entity, notably by encouraging Jewish immigration and "close settlement on the land." The tiny Jewish community of Palestine, composing about 10 percent of the country's population at the time, was thereby placed in a distinctly privileged position. By contrast, the Arab majority, constituting 90 percent of Palestine's population, was effectively ignored as a national or political entity. While the Mandate's twenty-eight articles included nine on antiquities, not one related to the Palestinian people per se: they were variously and vaguely defined as a "section of the population," "natives," or "peoples and communities." As far as Great Britain and the League of Nations were concerned, they were definitely *not* a people.[4]

In consequence of the imposition of this peculiar constitutional structure, the Palestinian people and their leaders faced a cruel dilemma throughout the Mandate period. Starting soon after the British occupation, they repeatedly pressed Great Britain to grant them the national rights, notably self-determination, and the political rights, notably representative government, they justifiably considered were their due. They claimed these rights on the basis of the American president Woodrow Wilson's Fourteen Points,[5] Article 4 of the Covenant of the League of Nations,[6] Allied promises to support Arab independence during World War I,[7] and their natural rights as a people. Each time they did so, however, they were told that they were obliged to accept the terms of the Mandate as a precondition for any change in their constitutional position. But these terms denied the Palestinians any of these rights, or at best subordinated them completely to the national rights of the Jewish people. Acceptance of the Mandate by the Palestinians would thus have meant their recognition of the privileged national rights of the Jewish community in what they saw as their own country, and formal acceptance of their own legally subordinate position, indeed of their nonexistence as a people. This was something that the Palestinians felt they could not do without denying their own rights, their own national narrative, and the evidence of their own eyes, which told them that Palestine was an Arab country and belonged to them, and to them alone.

Perfectly illustrating the situation the Palestinians faced, the British colonial secretary, Lord Passfield, meeting with a Palestinian delegation visiting London in May 1930, responded to its demand for a parliament "elected by the people in proportion to their numbers, irrespective of race or creed" as follows:

> Of course, this Parliament as you call it that you ask for, would have to have as its duty the carrying out of the Mandate. . . . the Mandatory power, that is the British government, could not create any council except within the terms of the Mandate and for the purpose of carrying out the Mandate. That is the limit of our power. . . . Would you mind considering our difficulty that we cannot create a Parliament which would not be responsible and feel itself responsible for carrying out the Mandate?[8]

The disingenuousness of Passfield's utterance is not what is most notable about his response.[9] Nor is its illogic, which was manifest to outside observers at the time, such as the veteran French foreign minister Aristide Briand, who wrote in a note on a secret French diplomatic verbatim report of the meeting: "La position de l'Angleterre apparait d'ailleurs comme un comble d'illogisme" (The position of England seems to be the height of illogic).[10] For how could a representative, democratic institution like a parliament be required in effect to negate the rights of the majority that had elected it? A member of the delegation, the mufti, Hajj Amin al-Husayni, tried to explain to Lord Passfield that Palestinian acceptance of a parliament charged with carrying out the terms of the Mandate would be "self murder." Passfield brushed his objections aside and tried to convince his interlocutors to accept an Arab Agency (along the lines of the Jewish Agency, which had been set up in accordance with the terms of the Mandate) instead of an elected representative parliament.[11] Passfield's response is most interesting for showing in the starkest terms the almost inescapable dilemma produced for the Palestinians by the Mandate system fashioned by the British, and the difficulties that the Palestinian leadership of the day faced in trying to cut this formidable Gordian knot.

As with comparisons in the social and economic spheres, it is all too easy for historians who mistakenly start from the false assumption that the two sides were on an equal footing vis-à-vis the British (or even worse, that the British favored the Arabs) to underestimate the extent of these legal and constitutional obstacles to the realization of Palestinian aspirations, and the difficulty of overcoming them. They may also fail to appreciate the tenaciousness and sheer doggedness of British governments throughout most of the Mandate period in resisting the principle of responsible, representative government in Palestine, and any constitutional modification that would have made this possible. From the beginning of the Mandate and until the end of the 1930s, the British obstinately rejected the principle of majority rule, or any measure that would have given a Palestinian Arab majority control over the government of Palestine.

This seemed to change with the White Paper of 1939, whereby, facing the 1936–39 revolt and the looming clouds of World War II, Britain finally accepted that it was simply not possible to suppress the Arab majority in order to make possible the growth of a Jewish majority, such that a "Jewish national home" would mean Zionist domination of Palestine. However, even when the British appeared to grant the form of a concession on this point in the 1939 White Paper, which envisaged an independent Palestine after ten years, the cabinet discussions at which this initiative was decided upon reveal the government of Prime Minister Neville Chamberlain to have been fully intent on withholding the substance of any such concession to the Palestinians. These discussions make it clear that the British intended to make any changes in the system whereby Palestine was governed totally dependent on the consent of a Jewish minority.[12] Of course by the end of the 1930s, the political leadership of the Jewish minority was fully intent on achieving nothing less than independent statehood in as much of Palestine as possible—although Jewish leaders would have preferred and fully intended to try to take all of Palestine for the Jewish state—and were already close to having the means to attain at least their minimal goal.[13]

From November 2, 1917, the date that the Balfour Declaration was issued, over four years before the Mandate for Palestine was granted, Britain was fully committed to the creation of a Jewish "national home" in Palestine, whatever that term meant precisely. The Jewish national home in fact meant quite different things to different British officials at different times, whereas for most Zionists, whatever they may have said for public consumption, it always meant ultimately transforming all of Palestine into a Jewish state.[14] What was fully clear throughout, however, was that successive British governments simply were not prepared to countenance any progress toward Palestinian self-determination, or toward the linked principle of representative government, that would enable the country's overwhelming Arab majority to place meaningful obstacles in the way of the Zionist project. They were committed to holding fast to such a position at least until immigration brought about a Jewish majority, at which stage it would become a moot point and perhaps democracy could be admitted.

There was a fully fleshed out, subtly racist rationale behind this British policy, one that certainly operated for the first part of the Mandate, and perhaps throughout it. It was that the Jews were important, were a people with significance, while the Arabs of Palestine were insignificant, could be ignored, and indeed were not even thought of as a people per se. This was put most clearly by Foreign Secretary Balfour, in a damningly frank confidential 1919 memo that deserves to be far better known: "Zionism, be it right or wrong, good or bad, is rooted in age-long traditions, in present needs, in future hopes, of far greater import than the desires and prejudices of the 700,000 Arabs who now inhabit that ancient land."[15] Note that, in Balfour's view, the "ancient" land of Palestine did not belong to the Arabs who constituted the majority of its population: these Arabs just happened to inhabit the country at that moment in time; and they did not have lofty "traditions," "needs," or "hopes" like the Jews; by contrast, they had the far baser "desires and prejudices." Above all, they were not a people. In view of these revealing words, one can easily identify the source of the discriminatory language of the famous declaration that bears Balfour's name, and of the Mandate document that he helped to negotiate.

To carry out this policy of rank discrimination against the Palestinian Arab majority, it was necessary for the British to resort to means that were unusual even for the leading colonial power of the day, which ruled over a huge area of the globe via a broad range of systems of direct and indirect rule, and had vast experience in thwarting the will of majorities in different countries. In order to protect the establishment of a Jewish national home in Palestine against the opposition of the majority of the population, the British were obliged to keep the reins of central state power in the mandatory administration entirely in their hands, even as they allowed the yishuv virtually total internal autonomy. This autonomy included full-fledged representative institutions, internationally recognized diplomatic representation abroad via the Jewish Agency, and control of most of the other apparatuses of internal self-government, amounting to a para-state within, dependent upon, but separate from, the mandatory state.

Palestine thus represented a striking anomaly among the Class A League of Nations mandates. These territories were all former parts of the Ottoman Empire that had been provisionally recognized in 1919 by Article 4 of the League's Covenant as "independent states," deemed to be in need solely of a period of external advice and assistance until they could take their place as full-fledged members of the international system. This process was completed with Iraq in 1932, when it attained independence and joined the League of Nations, and belatedly with the other Class A mandates (with the exception of Palestine): Lebanon and Syria obtained their independence in 1943, with Transjordan in 1946, and with Israel in 1948. Although Article 4 of the League of Nations Covenant was cited in the preamble to the Palestine Mandate, its full implications for the governance of the country were otherwise ignored in the rest of that document, as they were in the policies that the British followed in Palestine in succeeding decades.

A comparison with countries in similar situations would be useful here. For most of the interwar period, the other Class A mandates were governed under their British and French high commissioners by a king and prime minister in Iraq, an amir and prime minister in Transjordan, and presidents and prime ministers in Syria and Lebanon. Even though the individuals in these positions were often no more than figureheads, they had at least nominal authority, and sometimes much more than that. In principle, they represented the sovereignty of these "independent states," which were supposedly only temporarily under foreign tutelage. In Palestine, by way of contrast, the British high commissioner was the highest, indeed the sole, source of authority in the land (although the Jewish Agency had a status guaranteed by the Mandate itself), there was no parliament or any other elected nationwide representative body, and no cabinet, nor were there any responsible Arab officials. The status of Palestine in this respect was thus anomalous even by comparison with many other parts of the vast formal and informal British Empire of the interwar period.

The Palestinian Arabs were thus in a situation that was relatively unusual in the Arab Middle East, of a new polity emerging without being allowed any of the attributes of stateness. In this respect, the Palestinians during the interwar years were totally unlike the peoples of Egypt, Iraq, Syria, Lebanon, and Jordan, and indeed unlike even the peoples in most other colonial and semicolonial domains in the Middle East and North Africa (the main exceptions being Algeria and Libya). Needless to say, they were also in this respect totally unlike the yishuv under the leadership of the Zionist movement. Specifically, the Palestinians had no international sanction for their identity, no accepted and agreed context within which their putative nationhood and independence could express itself, and their representatives had no access whatsoever to any of the levers of state power.

In fact, access to those levers was systematically denied to anyone of Arab background. The low ceiling that Arab functionaries came up against is best illustrated by the case of George Antonius, an urbane, articulate Cambridge-educated (but Lebanese-born) official of the mandatory government, who performed ably in the positions he held in the Education Department, but was repeatedly passed over for responsible posts, as mediocre British subordinates were promoted over his head, until he finally resigned in disgust.[16] Similar limitations did not apply to Jewish officials, if they were British by origin rather than Palestinian: among them were the first high commissioner, Sir Herbert Samuel, and Norman Bentwich, attorney general of Palestine until 1930, both deeply committed Zionists. By way of contrast, although a few senior British officials might well be considered anti-Zionist, pro-Arab, or even anti-Semitic, from the beginning of the British occupation of Palestine in 1917 until its bitter end in 1948, none of the top appointees of the mandatory administration outside the judiciary were Arabs.

Once again, the contrast with the situation of other Arab countries is highly illustrative: by the early 1930s, Yemen, Saudi Arabia, Egypt, and Iraq were already independent states, with Arab ministers and senior functionaries throughout the machinery of state. In Syria, Lebanon, and Transjordan during the same period, there were Arab government officials up to the rank of ministers, parliaments existed, and many of the trappings of power were in Arab hands, although France and Britain still retained substantive power. As we have seen, by 1946 the latter three countries were also independent (even if the independence of all seven was hedged around with drastic limitations).

Meanwhile, although Morocco, Tunisia, the Sudan, and all of the Arabian Peninsula's shaykhdoms, emirates, and sultanates (which later became the independent states of Kuwait, the United Arab Emirates, Qatar, Bahrain, Oman, and South Yemen, the latter eventually incorporated into the Arab Republic of Yemen) were under a variety of forms of indirect European control until the 1950s, all were ruled in some measure by their own indigenous governments.[17] These Arab states had recognized indigenous state structures staffed by Arab functionaries, even though the colonial powers maintained a high level of supervision through the imposition of restrictive and intrusive controls, backed up with the highly unpopular stationing of their military forces throughout the Arab world during the interwar period, even in Iraq and Egypt, both nominally independent states.[18] These indigenous state structures operated autonomously throughout most of the colonial period, albeit in many cases under the supervision and control of omnipresent, and sometimes omnipotent, European colonial officers or "advisors." The sole exceptions to this pattern in the entire Arab world were Mauritania, the Spanish Sahara, and the Aden Crown Colony, as well as Libya and Algeria, which two not coincidentally were sites of settler colonialism, like Palestine. Settler colonialism, which involved replacement of the indigenous population by a new one, or at least the subordination of the former by the latter, denied any form of representation or control over governance to that indigenous population. It could not have been otherwise, since no indigenous majority would have voluntarily ceded its country to a settler minority, and settler colonial projects in consequence necessarily had to be executed by force.

These differences were largely a result of the fact that the terms of all the other mandates, and the positions of the colonial powers in most other Arab countries (again, with the notable exceptions of Libya and Algeria), and indeed even the position of Britain in many of its colonies such as India, were predicated on the assumption that in each of these countries there was a people either already in existence or "in emergence," with the eventual right to independence and statehood. This was held to be true even though in some cases independence was envisaged by the colonial power as taking place in the distant future. In the case of Palestine, however, this national existence was explicitly recognized only for the Zionists in the terms of the Mandate, which as we know reprised the wording of the Balfour Declaration in speaking of a "Jewish people" with a right to a "national home," whose right to independence was implicitly recognized.

Meanwhile, as we have seen, the Palestinians were, both explicitly and by omission, denied the same recognition. Thus after having been part of the independent Ottoman Empire, with a parliament to which they had elected deputies in 1877, 1908, 1912, and 1914, the Palestinians thereafter found their country in a position that was far worse than that of all the other Class A mandates, and worse even than that of many colonies. At the May 1930 London meetings with a delegation of Palestinian leaders, both Lord Passfield and British prime minister Ramsay MacDonald brushed aside as irrelevant Palestinian arguments based on Article 4 of the Covenant. When Passfield went on to stress the unfavorable position of the Palestinians, saying, "Your position is inferior to that of a colony and it is our duty under the Mandate to endeavor that you should rise to the point of a Colony," some of his Arab interlocutors were shocked. "Do you mean that we are below the Negroes of Africa?" expostulated the mufti. Passfield reassured him that they were not, but that they were "less than" some other colonies like Australia and Canada. To that, another delegate, Raghib Bey al-Nashashibi, responded, lamenting that "we had a government of our own in which we participated. We had Parliaments." He was referring of course to the Ottoman Parliament before the British occupation, in which, incidentally, al-Nashashibi himself had been an elected deputy for Jerusalem. Passfield answered by bringing the discussion back once again to the grim necessity of his interlocutors accepting the terms of the Mandate, which the Palestinian leaders present simply could not do.[19] Get back into the iron cage, they were being told.

In consequence of this unyielding British position, the Palestinian Arabs were allowed neither access to control of the Mandate government, nor the right to build up their own powerful, autonomous, internationally recognized para-state structure, as the Zionists were with the Jewish Agency. Thus, the group of leaders who met with Passfield and MacDonald, which included six of the most prominent Palestinian political figures of the day, among them Muza Kazim al-Husayni, head of the Arab Executive (elected by the Third Palestinian Arab Congress, a nationalist body that met in December 1920, but never officially recognized by the British), Hajj Amin al-Husayni, the mufti, and al-Nashashibi, the mayor of Jerusalem, were not recognized by the British as acting in any official capacity. In the official British minutes of the meeting they are described as a "Deputation to the Prime Minister and the Secretary of State for the Colonies from Arab Palestinian interests regarding the position of Palestine."[20] The six most important leaders of a people constituting the overwhelming majority of Palestine's population were thus seen as representing no more than "Arab Palestinian interests regarding the position of Palestine."

This was consistent with a British position denying the representative nature of any body purporting to speak for the Palestinians, unless as a precondition it accepted Britain's policy of support for the Jewish national home and the concomitant denial of Palestinian national rights. Thus, as early as 1920, Wyndham Deedes, chief secretary of the Palestine Government, responded to a protest memo sent to him by Musa Kazim al-Husayni on behalf of the Third Palestinian Arab Congress, by "disputing the representative nature of the Congress."[21] When Herbert Samuel met with the Arab Executive elected by the Congress, to stress that they must accept the Jewish national home policy embodied in the Mandate "as a condition of recognition by the government," they reminded him that he had accepted to meet with them in spite of their protests against this policy. Samuel stated coldly: "Yes, but I meet with you in a private capacity only."[22]

Even when the British purported to redress this egregious imbalance, via proposals for a legislative assembly or for an Arab agency, these offers, like that made by Lord Passfield during the 1930 meeting, were fatally compromised in the Arabs' eyes by the absolute precondition that they accept the terms of the Mandate, which enshrined their inferior status by comparison with that of the Jews. In other words, Britain did not accord the Palestinian Arabs the right of national self-determination and representative self-government, as it did to the Jews of Palestine, and as the other mandates promised, and ultimately belatedly provided, the peoples of Syria, Lebanon, Iraq, and Transjordan. Instead, in the British view they might at best be allowed to share with the Jews in some of the functions of government. However, unlike them, the Arabs were to do so not by right, nor as a national entity, as was laid down regarding the Jews in the documents defining the Mandate, but as supplicants, and on sufferance, as it were.

These are not insignificant matters. In consequence of these fixed British positions, the Palestinians did not have any form of organized access to the supposedly uncontested, "neutral," and universally accepted forum that a state, even one still under a greater or lesser measure of foreign control, provides to a polity. For in many colonial situations, even if the state is still essentially dominated by the imperial power, there exists a shared assumption between the colonizer and the colonized (except in the case of settler colonialism) that the latter will ultimately be the heirs of the structures of this state. So it was for the yishuv, and for the Arab peoples living in the other countries under Class A mandate, in all of which the transition took place either more or less smoothly. Indeed, it is striking how easily the new state of Israel took over most of the levers of the administrative structure left behind by the British in May 1948, and how access to them was even at that late stage largely denied to the Palestinians.[23]

Beyond this, the forum of the state proved invaluable to the colonized in most "normal" colonial situations as an axis around which the polity could coalesce, or as a focus for its action, even if complete control over the structures of the state or over national sovereignty was denied by the colonial power. Access to a state also provides leverage over the monopoly of armed force that only the state can claim, and over the educational system, state-controlled media, and other means of influencing and shaping public perceptions. It was just these assets of the state that Egyptian and Iraqi nationalists found so valuable when they finally began to wrest control of them from the colonial power in the 1920s and 1930s.[24] A further problem facing the Palestinians is well summarized by the political scientist Issa Khalaf: "More fundamentally than self-governing institutions, the lack of effective power over the State meant that the Palestinian Arab notability which headed the national movement would be unable to use the resources of the state to centralize power in its hands and thereby develop into a cohesive stratum."[25] This lack of even a minimal level of cohesion by comparison with other Arab elites, resulting in some part from the systematic British denial of access to power over a state mechanism, would long continue to plague the Palestinian leadership, even after the catastrophe of 1948.

Nor did the Palestinians even have a para-state structure like the Jewish Agency, since the British would only recognize an Arab Agency, as Passfield suggested they might in 1930, on condition that they accepted the terms of the Mandate. We have seen that the Palestinians considered the Mandate to constitute the negation of their national existence as a sovereign people in all of their country. An earlier British proposal, made in 1923, for an Arab Agency to be appointed by the high commissioner (rather than elected as in the Jewish case) was, in the words of Ann Mosely Lesch, "a pale reflection of the Jewish Agency," without most of its power and functions, without sanction in the Mandate, without independence, and without international standing.[26] This latter point is extremely important, for by the terms of the League of Nations Mandate, the Jewish Agency was "recognized as a public body for the purpose of advising and cooperating with the Administration of Palestine." The resulting recognized international standing of the Jewish Agency meant that the Zionist movement was entitled to diplomatic representation in Geneva before the League of Nations Permanent Mandates Commission, in London, and elsewhere.

By contrast, the Palestinians had no international standing whatsoever, and indeed were often dependent on the hostile and unsympathetic British for such unsatisfactory diplomatic representation as they could obtain in Geneva and elsewhere. As 'Auni 'Abd al-Hadi, a member of the 1930 Palestinian delegation, complained to Passfield when the latter suggested that the delegation take their grievances to the Permanent Mandates Commission in Geneva, rather than addressing them to the British: "When we submit a petition to the League of Nations it is carried by His Majesty's Government who is there our antagonist, we are not represented there, and our case is being made by our opponents."[27] The significance of the quasi-official diplomatic status accorded to the Jewish Agency by Britain and the League of Nations through the Mandate thus cannot be overemphasized. It gave the Zionist movement an international legitimacy and guaranteed it invaluable access in world capitals, besides providing the framework within which the Zionist para-state that ultimately became Israel could be constructed without hindrance, and indeed with ample British and international support.[28]

Palestinian politics were thus condemned to an even higher level of frustration than politics in the other Arab countries. In the other mandates, there was a constant struggle between the mandatory authority (which was nearly always reluctant to cede any of its authority) and the local nationalist forces that composed the national movement, over the powers to be accorded to the national government. In none of them, nor in Egypt, which was under some form of British occupation from 1882 until 1954, however, was there any question about the existence or potential sovereignty of this government. In Egypt, the British and their allies within the Egyptian system, including the king and his cronies, managed to keep the hugely popular Wafd Party out of power for all but twelve of the thirty years from nominal independence in 1922 until King Farouk was deposed and the parliamentary system came to an end in 1952. Vital elements of state power were nevertheless in some sense in Egyptian hands. Similar manipulations of the political and electoral systems by the colonial power, often in collusion with its local political clients, occurred in Iraq, Syria, and Lebanon. Even though the European powers maintained military forces in most of the Arab countries against the will of their populations during the interwar period, the struggle against these powers and their unwanted military presence was nevertheless directed from within the state, or could be when control of the state could be won.[29] The Palestinians never had any such advantages. And they proved unable to create their own autonomous forum from which to challenge the colonial authority and its Zionist protégés.

A question remains: Why were the Palestinians unable to create such an independent structure, notwithstanding British obstruction and nonrecognition? For even if it were obliged to operate initially in spite of a lack of British and international recognition, such a unified national structure could have served as an alternative pole of legitimacy to the mandatory state structure, which the Palestinians perceived as illegitimate because it was based on the discriminatory terms of the Mandate. Although the Egyptians and Indians faced completely different (and no doubt less daunting) challenges, creation of an alternative structure was done with no little success by the Egyptian national movement through the Wafd Party during the years after 1919 and until Egypt gained its nominal independence in 1922. The Indian independence movement did it even more successfully via the Congress Party during the same period and afterward. Denied access to the levers of state power, and denied full representative government, both national movements broke decisively with the British and created alternative sources of legitimacy. In both cases, this approach was successful in achieving major concessions, including aspects of representative government and commitments to self-determination.[30]

This is a crucial question, to which we will return as part of an analysis of Palestinian critiques in the late 1920s and early 1930s of the approach followed by the Palestinian leadership, which was dominated by traditional elites, or notables, of refusing to separate themselves from the British until they had no choice, and by then it was probably too late. There is ample illustration of this tendency in the minutes of the many meetings between Palestinian delegations and British officials. A plaintive, almost piteous, tone emerges from the statements of Palestinian representatives. Their legalistic arguments for independence, sovereignty, and representative government, often grounded in Article 4 of the League of Nations Covenant, which referred to Palestine as "independent," were constantly tuned aside by patronizing British officials. In spite of facing this unyielding stonewall of British rejection of their national claims, and indeed of their national existence, these Palestinian notables were for far too long unable to find a means to disentangle themselves and their people from the legal and constitutional constraints that Great Britain had forged for them. They could never get out of the iron cage fashioned by their British masters.

What British officials wanted from the Arab leaders with whom they dealt was crystal clear, and they were explicit in spelling it out, privately and publicly. In the words of Ramsay MacDonald, it was to "co-operate together in pacifying legitimate opinion in Palestine." This meant one thing: bringing Palestinian elites to acquiesce in Britain's policy of establishing a Jewish national home in Palestine. The Palestinian notables MacDonald was trying to convince understood precisely what was required of them; in the words of the mufti, what the British wanted them to do was "to cooperate with them for our detriment."[31] This is what most of these notables in effect did for the better part of the first two decades of the British occupation of their country. All the while, as they went along with the British, they protested loudly at being obliged to do so. Presumably, members of this elite, drawn largely from the old notable class, assumed that sooner or later the British would come to their senses and deal with them as the "natural rulers" of Palestine. Whatever the thinking behind this doomed policy of de facto cooperation with a mandate designed to extinguish Palestinian rights, the Palestinian notables continued along this fruitless path until pressures from below that both they and the British proved unable to contain exploded into the bloody revolt of 1936–39. How and why the Palestinian leadership went along with the British, and why the inevitable explosion was so long in coming, are in part explained by the impact of some of the institutions, notably religious, created by the British in lieu of the political, representative, and national structures demanded by the Palestinians.

The Communitarian Paradigm: Invented Religious Institutions

The British colonial undertaking in Palestine did not begin from a tabula rasa, even if the unique ingredient of Zionism made it an unprecedented experiment of sorts. Very little that Great Britain did in Palestine, or in any other colony, mandate, possession, or sphere of influence, was without a referent to its rich colonial heritage, notably in India and Ireland. In particular, the colonial practices that British officials brought to bear in the different parts of the far-flung empire they controlled were profoundly inflected by hundreds of years of experience accumulated by the British governing classes in ruling over the Irish and the Indians. Historian Roger Owen has deftly shown how the regime Lord Cromer imposed from the early 1880s onward on one of Britain's most important possessions, Egypt, was patterned largely on the system he had earlier helped run in India as an assistant to his cousin, the viceroy Lord Northbrook, and a later viceroy, Lord Ripon.[32] The same was true for Palestine, mutatis mutandis,[33] and there are plentiful examples of similar borrowings elsewhere in the British imperial experience, such as replication of some of the forms of indirect rule practiced in some parts of the British Indian empire in the Persian/Arabian Gulf region and in British West Africa.[34]

Similarly, in dealing with nationalist movements among the Indians, the Palestinians, and others, British politicians and officials were deeply imbued with what they took to be the lessons of their lengthy and unpleasant experiences with Irish nationalism (needless to say, these experiences were mutually unpleasant, and indeed undoubtedly more unpleasant for the Irish). The stratagems the British developed in dealing with the Irish, and in particular the rhetorical styles and patterns of derogatory discourse they deployed—such as utilization of the term "terrorist," or in an earlier era, "criminal"—were the prototypes for their efforts to control, diminish, and denigrate other peoples, and disrupt the national resistance.[35] It should not surprise us to learn that on the other side of the colonial divide, leaders of some nationalist resistance movements sought to learn from others who had experience in confronting British colonial rule. Certain Palestinian and Egyptian nationalists, for example, saw the Indian Congress Party as an exemplar during the interwar period, and there was often cooperation between nationalists from different colonial possessions abroad.[36]

The cases of Ireland, India, and Palestine, three countries ruled by Britain and which all ultimately suffered bloody twentieth-century partitions heavy with consequences for their later history, furnish a number of general lessons about how colonial powers maintained control of populations characterized by deep internal divisions.[37] These examples provide a particularly illuminating comparative perspective on the history not only of countries that were colonized by Great Britain, but also of those ruled by other colonial powers. Notably, the other great colonial power of this period, France, assiduously applied lessons learned in its North and West African and Southeast Asian colonies, protectorates, and possessions before World War I to the mandates that it acquired after the war in Syria and Lebanon. As elsewhere in its colonial empire,

French rule in the latter two possessions was based on a reductive representation of the colonized societies as primitive or backward,[38] but especially their representation in religious terms, and their control through the manipulation, modification, and often even construction of religious, ethnic, and other identities.[39]

One of the most notable results of the manipulation of religious identities was the creation of "Greater Lebanon," which became the modern state of Lebanon, out of Mount Lebanon and its environs. Mount Lebanon had a long history of the involvement of Western powers, notably France and Britain, in support of the latter's local clients.[40] Over time, its mainly Maronite (a mainly Lebanese Christian sect in communion with Rome) ruling strata became eager to create a larger entity centered on Mount Lebanon that would include many non-Maronite areas, and would be intimately linked to France.[41] The Sunni and Shi'ite Muslims, Greek Orthodox, and Druze who formed the bulk of the areas thereby annexed were largely unfavorable to being included in the new Greater Lebanon, and the resulting intercommunal tensions dominated much of the history of Lebanon for the rest of the twentieth century. These tensions neatly served the divide-and-rule purposes of the French colonial party. Variants of this approach were utilized with considerably less success in Syria.[42] As we shall see, a similar approach, used extensively throughout the British Empire, was crucial to the effort in Palestine.[43]

It is now well established that in the colonial era, one of the most crucial forms of control developed by Britain for maintaining hegemony over a vast empire with relatively modest military forces was the management, and sometimes the encouragement, or even the creation, of religious and ethnic difference. The British did this in a manner not at all dissimilar to that followed by the French in Lebanon and elsewhere. This process was often grounded in existing distinctions within the societies the British ruled over, but it frequently involved the development and refinement of these existing differences, and sometimes even the production of new ones.[44]

The net result was often a highly developed and systematized communitarian structure, within which the British could play their favored role of arbiter, and ideally be seen as above or outside a "local" conflict, rather than as part of it, or even the creator of it, as they were in many cases.

Of course official Britain, whether in the nineteenth century or the interwar period, was always pleased to be invisible in these sordid matters, or as close to invisible as was possible. The preferred posture of the greatest power of the age was to pose as the impartial external actor, doing its levelheaded, rational, civilized best to restrain the savage passions of the wild and brutish locals. One cannot read the memoirs or many of the official reports of British officials in mandatory Palestine—an entity that in its then-current form the British themselves had created, and that was riven by political conflicts they themselves had fostered—without being repeatedly struck by this tone of innocent wonderment at a bizarre and often tragic sequence of events for which these officials rarely if ever acknowledged the slightest responsibility.[45]

Another form of imperial control involved a reliance on indigenous elites, and sometimes other social strata, to participate in structures of indirect rule. This device relieved Britain of some of its more onerous duties and responsibilities, while distributing a limited amount of power, as well as a significant degree of prestige and status. These elites could be existing aristocracies, as in the princely states in India, or invented aristocracies, as in many of the Gulf principalities.[46] On another level, these groups could be segments of the dominated society chosen by the British for specific tasks, but rigorously restricted to those tasks and otherwise kept strictly in their place.[47] One example was the "martial races" that were utilized to help fight Britain's wars for the empire.[48] These included the Sikhs and Pathans of India's North-West Frontier, the Gurkhas of Nepal, the Bedouin of the Arabian and Syrian deserts, and other groups deemed "virile" enough to serve their British colonial masters in this way. Indeed, the British-officered and -controlled Transjordanian

"Arab Legion," raised from the latter groups, played a crucial role in maintaining British control over Palestine, as well as in suppressing the Iraqi revolt of 1941, and overcoming the Vichy French forces in Syria and Lebanon in the same year. In its dependence on colonial auxiliary forces to maintain its global strategic position, Britain was little different from France and other colonial powers.[49]

In Palestine, where the British had taken on the daunting responsibility of creating a Jewish national home in an Arab land with a 90 percent Arab majority, they faced an especially difficult task. In keeping with their hierarchical view of all societies, particularly subordinate ones, the British saw that one essential precondition for achieving this task was preventing the resistance to the Zionist project by a critical mass of the Palestinian elites, the notables who dominated Arab society and had previously served as intermediaries between that society and the Ottomans.[50] While refusing the notables any official standing, and frustrating their national aspirations along with those of the rest of the Palestinians, the British nevertheless treated them with a certain ostensible deference, and were careful to allow them a limited role as intermediaries for the rest of Palestinian society, as well as certain other prerequisites. This was in line with the well-established British predilection, already mentioned (and seen most spectacularly in India, but also elsewhere in the British Empire), for developing privileged relations with real or invented aristocratic elites, rather than political formations rooted in the middle classes or the mass of the people. Among the most successful means for achieving this end in Palestine was the establishment and empowering by Britain of refashioned, as well as entirely new, Islamic institutions dominated by some of these traditional notables: institutions like the shari'a court system, the network of public charitable foundations, and the administration of Muslim holy places in Palestine.

The need for the creation or refashioning of some of these institutions originally emerged from the transition in Palestine from an Ottoman state that, even after the reforms of the nineteenth and early twentieth centuries, was still at least nominally Islamic, to a mandatory state dominated by a Christian power. Historian Uri Kupferschmidt has well described the dilemma the British faced: "Here was a Christian mandatory power, committed to the establishment of a Jewish national home, controlling a Muslim majority in a country considered holy to the three main monotheistic religions."[51] Under the system in the late Ottoman Empire, religious officials, notably the *qadis,* or judges in the Islamic religious courts, and the muftis, who rendered consultative opinions in legal cases, had been appointed by the Ottoman central government. Public endowments, what were known as *al-awqaf al-'amma*[52]—whose revenues went for the support of schools, soup kitchens, hospitals, mosques, and other public purposes—which had been established over many centuries of Islamic rule, had also formerly been administered as part of a bureaucracy whose apex was in Istanbul, headed by the Shaykh al-Islam, who was both the mufti of Istanbul and a cabinet-level minister. Those who created the institutions of the new mandatory regime felt that as a non-Muslim power, it would be inappropriate for Britain to be seen to usurp directly these functions of the Islamic Ottoman state. So, making a virtue of necessity, they resorted to the principle of indirect rule borrowed from India, and already being implemented in other parts of the Arab world that had just come under their control, around the turn of the twentieth century and at the end of World War I.

In so doing, the British architects of the mandatory regime in Palestine were operating on the basis of a worldview rooted in their earlier colonial experiences, notably in Ireland and India, with a crucial Egyptian admixture. This was a worldview that almost invariably perceived colonized societies in religious and communitarian rather than in national terms, and as profoundly divided internally rather than as potentially unified. In many ways, the most relevant parallel is to the way the British and other European observers saw Egypt. Indeed, the Egyptian example was drawn upon liberally by several of the earliest British administrators of Palestine, including Sir Ronald Storrs, Brig. Gen. Sir Gilbert Clayton, and Col. Sir Wyndham Deedes, all of whom had served extensively in Egypt, whether in the Arab Bureau, in military intelligence, or in other branches of the British regime there. The view of Egyptian society that formed the intellectual underpinning for the British regime of indirect control there, which lasted in one form or another from the occupation of 1882 until the evacuation of 1954, received its fullest exposition in Lord Cromer's magisterial *Modern Egypt*. In this book, published immediately after Cromer's retirement, the first British proconsul on the Nile set out the results of his decades of Egyptian experience.[53] Cromer was categorical in asserting that there was no Egyptian nation; that Egypt was a congeries of disparate and incompatible religious and ethnic groups; and that these competing groups would be at one another's throats were it not for the benevolent presence of the British.[54] As an apology for colonialism, this description served perfectly. However, as an analysis of Egyptian society, it was obviously somewhat lacking, particularly in an era of rising Egyptian national feeling, and a growing sense of national unity against the occupier. This was demonstrated in 1906 during the Dinshwai affair, when Egyptian villagers were executed for the accidental death of a British officer, and the 'Aqaba crisis with the Ottoman government over the eastern frontiers of Egypt, and more tangibly during the great nationwide Egyptian revolt against the British in 1919. Nevertheless, in many ways this distorted and self-serving model of Egyptian society served as a template for what the British chose to see in Palestine: a land composed of three religious communities, only one of which, the Jews, had national rights and status.

However, in order to complete this vision of a sort of modified Ottoman *millet* system,[55] with each group enjoying a certain element of autonomy, something in the way of religious institutions for Muslims and Christians to match the Jewish community's newly recognized national institutions was needed. These would have to be offered in place of the Arab national institutions that

Palestinians, both Muslims and Christians, were clamoring for soon after the British occupation, citing British promises of independence to the Arabs and Article 4 of the Covenant of the League of Nations. Such national institutions the British were resolutely determined to deny the Arabs; complicating the task facing the British in constructing religious institutions to substitute for them was the fact that many members of the Palestinian middle and upper classes had lived, studied, worked in, or visited Egypt. They were therefore well aware of the Egyptian precedents, and of Britain's notorious predilection for the politics of divide and rule, generally on a religious basis.[56] Thus, early after the British occupation, Palestinian political figures set up Muslim-Christian Associations (and later a Palestinian Arab Congress) in major cities and towns all over the country as a means of countering an attempt to use this approach to divide the Palestinian Arabs along religious lines. This did not stop the British, who proceeded in the haphazard, nonsystematic fashion of British colonialism to construct an entirely new communitarian system that denied national rights to the Arabs while preserving them for the Jews.

What this meant in practice was the creation in Palestine of "Islamic" institutions that had no precedent in that country's history, or indeed in the entirety of Islamic history. Among them was the Supreme Muslim Council (SMC), al-Majlis al-Islami al-A'la. This entirely new body was given a variety of duties, including control over the revenues of Palestine's public awqaf, which were generally supposed to go to charitable and other public service purposes. These considerable revenues had formerly been controlled by the Ottoman state's central religious bureaucracy. To the SMC also accrued the significant patronage that came from control of appointments in an extensive religious bureaucracy that included qadis, members of the shari'a court of appeal, local muftis, as well as the employees of numerous schools, orphanages, religious centers, and other institutions. The council also had the power to hire and fire all awqaf and shari'a court officials employed with awqaf funds.[57]

For all the influence of Palestine's notables at different times in the past, never in the preceding several hundred years of Ottoman rule had such power over religious institutions and the resources they allocated been concentrated in local hands. Formerly, qadis had always been appointed from Istanbul, awqaf funds and other revenues had been disbursed by the Ottoman bureaucracy, and tight control was always maintained over all aspects of Sunni religious orthodoxy.

Another such refashioned Islamic institution was the office of mufti of Jerusalem for the Hanafi rite (which of the four Sunni legal and religious rites had the largest following in Palestine, and had been the official rite of the Ottoman state). The British themselves changed this title to *mufti filastin al-akbar,* "Grand Mufti of Palestine," most likely following an Egyptian precedent.[58] The position of Hanafi mufti of Jerusalem had always been an important one in the past, but it had been limited both in terms of geographical scope and authority. For example, the holder of this position traditionally had no power over muftis who served in other major Palestinian cities, although he certainly had greater prestige than any of them. This new title, and the job description for it that developed over time, considerably expanded both the scope and the authority of the position. The first British high commissioner in Palestine, Sir Herbert Samuel, offered this powerful post to Hajj Amin al-Husayni. The al-Husaynis were one of the richest and most powerful families in Jerusalem, and their members had held the position of Hanafi mufti of Jerusalem for most of the preceding two centuries.[59] Until his death in 1921, Hajj Amin's half-brother, Kamil, had been the mufti, in which post their father and grandfather had preceded him. Other members of the prominent al-Husayni family had served as mayors of the city and members of parliament during the Ottoman era, and one of them, Salim Bey al-Husayni, had been mayor when the British occupied Jerusalem in 1917.

Sir Herbert Samuel chose Hajj Amin al-Husayni even though he was quite young and not particularly well known for either religious learning or zeal. Moreover, he had received the fewest votes of the four candidates for the post from the Jerusalemite Islamic religious leaders who were polled in accordance with the Ottoman-era system for selection of a new mufti. While he had received two years of religious training in Cairo at the prestigious al-Azhar before the war, most of al-Husayni's background was decidedly secular: he had served as an officer in the Ottoman army during the war, had been an official of King Faysal's short-lived government in Damascus, and had been sentenced in absentia to ten years imprisonment and banned from Palestine by the British because of his alleged involvement in the anti-British and anti-Zionist Nabi Musa disturbances of April 1920, when Zionists and Arabs clashed on the Muslim feast day of the prophet Moses. With the blessing of the British, however, al-Husayni was forgiven for his "crimes," nine months later became mufti, and came to head the Supreme Muslim Council as well. This led to a situation unheard of in Islamic jurisprudence, where a mufti in effect appointed the qadis.

In the Ottoman and every other Islamic system, the post of mufti was invariably subordinate in power and prestige to that of the qadi.[60] The qadi had normally been appointed by the Ottoman state from the ranks of the central Ottoman religious establishment, and because of the importance of the position was not supposed to come from a local family, in order to prevent conflicts of interest and local favoritism. The mufti, as well as the qadi's deputy, the na'ib (who was also chief secretary of the shari'a court), was by contrast almost always of local origins.[61] Under the Ottomans, therefore, there was always a certain balance between these positions, although the post of qadi was clearly preeminent. This system was completely restructured and in effect turned upside down by the British, who in practice placed the newly styled "Grand Mufti of Palestine" above all other religious officials in Palestine.

The seemingly strange choice of the young Hajj Amin al-Husayni for this powerful new post was in fact a shrewd one, if one keeps in mind what the British intended these institutions to do.

In a situation in which, by the terms of the Mandate for Palestine, only one party, the Jews, was formally recognized as a political or national entity, it was absolutely essential to British purposes to divide, distract, and divert the opposition of the other party representing the overwhelming majority of the country's population, the Palestinian Arabs. It was equally essential to prevent them from uniting on a national basis against the British and their Zionist protégés. As we have seen, the British also saw that it was essential to avoid giving the Arab majority national or representative institutions, or any other form of access to state power.

The British carried out this diversion in part by providing the Palestinian Muslim elites with entirely new communal structures recognized by the mandatory state, involving a certain degree of autonomy, and enjoying significant revenues. These Muslim institutions were created out of the bits and pieces of the previous Ottoman religio-political system, and were housed in the same locales previously utilized for analogous purposes, thereby constituting a peculiarly brazen form of "invented tradition."[62] The Muslims could consider these new religious institutions "their own," which in a sense they were, but they were devoid of power or authority outside of the purely religious and communal sphere (the most important legal cases were decided by three-man appeals courts on which sat a British and a Jewish, as well as a Muslim, judge).

There was a clear bargain involved in accepting positions within this and other British-devised structures in mandatory Palestine. In exchange for official recognition and status, well remunerated quasi-official positions, the possibility of considerable patronage, and a certain restricted level of communal autonomy, those leading Palestinian figures who accepted such posts were obliged to refrain from openly opposing the Mandate, its commitment to support a Jewish national home, and the concomitant denial of Palestinian self-determination. These restrictions were imposed as well on officials who were on the payroll of the mandatory government but were outside the religious structure that was controlled by the mufti, including the mayors and a variety of employees within the mandatory administration, such as the health and education systems that served the Arab population. However, the greatest coup for the British in the first decade after their occupation was to have inveigled Hajj Amin al-Husayni, a leader of the most prominent family in the most important city of Palestine, a man with familial, religious, social, and political prestige, into accepting such a position as part of an implicit bargain of this sort.

In making this decision, British policymakers could not but have been aware of the fact that a few months earlier, in December 1920, al-Husayni's older relative, Musa Kazim al-Husayni, who had been removed from his post as mayor of Jerusalem after the 1920 Nabi Musa riots, had been elected head of the Arab Executive of the Palestine Arab Congress. The latter was a nationwide body that demanded national rights for the Arab majority; the British contested its legitimacy and representative nature and never officially recognized it. The British were well aware that in this capacity Musa Kazim al-Husayni was perhaps the most prominent opponent of their policy. By appointing a relative of his to an important position that was in their gift, they undoubtedly hoped to weaken Musa Kazim al-Husayni and undermine his credibility in opposing them. In thus playing members of the same prominent family against one another, the British were drawing on both their own imperial tradition and the patterns earlier followed by the Ottoman authorities in order to maintain control of far-flung provinces of a large empire.[63] As the British had probably hoped, the two men, who came from different branches of the large al-Husayni family, remained rivals until Musa Kazim al-Husayni's death in early 1934, when the mufti became the paramount, if often challenged, leader of the fractured Palestinian national movement.

The British high commissioner who decided to make this appointment, Herbert Samuel, a committed Zionist, a former cabinet minister, and an extremely shrewd politician, interviewed the youthful Hajj Amin al-Husayni himself before making up his mind.

He only did so (over the reservations of some of the most committed Zionists among his officials) after the future grand mufti assured him of his "earnest desire to cooperate with the Government and his belief in the good intentions of the British Government towards the Arabs," and that "the influence of his family and himself would be devoted to maintaining tranquility."[64] These were weighty words, not lightly uttered, and they were taken seriously by the British authorities. For all the Zionist criticisms, then and later, of the British for this appointment, and of the mufti and other Palestinian leaders for not showing consistent and total submissiveness to the British Mandate and the Zionist movement, for a decade and a half the mufti kept his side of the bargain, as did the British their side. In consequence, for many years this connection proved to be very advantageous for both.

Sir Herbert was clearly gambling that this young firebrand with impeccable nationalist credentials, only recently pardoned for his "radical" activities, would serve British interests by preserving calm in return for his elevation to a post whose prestige, resources, and importance the British were greatly enhancing. Despite constant, bitter Zionist complaints about the mufti, Samuel's gamble paid off for the British until the mid-1930s, when al-Husayni could no longer contain Palestinian popular passions. While he built up a position of considerable power and influence for himself, thereby angering the Zionists, who understandably feared any autonomous representation of the will of the Palestinian Arab majority, the mufti was generally quite careful not to alienate the British, without whose constant support he could not have retained his position.

It was a mark of the mufti's skills that he was able to manage this difficult balancing act for so long. These skills were demonstrated as well by his lengthy survival near or at the top of the harsh world of Palestinian politics. Soft-spoken, reserved, but generating a charismatic aura in small groups,[65] Hajj Amin al-Husayni was far from the archetype of the Arab nationalist leader of the interwar period. He was not a noted public speaker, like Sa'd Zaghlul and

Mustafa Nahhas in Egypt, or 'Abd al-Rahman al-Shahbandar and Shukri al-Quwwatli in Syria. Nor was he a self-made man, who had risen to prominence mainly because of his personal qualities and his leadership abilities. Very much an aristocrat, self-consciously a member of the Palestinian notability, the mufti adeptly managed to use the religious institutions he had been placed at the head of to build up a large popular following drawn from the network of traditional clients of the al-Husayni family, nationalists yearning for a paramount leader for their movement, and beneficiaries from the large network of patronage he dominated.

Among all the other leaders of national movements in Arab countries during the interwar period (with the sole exception of Libya), and among Palestinian leaders as well, the mufti was alone in being a religious dignitary, whose base of power was a "traditional" religious institution, albeit a newly invented one, created and endowed with resources by the colonial power. In this unique institution, created by Britain in the singular circumstances of this specific mandate, we find one of the crucial differences between Palestine and Arab countries like Egypt, Syria, Lebanon, and Iraq. There, largely secular political parties and other movements, however weak or poorly organized they may have been, were the primary vehicles for nationalist leaders, until control over the state and its resources could be achieved.[66] The Wafd in Egypt, the National Bloc in Syria, and various groupings and movements in Lebanon and Iraq played this function. There was no true analogue to them in Palestine, although political parties began to be founded in the late 1920s and early 1930s.

In part because of the considerable assets that Britain had put into his hands, but largely due to his consummate political skills, within a little more than a decade Hajj Amin al-Husayni had become the dominant Palestinian political leader, and as such a lightning rod for the dissatisfaction of the Zionists. Here, too, there is an amnesiac element in the vilification of the mufti in much Zionist and Israeli historiography. This is no doubt influenced by his subsequent career, when in the mid-1930s al-Husayni became paramount leader of the Palestinian national movement in actively combating both the British and the Zionist movement. To add to his notoriety, the mufti ended up in Germany as an ally of the Nazis during World War II, after his escape from Palestine in 1937 following repeated failed British attempts to arrest him, as they did most other Palestinian nationalist leaders at that time.[67]

This subsequent history of open resistance to Britain and Zionism notwithstanding, for the first decade and a half after his appointment, Hajj Amin al-Husayni served the British exceedingly well in keeping Palestinian opposition to the mandatory regime within "moderate" limits, showing the devotion "to maintaining tranquility" that he had promised Herbert Samuel in 1921. This certainly continued to be the case until the mid-1930s, when the mufti felt obliged to align himself with a growing popular rebellion against his former British masters, and reluctantly abandoned his balancing act between them and the popular forces that threatened to leave him and the rest of the traditional leadership behind. One indication of how valuable the British perceived the mufti to be is the willingness of the notoriously tightfisted mandatory administration to subsidize him out of their own revenues, in addition to those produced by public awqaf properties. When the largely agricultural revenues of the latter declined after the Great Depression of 1929 knocked the bottom out from under the prices of agricultural products, leading to a decline in the revenues of the Supreme Muslim Council, they were supplemented by direct British subventions starting in 1931. These were naturally kept secret, in the interest of both parties.[68]

We have seen that the British rigorously denied the Palestinians access either to the forum of the state, or to a nationalist para-state structure, and that the Palestinians themselves ultimately failed to develop their own institutions that might serve this purpose. It was not through lack of trying, for the Palestinian national movement repeatedly attempted to create some such institutions, through the establishment of Muslim-Christian Associations and the founding of the Palestine Arab Congress and its offshoot, the Arab Executive. None of them grew into the kind of structure that might have served as the nucleus of a state, or as an alternative to the mandatory state, from whose higher ranks Arabs were systematically excluded. Indeed, at times efforts to refashion these institutions in such a manner appeared halfhearted, partly because of the inability or unwillingness of the notable leaders of the Palestinian national movement to create mass-based political groupings, along the lines of the Wafd Party in Egypt and others in the Arab countries, India, and elsewhere in the colonized world. Beyond this there was the unremitting hostility of the mufti to any institution or any individual that threatened to challenge the power and prestige of the extensive religious institutions he controlled.

This jealousy obviously extended to the Municipality of Jerusalem, formerly headed by a member of the al-Husayni clan but controlled from 1920 until the mid-1930s by one of the mufti's leading rivals, Raghib Bey al-Nashashibi.[69] As we shall see later, the mufti's jealousy also affected nascent political parties and other groupings that emerged in the late 1920s and early 1930s (such as the Istiqlal Party), especially if they were not dominated by his own partisans. Lacking effective vehicles for building toward statehood, either preexisting, provided by the British, or developed by the Palestinians themselves, the Arab population of Palestine was instead granted a religious leadership, authorized, encouraged, legitimated, subsidized, and always in the end controlled by the British. This new creation was very much in keeping with the British vision of a Palestine composed of three religious communities, only one of which, the Jews, had national rights and status. It served the purposes for which the British had created it admirably until the mid-1930s, when the Jewish national home was already virtually a fait accompli. This important fifteen-year period, during which the basic dynamics for the rest of the Mandate were established, is easily forgotten, since once the mufti was pushed into serious opposition by the popular explosion of the mid-1930s, he became a deadly, albeit ultimately ineffective, foe of both the British and the Zionists. Nevertheless, as we shall see, for a time the British did not entirely give up hope of recuperating him, nor did he, apparently, of reestablishing a relationship with them.

On close examination, the primary effort of the notables who dominated the Palestinian national movement, who undoubtedly sincerely wished to liberate their country, was an ineffectual beseeching of various British government ministers, including Ramsay MacDonald and Lord Passfield, successive high commissioners, from Herbert Samuel onward, and other British officials, to grant the Palestinians their national rights, in endless, repeated, fruitless meetings. The futility of this approach became clear to many other Palestinians, who in time demanded a different course in dealing with the British. In the end, the notables were capable neither of providing the alternative approach that the Palestinians so sorely needed, nor of diverting them from the tragic course that led to the sacrifices of the 1936–39 revolt, the crushing of which marked the beginning of the end of Arab Palestine.

To escape the fiendish iron cage devised for them by the British, should the Palestinians have accepted the national aspirations of the Jewish people—most of whom, the Europeans among them, they saw as foreigners and intruders—in exchange for recognition of their national rights? Could they have done so, given that at the time most of them (and many others, including many Jews) saw Judaism as a religion and not as the basis for a nationality, and thus did not accept the core premises of political Zionism? Had they done so, would the Zionists have recognized their national rights or the prerogatives that should have gone with their majority status? And what of Britain, whose leaders were committed to exclusive support of a Jewish national home, as much out of perceived self-interest as out of belief? These are questions that, while they cannot be answered with any certainty, suggest the depths of the dilemma the Palestinians faced.

3
A Failure of Leadership

Rivalries among the Notables

Histories of Palestine under the British Mandate almost invariably focus on the disputes among Palestinian Arab leaders and the factions they headed. Quite frequently, attention to these and other aspects of political history comes at the expense of the underlying economic, demographic, and constitutional realities, which were briefly examined in the last two chapters. The factions that are the subject of this attention were indeed important. They were sometimes based on long-standing groupings centered on notable families, such as that headed by the al-Husaynis of Jerusalem. The al-Husaynis possessed relatively large landholdings, had far-flung networks of clients, and had traditionally held prestigious religious and political offices, such as those of Hanafi mufti of Jerusalem, and the posts of mayor and parliamentary deputy for the city in the late Ottoman era. Other factions were more recent in origin, or were no more than coalitions of leaders, families, and village groupings. Conflicts among these and other local factions in Palestine and elsewhere in the region had once been quite important. They diminished in both intensity and significance beginning in the mid-nineteenth century as a consequence of the growth in power of a modern central Ottoman state and the decline in local autonomy, and later with the emergence of mass politics. However, both factionalism and factional rivalries grew more potent during the British Mandate.

Among the various inter-elite rivalries during the Mandate period, one primary cleavage stands out. This was the deep gulf between two groups that ironically were both sustained and encouraged, albeit in different ways, by the British mandatory authorities. The first was made up of supporters of the "grand" mufti, Hajj Amin al-Husayni, who came to be known as the al-Husayni faction, or as *majlisiyun*, partisans of the Supreme Muslim Council (al-Majlis al-Islami al-A'la), the institution invented by the British, discussed in the previous chapter. The second group was known as the *mu'aridun* (the opposition), and was headed by Raghib Bey al-Nashashibi, whom the British had appointed mayor of Jerusalem after the Nabi Musa riots of 1920, replacing the mufti's distant cousin, Muza Kazim al-Husayni.

While this rivalry certainly dominated the politics of Arab Palestine, particularly in the latter half of the Mandate period, there were many other cleavages in Palestinian politics. For example, until the death of Musa Kazim al-Husayni in 1934, he and his much younger cousin, the mufti, were often engaged in discreet competition. Especially after the disturbances of 1929, this came to reflect generational, intrafamilial, institutional, and other tensions. Over time, moreover, numerous challenges were launched by other sectors of society against what was perceived as the overly conciliatory approach toward the British that was taken by all the notable leaders. This was contrasted with the empty militant rhetoric of the rival leaders, most of whom were correctly perceived by Palestinian public opinion to be surreptitiously cooperating with the British. Both the mufti and al-Nashashibi, of course, had been appointed to their positions and were sustained there by the British authorities.

The rivalries between the two leading factions were often very real, and at times became exceedingly fierce.[1] By the later phases of the great 1936–39 revolt, this conflict had degenerated to the point that some al-Nashashibi supporters and others organized by the British in so-called peace bands were actively engaged alongside British troops in the massive campaign to hunt down partisans of the mufti's faction and other armed rebels. Meanwhile, several supposed collaborators with the British from among the ranks of al-Nashashibi's partisans were assassinated, presumably by followers of the mufti. Homes were burned, and key opposition figures were forced into exile.[2] The deep political differences between these two factions continued after the termination of the Mandate. When Jordanian troops took control of the eastern part of Jerusalem during the 1948 war, al-Nashashibi was named military governor of the city by Amir (later King) 'Abdullah of Transjordan. Al-Nashashibi's supporters and allies thereafter voted at a special congress convened in Jericho by Amir 'Abdullah in December 1948 for the incorporation of the West Bank into what became the Hashemite Kingdom of Jordan. Many of them were thereupon absorbed into the new Jordanian administration. By contrast, in areas under Jordanian control the mufti's followers were disarmed and many were proscribed and hunted by the Arab Legion beginning on May 15, 1948. Some of them were later plausibly accused of involvement in the assassination of King 'Abdullah while he was on a visit to Jerusalem in 1951.

Important though the internecine rivalries within Palestine's Arab elite were, one of the most tedious aspects of the standard version of pre-1948 history is an obsessive focus on these rivalries, sometimes to the exclusion of much else of importance.[3] It is partly a function of the long-standing tendency of historians of the Middle East to concentrate on political history at the expense of economic, social, cultural, and intellectual history, and on elites rather than other segments of society.[4] This tendency appears to be diminishing in the treatment of the modern period.[5] While the notables had great importance as a group, and are certainly worthy of attention, a persuasive argument can be made that there has been an overemphasis on them in the literature, to the detriment of the examination of other social groups and other problematics.[6]

Beyond this broader general concern, there is reason to be skeptical about the sometimes mean-spirited and often condescending contemporary depictions by some outsiders of the pettiness of Palestinian inter-elite rivalries, especially during the Mandate period. There is no question that some of these rivalries were personal or trivial. Nevertheless, the subtle, and at times not-so-subtle, racial attitudes that characterize the remarks about Arab politics of many of these contemporary outside observers should cause us to treat their views with caution. Examples of such attitudes from this period are legion: the head of the Education Department in Palestine, Humphrey Bowman, noted of two of his British subordinates that one had "contempt" for "people in the East," while the other "rather despises the Arabs."[7] Similarly, the Hebrew writer Josef Chaim Brenner described the "degeneracy and savagery" of the Arabs, who could only become part of "the human fellowship" through the efforts of the Jews of Palestine.[8] Meanwhile, contemporary French observers, such as the young intelligence agent Lt. Pierre Rondot, later to become a noted scholar, often referred to the *tendances fanatiques* of the Palestinians.[9] In spite of such problems, these observations by frequently ill-informed outsiders, whether contained in contemporary diplomatic dispatches, intelligence reports, private letters, or journalism, are among the main sources we have for the period. And it is beyond question that these rivalries played a major part in the politics of the period, even if they may have been exaggerated, distorted, or misunderstood as a result of such attitudes on the part of Western observers.

It is not just in the secondary works that deal with this period that one finds a heavy emphasis on conflict within the Palestinian elite. While these differences are naturally featured in the Arabic-language press, much of which was aligned with one or another faction, contemporary British and Zionist records also focused intensely on this topic, both because it was of importance in and of itself and, crucially, because the existence, and if necessary the encouragement, of internal Palestinian differences were critical to the achievement of British and Zionist aims in Palestine. The extent to which these internal Palestinian differences were actively fostered and encouraged by outside actors is an aspect of the history of the period that is all too rarely emphasized by scholars.

We have seen one instance of the manipulation of internal Palestinian differences by the British in the appointment of Hajj Amin al-Husayni as "grand mufti" by Sir Herbert Samuel. As already noted, this was an extraordinary action: al-Husayni had been sentenced in absentia to ten years in prison for fomenting the Nabi Musa riots of April 1920. And we have seen that the appointment was partly motivated by the desire of the British to establish Hajj Amin as a rival to his older relative, Musa Kazim al-Husayni, who had been removed from office as mayor of Jerusalem in the wake of these riots. Musa Kazim al-Husayni subsequently became head of the Arab Executive elected by the Palestinian Arab Congress of 1920, and was thus the most senior Palestinian leader opposing the British. At the same time, the British desired to conciliate another branch of the large and influential al-Husayni family, that from which holders of the position of Hanafi mufti of Jerusalem had been drawn for four generations.[10] The appointment of Raghib Bey al-Nashashibi as mayor of Jerusalem after the British removal from that post of Musa Kazim al-Husayni was another example of this divide and rule policy. According to one account, "Nashashibi's acceptance of the mayoralty in succession to Musa Kazem Pasha al-Husseini highlighted the feud between supporters of the two rival families—a dispute which was to dominate the politics of Arab Palestine during much of the mandatory period."[11] It can be surmised that among the reasons for the British to appoint al-Nashashibi was the objective of inflaming that preexisting feud.

As we have seen, the British and the Zionists made efforts to play Palestinian leaders off against one another in order to exacerbate old rivalries, or create new ones as part of a strategy of divide and rule. That some of these rivalries existed before the British arrived is unquestionable, as is the fact that the Ottomans consistently played one notable faction off against another.[12] The British themselves were of course steeped in the time-honored imperial tradition of *divide et impera,* in Palestine and elsewhere.[13] It is difficult to verify the scope of such efforts, however, as the underhanded methods employed by officials in inflaming local tensions were generally considered highly confidential. Solid evidence of this type of activity is scant, thus the subject is rarely addressed in the literature on the period.

Another problem all too rarely addressed in the literature is that beyond the generalized racism already mentioned, most contemporary British and Zionist observers, as well as other Europeans, revealed an attitude of superiority toward Arabs of all classes, ranging from casual condescension to outright contempt. In a typical example, the British colonial secretary, the haughty former viceroy of India, Lord Curzon, is described in 1921 by the French ambassador to London as "admitting [later Iraqi King] Faysal's mischievousness, but considers it common to all Orientals and thus of no importance."[14]

The consequence of such widespread prejudice is that what purports to be political analysis often amounts to no more than uninformed gossip. Thus a French diplomat in 1932 flatly describes "all the Muslim politicians in Palestine" as venal, unprincipled, anti-European, anti-Jewish, and anti-Christian, and ready to sell both their lands and themselves at the first opportunity.[15] While some of these accusations may have been true of some Palestinian leaders, they were certainly not true of *all* of them. Nevertheless, this comment gives an indication of the mind-set of many European observers, who were ignorant of the local language and remained outsiders in the societies they described, but on whose observations we are obliged in some measure to rely as sources. Finally, beyond what may have resulted from prejudice or ignorance, there was always the possibility of perfectly innocent behavior being misinterpreted, whether unintentionally or willfully, in the sources produced by these British, Zionist, and other European observers, who themselves were often active participants in the events they record. In dealing with materials from European and Zionist archives, and generally with the observations of Europeans in this era, their conviction of Arab "venality" was so strong, and the general distaste for "Orientals" (a category that often included Jews) so prevalent, that one must use them with care when there is any reason to doubt a given observer's judgment on this score. Nevertheless, such sources often contain material of great reliability and significant value.

We have already established that there was some degree of manipulation of Arab internal rivalries in Palestine by outside forces, particularly on the part of the British. It emerged very early on during British rule that in order for Britain to maintain control of an overwhelmingly Arab country in which it proposed to establish a thoroughly unpopular Jewish national home, it was absolutely necessary to divide the Palestinian population. In the wake of the virtually universal Palestinian rejection of the Balfour Declaration, of Zionist objectives in Palestine, and of the document that embodied both, the League of Nations Mandate for Palestine, and after the anti-Zionist and anti-British riots in Jerusalem in 1920 and in Jaffa in 1921, this necessity was apparent to even the dimmest and most unperceptive British officials. The corollary to this proposition, that if dividing the Palestinians failed, it would be necessary for Britain to have recourse to massive force, was not as widely understood among British officialdom, especially in London.

However, successive British governments from 1917 until at least 1939 were firmly committed to Zionism for reasons rooted partly in strategic considerations, partly in Christian Zionism, and partly perhaps in a subtle form of anti-Semitism that supported the national rights of Jews in Palestine while remaining silent about discrimination against them elsewhere.[16] Given this commitment, and given a certain degree of obstinacy in London in avoiding confronting the costs that would eventually flow from such a policy, those officials in Palestine who had their doubts as to its viability generally kept their views private. The few who voiced them publicly in the Palestine administration often found themselves branded as anti-Zionists, or worse, as anti-Semites, by those back home in Britain who refused to recognize these realities on the ground.[17]

These accusations were leveled in particular against some officials of the British military administration that controlled Palestine in the years until Sir Herbert Samuel was named high commissioner and the Mandate was finally implemented, and later against others under the Mandate. Some of these individuals were anti-Semitic (many of them, indeed, loathed all "Semites" equally, including the Arabs),[18] but this did not vitiate the acuity of their analysis that massive force would have to be employed in order to impose a Jewish national home on the unwilling Arabs. The leader of the radical Revisionist Zionist movement, Ze'ev Jabotinsky, nearly alone among his peers, recognized this fact from the very beginning. As early as 1925 Jabotinsky wrote: "If you wish to colonize a land in which people are already living, you must provide a garrison for the land, or find a benefactor who will maintain a garrison on your behalf.... Zionism is a colonizing venture and, therefore, it stands or falls on the question of armed forces."[19] Jabotinsky and the few British officials who agreed with him were in fact right, although this was only unequivocally proven to be the case during the Arab revolt of 1936–39, and the bloody fighting of 1947–48. In the intervals, many British officials in Palestine and London preferred to bury their heads in the sand.

It was therefore a vital objective of the British to keep the Palestinians from uniting against them and their policy of support for Zionism in order to prevent or at least delay the inevitable Arab backlash against this policy. This necessarily involved accentuating existing differences, and in some cases creating new ones. A variety of means were used to achieve these ends, with considerable success at least until the mid-1930s. As we have seen, British efforts to manipulate Palestinian leaders and factions could take the form of official appointments in the gift of the mandatory power, whether these were within the administration or in semiofficial institutions such as the Supreme Muslim Council. While other forms of blandishment and punishment were employed, there was often little need to resort to such extremes, as the power of the mandatory government was so great that it could seriously harm the interests of those it chose to punish, and richly reward those whom it wished to favor, simply via the utilization of the considerable authority at its disposal. The power to hire and fire employees in government and semiofficial jobs, the existence of government censorship, the power to allow or ban meetings, demonstrations, and the organization of groups and associations, the authority to impose administrative detention and internal and external exile, and myriad other overt and covert means enabled the British to exert enormous influence over Palestinian society. The individuals receiving these benefits may have believed that they were outsmarting the British, and that they were getting the better part of the bargain. The mufti most likely felt this to be the case, as he built the Supreme Muslim Council and the other institutions he controlled into an alternative political base for himself and his supporters. But such deals were a devil's bargain since, as we shall see, the political leaders who entered into them were fatally limited in their freedom to oppose British policies in the 1920s and 1930s.

Meanwhile, representatives of the Zionist movement appear to have paid subventions to certain leading Palestinian figures, at least through the mid-1920s and in some cases afterward. This seems clearest in the case of newspaper owners and publishers, since we know that as early as the pre–World War I period, subsidies were paid to a few individuals to produce pro-Zionist articles, whether in Palestine or Egypt or elsewhere.[20] The means of influencing the press included as well the purchase of large numbers of subscriptions (something quite valuable in a time and place when paying readers were hard to find), and steering lucrative advertising to "cooperative" newspapers.[21] The evidence is murkier for later periods, and for instances of direct subventions to politicians.[22] As with the touchy issue of land sales by Arab landlords to Zionist land-purchase agencies or to individual Jewish buyers, all concerned carefully wreathed these activities in secrecy, with multiple intermediaries sometimes involved. On the other hand, as any allegations in this regard, even unfounded ones, were enough to harm the reputations of nationalist Palestinian politicians, they could be a potent political weapon for all and sundry, and even today these allegations must be examined carefully. We shall see later in this chapter how the nationalist leader 'Auni 'Abd al-Hadi came to be affected by just such allegations when his opponents perceived his activities to be dangerous.

The main sources that reveal to us the payment by the Zionist movement of subsidies to Palestinian political figures are official reports or private papers and diaries in the Zionist archives. Typically, Chaim Kalvarisky, a leading official in the Zionist movement, in 1923 reported that Fakhri al-Nashashibi, Raghib Bey's cousin and deputy, had asked for funds to help set up a political party in opposition to the Supreme Muslim Council and the Arab Executive.[23] There is similar information in the British archives, and suspicions regarding Zionist payoffs to leading Arab figures, occasionally unfounded, in other sources that may or may not have been well placed to know what was going on. These include the diplomatic and consular correspondence of other powers, such as that of the French. Thus the French consul general in Jerusalem reported, giving no evidence for this allegation, that the nationalist leader Mu'in al-Madi had secret contacts with the Zionists, who were trying to win him over, presumably with financial inducements.[24] To take a parallel issue of similar sensitivity, Zionist sources reported land purchases in terms of the original seller and the final ownership of a piece of property. It is not clear from these sources whether these sales took place in an active market for land, such that a given piece of land may have passed through several hands before ending up in Zionist ownership.[25] Similarly, it is not always clear whether the middlemen who were frequently involved were so well disguised that sellers might have had no idea to whom their property was ultimately being ceded. On the other hand, in many cases the only possible purchasers were Zionist organizations, or sellers were aware of the identity of the purchasers.[26]

It appears that direct payments were made to a number of Arab politicians, but sometimes we do not know by whom, in what guise, or what the recipients thought they were being paid for. This should lead us to use with caution some reports on this topic. Moreover, it is rarely mentioned by historians who note this practice that it seems to have been abandoned as a general policy in the mid-1920s when its inefficacy became manifest.[27] As Tom Segev correctly points out, much of this effort was dedicated to "fanning inter-Arab rivalries."[28] There was another objective besides subversion that drove many of the key Zionist figures involved in these efforts: intelligence gathering. The historian Benny Morris notes that these individuals saw "links with Arabs as both attempts at conciliation and as the cultivation of sources of information."[29] Thus the ubiquitous Chaim Kalvarisky, active in land purchase, bribery of Arab notables, and political negotiations, was "a key Yishuv intelligence officer."[30] Morris names four other key figures in the Zionist movement involved in the same efforts; they, too, wore several hats, including work in espionage. Perhaps the most eminent of the four, Reuven Zaslani, eventually became the founder of Israel's external espionage agency, the Mossad. Zaslani later changed his name to Shiloach, and the Middle East Center at Tel Aviv University (now the Moshe Dayan Center) was named for him for a time. The two names that this center has borne illustrate the intimate (and thoroughly unselfconscious) relationship within Israeli institutions between academic study of the region on the one hand, and both intelligence work and warfare directed against the Arabs on the other.[31]

Radical Challenges to the Notables

While there existed rivalries among Palestinians that external forces sought to exploit for their own purposes, rivalries also existed between the imperial powers, which local actors attempted to exploit, with greater or lesser degrees of success. In the interwar period, the most noteworthy of these was the long-standing Anglo-French competition for influence in the Middle East, which had been particularly acute before World War I. The 1904 entente whereby France acquiesced in Britain's preponderant position in Egypt (and

Britain accepted France's dominant standing in Morocco) at least nominally resolved those two aspects of this rivalry. With respect to Syria, the competition for influence between the two powers was supposedly settled by a series of diplomatic exchanges in 1912 and subsequent Anglo-French railway understandings, later formalized in the 1916 Sykes-Picot accords, which promised France a hegemonic position in the areas that were to become Syria and Lebanon.[32]

The granting of mandates to Britain and France over the new entities they created out of the Arab provinces of the Ottoman Empire after World War I ostensibly put a final end to this rivalry. However, it was not easy for the French and British officials of the new mandatory regimes, many of whom had long careers in colonial affairs in the Levant, and all of whom were steeped in a heritage of over two centuries of acute worldwide Anglo-French imperial competition, to unlearn the lessons engendered by such prolonged suspicion and dislike of one another's policies and methods. And even after the formal resolution of the differences between them, there were still clear conflicts between the interests of the two powers in the Levant. A great deal of resentment consequently ensued among officials on both sides. This could be seen especially when Britain's protégés in the Jordanian government gave refuge to rebels fleeing French repression after the failure of the 1925–26 revolt in Syria. France thereupon returned the favor via its protégés in the Lebanese and Syrian governments by harboring Palestinians fleeing British repression during the 1936–39 revolt in Palestine. Because of the resulting tensions, British diplomatic dispatches regarding Syria can be particularly revealing (and highly critical) as regards aspects of French policy.[33] The same is often true of what is written by French observers regarding both the policy of the British in Palestine and the activities of their local allies and clients, both Zionist and Arab.

The French, for example, were highly skeptical of the bona fides of those among the Palestinian elite who had the closest ties with the British. They generally saw them as no more than weak collaborators with a power trying to impose an untenable policy of support for Zionism that was understandably opposed by the vast mass of the population. From very early on in the Mandate, French consular sources, reflecting the now-buried, but still smoldering, old rivalry between the two powers, were explicit and consistent in describing the near-universal nature of Palestinian Arab hostility to British policy. One French official in Palestine wrote in 1921: "One should not have any illusions: the anti-Zionist movement that was recently launched in Jaffa has deep roots."[34] A French intelligence agent in 1921 reported strong anti-British (and pro-French!) feeling in Palestine because of Britain's support for Zionism, noting at this early date that the influence of the notables on public opinion was waning and that *les gens du peuple* were increasingly in control of events.[35] A 1932 dispatch was even more unequivocal:

> This hostility is already an undeniable fact, and it will increase. Except for a small group of profiteers around the Mayor of Jerusalem, Ragheb Bey Nachachibi, who desire to share the few places allowed to the locals, the entirety of the Palestinian Arab world is currently turned against the mandatory power. Until now the slogan (insofar as politicians so undeveloped and unconvincing can have one) has been: "Against Zionism." Now it is: "Against England, which is responsible for Zionism."[36]

Raghib Bey al-Nashashibi and his allies were thus perceived by the French to be a tiny and isolated group, without support within Palestinian society, and essentially kept afloat by British support and Zionist subventions. French diplomats were quite unequivocal in this regard. Another dispatch, from d'Aumale, the French consul general in Jerusalem, repeated allegations by the mufti that the Nashashibi faction was in the pay of the Zionists and added:

> My information tends to lead in the very same direction. The Palestinian Muslim opposition [to the mufti] is dependent

upon the Zionists. . . . [They] are all grasping landlords, to whom
the Jews offer good money. . . . This opposition to the Mufti does
not involve either financial power, or moral values, and it has no
Islamic significance whatsoever.[37]

After reading these and other French comments disparaging
Raghib Bey al-Nashashibi and other leading members of his faction,
one is left with the question: how politically important was this
group in reality? Were they any more than a clique of protégés of the
British colonial power, unrepresentative of their own society, and
for some time at least in receipt of clandestine funding from the
Zionist movement (which is largely the view of them reflected in
much of the Arab-nationalist-influenced historiography)? Or was
the French reporting as unobjective and biased as some other reporting by outsiders? As we have seen, French observers clearly considered that the degree of support that this group could muster
for their positions on the popular level was very small. At the same
time, however, it should be noted that by the 1930s there were many
Palestinians who were highly critical of the mufti and his faction,
because they, too, were seen as having close links with the British,
and because they were perceived to be just as responsible as the
Nashashibi faction for the passiveness, torpidity, and general ineffectiveness of the notable leadership of the forces that composed
the Palestinian nationalist movement.

In fact, in fairness to al-Nashashibi, until the mid-1930s his public position vis-à-vis the British (to be distinguished from what he
might have said and done in private) was no more and no less conciliatory than that of the mufti. Indeed, until only a few years before
the outbreak of the 1936–39 Arab revolt in Palestine, virtually the entire Palestinian leadership remained individually on relatively cor-
dial terms with senior British officials. Their actions indicate that for
well over a decade they believed that by simply continuing to negotiate with British officials, combined with a little genteel pressure,
they would eventually be able to persuade Britain to change its pol-

icy and hand over the reins of power to the country's "natural" rulers, that is to say themselves. This comes through clearly in the entirety of the records we have of meetings between Palestinian leaders and the British, such as the London meetings of 1930 described in Chapter 2. The mufti shared fully in this approach; indeed, he was a leading member of the 1930 delegation that met with Lord Passfield.

But beyond that, in the last analysis the mufti was fatally compromised in the eyes of many Palestinians by being no more than a functionary of the British mandatory administration. His status as a dependent of the British is reflected in another French dispatch reporting on what they probably exaggeratedly estimated to have been the resounding success of the Islamic Conference that he organized in Jerusalem in 1931 in order to garner support from the Muslim world for the Palestinians and for his own position as a national leader:

> From President of a small corps of Palestinian ulemas whose name, "The Supreme Muslim Council," is pompous, but which was nothing more than a fabricated council of a holy mosque, Hajj Amin has become the authorized spokesman of the entire Islamic world. He is no longer a simple British functionary. ... The British authorities, who have given him free rein, hoping one day to make use of him, find themselves overwhelmed. ... Many of them have told me of their apprehensions and their regrets at having taken this little cleric without a future out of a lowly position and of having themselves created an element of trouble in Palestine and in India.[38]

This is undoubtedly an overestimation of the degree to which the mufti's position had been enhanced as a result of the holding of the Islamic Congress.[39] Nevertheless, this French account sums up accurately the invented nature of the Supreme Muslim Council, the fact that the mufti was in a certain sense no more than an employee of the British mandatory administration, and his relatively modest standing before his rise to prominence following his selection as mufti by Sir Herbert Samuel. It also accurately depicts an early stage in the process whereby Hajj Amin al-Husayni gradually became a nationalist leader who no longer did the bidding of the British.

We are left with a picture of a Palestinian elite that was hopelessly divided internally, and many of whose most prominent members had a variety of more or less entangling connections to the British overlords of the country, while some had links to the Zionists as well. The primary modus operandi of these Palestinian leaders vis-à-vis the British differed little from one individual to another, in spite of their apparent political differences and whatever else may have divided them: negotiate courteously, not to say obsequiously, with the British in private, while criticizing their policies loudly in public, and doing very little else to oppose them. They generally eschewed giving speeches, leading demonstrations, and other manifestations of mass politics. By contrast with Syria and Egypt, where political parties were well established in the 1920s, and where the decade after World War I was punctuated by a series of violent revolts, demonstrations, and continuous mass actions, the first such parties in Palestine were set up in the 1930s, and most were no more than vehicles for the ambitions and aspirations of a single leader or a family group.[40] Moreover, with the exception of a series of anti-Jewish and anti-British outbreaks in 1920 in Jerusalem and 1921 in Jaffa, and the upheaval of 1929 when about 250 people were killed, Palestine was less disturbed by political turbulence than these two countries. Indeed, for the first fifteen years of British rule, Palestinian leaders repeatedly assured their official British interlocutors that they were working to calm their followers.

Again, this situation can in part be explained by the fact that the men who dominated Palestinian politics at this stage felt themselves to be the natural rulers of the country. Like their fellow notables in other Arab countries, they considered themselves to be the legitimate heirs to the Ottoman dominion. Many of them had served this dominion with distinction, or had received training in its leading institutions: Musa Kazim al-Husayni was an Ottoman pasha who had served as governor of Yemen; Hajj Amin al-Husayni had served as an officer in the Ottoman army for the entirety of World War I, as had Dr. Husayn al-Khalidi, later mayor of Jerusalem and leader of a political party (who was wounded in one of the last battles of World War I in Syria); Musa al-'Alami, an important figure in the Palestinian leadership, was the son of a prominent Ottoman official; Raghib Bey al-Nashashibi had served as a deputy for Jerusalem in the Ottoman Parliament from April 1914 until the end of World War I; while 'Auni 'Abd al-Hadi had been educated at the prestigious Mekteb-i Mülkiye-i Sahane—the Imperial Civil Service School in Istanbul.[41]

These men and their peers were accustomed to command, and felt themselves the equals of the other post-Ottoman elites in the Arab world, with whom they had long-standing personal, educational, and family connections. They noted with bitterness that in spite of its relatively high level of development compared with other parts of the Arab world, Palestine remained under the most oppressive form of direct British rule (with the exception of the yishuv, which had complete autonomy and self-rule), while a realm they considered to be backward, Transjordan, had obtained self-government from the British. Iraq, Syria, and Lebanon had all managed to obtain a measure of self-rule from the French, while Egypt had been nominally independent since 1922. Yemen and Saudi Arabia, of course, had never been under any form of European control, and were fully independent countries.

Seeing this strikingly disparate behavior on the part of the colonial powers, however, the primary response of the Palestinian elite (unlike many of their counterparts in Egypt and Syria) was to beseech, petition, and beg the British to give them what they considered to be their natural entitlement. The idea of mobilizing the Arab population of Palestine against the British on a sustained basis was thoroughly alien to most of them, for notwithstanding their modern Western educations, they were deeply imbued with the top-down traditions that permeated Arab society and the Ottoman political system, and were strongly influenced by their upper-class origins, and by the networks of ties with the British mandatory authorities that had developed since 1920. When such mobilization took place, it was generally spontaneously generated, and came from below, not orchestrated by this elite. This was true of the earliest outbreaks of violence against the yishuv and the British, in 1920, 1921, and 1929, and of the great Palestinian revolt of 1936–39.[42]

However, after over a decade of British occupation, the futility of the gentlemanly approach employed by the elites was manifest not only to foreign observers like the French. Increasing numbers of ordinary Palestinians, particularly the increasing numbers of educated youth, were chafing at the ineptitude and ineffectiveness of this leadership and its obvious inability to bring Great Britain to change the terms of the Mandate, to grant representative government, or to modify its support for Zionism in any significant way, let alone to grant Palestine independence. They were also growing impatient at the heavy-handed domination of the country's politics by the notables. This increasing popular discontentment with the course of the Palestinian national struggle at the end of the 1920s and in the early 1930s was visible in a number of ways.

The first was the growth of more radical forms of opposition to the British, based in new groupings, parties, and forms of association, such as boy-scout and other youth organizations with a nationalist or religious political orientation, the Young Men's Muslim Association, labor unions, and professional associations. Some of these groups called for boycotting the British entirely, taking the successful tactics of the Congress Party in India as their example and demanding immediate independence. Needless to say, such an approach horrified most members of a notable leadership that was almost without exception deeply involved with the British, and many of whom were directly on the payroll of the Mandate. Other grassroots groups, most notably one under the influence of the dynamic and popular Syrian shaykh 'Iz al-Din al-Qassam in the Haifa area, began laying the groundwork for the underground armed militant networks in the Palestinian urban areas and countryside that would later constitute the backbone of armed rebellion against the British, although this eventuality still seemed quite far off in the late 1920s.[43]

The most significant of the new formations to arise at this time was probably Hizb al-Istiqlal al-'Arabi, or the Arab Independence Party, whose first precursors developed in 1930, and which was formally founded in 1932.[44] Istiqlal was not an entirely new phenomenon, but rather the outgrowth of Pan-Arab groupings and tendencies that had long existed in Palestine and elsewhere. The leading members of the party had an involvement with Pan-Arab causes that went back to the Arab secret societies of the late Ottoman period, via the Istiqlal Party founded in Syria during the period of Faysal's Arab kingdom there (and of which the Palestinian party saw itself as a continuation). Its preeminent figure in Palestine was 'Auni 'Abd al-Hadi, a member of an aristocratic family educated under the Ottomans, who had been a leader of the prewar secret societies and of the Istiqlal Party in Syria, and a confidant of King Faysal's there. Lacking personal charisma, and practiced in backroom politics, 'Abd al-Hadi was a charter member of both the Palestinian and Arab elites. He differed from other members of the notable class who dominated Palestinian politics only in the uncompromising nature of his commitment to Arab nationalism and Palestinian independence, and in his unwavering opposition to the British.

The Palestinian Istiqlal Party aspired to be a mass-based political formation (although it never grew very large) that advocated an adamant anti-British and Pan-Arab stance and rejected the conciliatory approach followed by the Palestinian national movement until that point. Beyond that, according to the historian Weldon Matthews, "It was...the first Arab party in Palestine to attempt mass, public organization."[45] In addition to its declaratory policy, the Istiqlal Party called for specific radical measures, such as a na-

tionwide boycott of the mandatory administration, noncooperation with the colonial authorities, and sometimes noncompliance
with their laws, along the lines advocated by the Indian Congress
Party, which was a source of inspiration for it.[46] Short-lived though
it was (the party effectively ceased to exist in 1934), Istiqlal was in
fact one of the only true Palestinian political parties in the full sense
of that term, meaning having a clear ideology, a broad membership,
and a national rather than a regional, local, or family base, which
was the case of virtually all the other Palestinian parties formed in
the 1930s. The party's formation was a clear sign of the dissatisfaction of many educated young people with the uninspired and un-
successful forms of struggle that were unvaryingly employed by the
national movement's notable leadership.

Paradoxically, although 'Abd al-Hadi, the paramount leader of
the Istiqlal Party, was himself an eminent notable figure, the formation of the party constituted an expression of a social, educational,
and generational divide. This divide separated most of the older
Palestinian notable leaders, educated and trained under Ottomans,
and who for the most part wore the red tarbush (the "fez") that de-
noted a certain generation and class background, and a respectable
status in society, from many of their younger, less-well-off followers. The latter were brought up under the British Mandate, had received a modern education and had often learned English, were
impatient with the tactics of their elders, and were at least as scorn-
ful of this earlier generation's corruption, self-serving maneuvers,
and ineffectiveness as were many outside observers. By contrast,
'Abd al-Hadi was older, had an Ottoman education, spoke French in
preference to English (though he knew both), and was in every way
a patrician. His age (he was born in 1882), his training as a lawyer,
his consequent involvement in business affairs, and his diffident,
aloof manner, all marked him off from the younger, more radical,
lower-middle- and middle-class core of the party's membership. As
we shall see, 'Abd al-Hadi's work as a lawyer was ultimately to ex-

pose him to damaging accusations, which in turn gravely harmed the image of the party he headed.

Needless to say, the Palestinian notable leadership, the British, and the Zionists, collectively perceived this and other radical new Palestinian political movements and forms of organization with deep concern. For many of the notables, a boycott of the British would not only have meant admitting the complete futility of the tactics they had followed for over a decade. Perhaps worse, it would also have meant losing the jobs on which many of them depended for their livelihoods. This involvement of so many educated Palestinian members of the country's elite in the British mandatory administration was ultimately highly damaging to Palestinian unity, as the condition for such involvement was acquiescing in, or at least not opposing, the Mandate policy of support for a Jewish national home. Many members of this elite who held such positions had to choose between their livelihoods and the social status and prestige that went with them on the one hand, and their beliefs and principles on the other. Whatever the outcomes in individual cases, the overall impact of this dilemma was to paralyze many Palestinians who would otherwise have played a leadership role in politics—yet another illustration of the iron cage the British Mandate created for the Palestinians, and into which some Palestinian leaders willingly entered.

An Arab policy of boycotting the British also posed problems for the Zionist movement. It would have meant that the Palestinians were changing their avowed focus from anti-Zionism—a stance relatively easy to conflate with anti-Semitism, thereby raising hackles in Europe, America, and among Jewish communities worldwide—to outright opposition to British colonialism, a much more difficult position for the Zionists to counter successfully. For the British, finally, such a radical shift would have revealed the bankruptcy of the pretense that they were evenhanded brokers between the two sides, or that the Jewish national home policy could be implemented without the employment of overwhelming force against the recalcitrant Palestinian Arab majority. It also would have meant that they were embroiled in confronting yet another frustrating anticolonial struggle in a world slowly growing less favorable to colonialism. It therefore became essential for the British to find the means of "weakening the Istiqlal Party's influence in Palestine."[47]

Another manifestation of Palestinian discontent with the failure of the national movement to achieve any of its objectives was a general increase in rebellious acts, whether directed against the British or the Zionists, or sometimes other Arabs. The authorities naturally described these acts in terms of "lawlessness" or "banditry," rather than in political terms, and sometimes they were nothing more than that, although as the eminent economic historian Eric Hobsbawm has shown, much more is often involved than mere unruliness where "banditry" is involved.[48] The mounting number of attacks on travelers or on isolated Zionist settlements was in some measure a function of the increasing landlessness of the Palestinian peasantry in some parts of the country. This was largely due to the rapid expansion of Zionist landholdings in the 1920s and early 1930s, and the gradual imposition by the Zionist movement of the policy of *avoda ivrit,* or "Hebrew labor," which was meant to replace Arab agricultural laborers with Jewish ones, and the consequent growing landlessness and unemployment among the Palestinian peasantry.[49] The 1930 report of the Shaw Commission, appointed by the British government to investigate the causes of the 1929 riots, in which 133 Jews were killed by Arab mobs and 116 Arabs were killed, mainly by the British in the ensuing repression, described the problem of landlessness in some detail.[50] What the British and Zionists called "banditry" continued in the wake of the 1929 riots, and there was an eventual increase in the incidence of attacks on the British and their Zionist protégés, as well as on well-to-do Arabs.

There was clearly a class element to this antagonism toward other Arabs, fueled by the fact that, as we have seen, some of those profiting from selling land to the Zionists belonged to the same notable class whose members purported to be the leaders in the resistance to Zionism. The core of the new political formations that posed a challenge to the leadership of the notables starting around 1930 was made up of young, radical men from the middle and professional classes, many of them educated in Mandate schools, from the new urban working class, from displaced agricultural workers who had drifted to the cities and the shantytowns on their outskirts, and from other disadvantaged or nonprivileged groups. From the latter groups also emerged the sometimes inchoate bands of rebels who took to the hills to fight the British or Jewish settlers starting in 1929. From these same sectors of the Palestinian population came those who later organized the six-month general strike of 1936, which marked the start of the great 1936–39 Palestinian revolt and formed the backbone of the nationwide armed resistance to the British during the subsequent phases of the revolt.

The anger expressed by Palestinian public opinion at the unchecked expansion, with British support, of the Zionist project grew exponentially in the mid-1930s. This was particularly the case after the flood of tens of thousands of new Jewish immigrants yearly in the wake of Hitler's rise to power transformed the fundamental dynamics of the demographic battle, to the deepening disadvantage of the Palestinians. This in turn fed the growth of British-described lawlessness, the development of grassroots organizations beyond the control of the traditional notables, and the adoption of new forms of struggle and new demands. These unprecedented pressures pushed many of the traditional leaders, notably the mufti, to do two contradictory things in the mid-1930s: they escalated their public political confrontations with the British authorities even as they tried as best they could to maintain their cozy private relationships with them.[51]

These confrontations with the British were initially verbal. However, popular anger and both spontaneous and organized demonstrations and protests over rapidly rising Jewish immigration, increasing Palestinian landlessness, and the absence of measures to respond to this ever more critical situation eventually forced the Palestinian leadership, spurred by the Istiqlal Party in particular, to organize public marches the likes of which had been banned by the authorities. During one of the biggest and most turbulent of these protests, in Jaffa in October 1933, twenty-two demonstrators and a policeman were killed, and the nominal leader of the national movement, the octogenarian Musa Kazim al-Husayni, was beaten to the ground by stick-wielding British security forces.[52] He died a few months thereafter, and with him passed a certain old-fashioned style of leadership, and much of the assurance of the notables in their ability to control their nominal followers, the Palestinian people. Musa Kazim al-Husayni had never managed to impose himself as an effective national leader, whether with his own people, the Zionists (who had at one point in the early 1920s apparently managed to bribe him) or the British: one official said condescendingly while describing his dismissal as mayor in 1920 that he had "proved himself on occasion a courteous Arab gentleman."[53] In consequence, after the 1929 riots he had gradually lost ground to his younger and more astute relative, the mufti.

Only two years after Musa Kazim al-Husayni's death, his son, 'Abd al-Qadir al-Husayni, followed the lead of Shaykh 'Iz al-Din al-Qassam and his followers and became one of the leading exponents and practitioners of armed resistance to the British and their Zionist protégés. This marked a major shift in Palestinian strategy from the cautious approach of playing both sides of the street with the British, typified until this point by Musa Kazim al-Husayni, the mufti, and most of the rest of the traditional Palestinian leadership. 'Abd al-Qadir al-Husayni's death in battle with Zionist forces in April 1948 during fierce fighting over the strategic village of al-Qastal on the road to Jerusalem symbolized as well a generational shift that was taking place in Palestine at this time.[54] The short, fiery trajectory of his career, ending as the military leader of Palestinian forces fighting in the Jerusalem area, contrasted starkly with that of his father, a gentlemanly figure whose ineffectual efforts were confined to the corridors of power until his death in the wake of a demonstration in which he seemed quite out of his element.

The second response of the notable leadership to the challenge posed by these new grassroots organizations and the new demands they represented was to try to undermine or co-opt their rising political and associational formations, which were challenging the notable's power. In at least one aspect of this endeavor, they found willing allies among both the British and the Zionist leadership. In his pathbreaking study, Weldon Matthews has shown clearly how both parties colluded with the mufti and his political associates to meet what they perceived as the most dangerous of the overt challenges to their dominance, that posed by the Istiqlal Party.[55] Thus, he reveals that at a dinner in his home in 1932, the British high commissioner, Sir Arthur Wauchope, asked Chaim Arlosoroff, the head of the Political Department of the Jewish Agency, to provide incriminating material on the involvement of Istiqlal Party leaders in land transfers to the Zionist movement. Clearly, the British and the Zionists were as deeply alarmed as the Palestinian notables by the rise of a Palestinian radical grouping with nationwide support and a Pan-Arab agenda dedicated to opposing British rule and defeating Zionism. In 1933 the mufti's cousin and political ally, Jamal al-Husayni, published an anonymous story in the Damascus paper *Alif Ba* (later reprinted in a paper associated with the mufti) about the role of the Istiqlal Party's figurehead, 'Auni 'Abd al-Hadi, in a complex deal involving ten thousand acres of land in Wadi Hawarith that thereafter resulted in its sale to the Zionists, in 1927. That this story had some basis in truth—whatever 'Abd al-Hadi's real role in this murky episode—did not make any more savory the spectacle of the mufti and his cohorts conniving with the British and the Zionists to block the rise of a more militant alternative to their failing leadership and incoherent tactics.[56]

But when radical change in the course of Palestinian political opposition to the British and to Zionism was firmly blocked by the determined resistance of the traditional notable leaders to any diminution of their inept control over the Palestinian national movement, frustrated popular discontent had to find another avenue of expression. It ultimately did so in a variety of even more radical forms. These included the abortive attempt of Shaykh 'Iz al-Din al-Qassam in November 1935 to launch an armed uprising in which he was killed (his funeral was the occasion for a huge popular demonstration, whose size astonished contemporary observers[57]), the nationwide six-month general strike in 1936, the longest in colonial history to that point, and the subsequent massive armed rebellion against the British that lasted until 1939. Although at the outset these were spontaneous, grassroots popular manifestations, eventually they were all in some measure co-opted by the notable leadership. The failure of their traditional tactics ultimately obliged these leaders to stand uneasily at the head of mass movements that they did not fully control, and whose tactics they undoubtedly would not themselves have voluntarily chosen. Their inept leadership ultimately helped to doom these movements as well.

The Challenge from the Press:
'Isa al-'Isa and *Filastin*

Linked to the notables, but also to some of the radical voices that derided their failures, was the Palestinian press. Beyond providing a forum for the views of different notable leaders, and a venue for some of the movements and forces whose emergence was touched on in the previous section, different organs of the press played a role in articulating a response to the growing predicament the Palestinians found themselves in during the 1920s and 1930s. The press is a particularly valuable source for understanding issues of identity. One of the best ways to gain an understanding of the linkage between local patriotism, anti-Zionism, and Arabism in the coalescence of Palestinian identity is via study of the burgeoning press in Palestine, whether during the late Ottoman or the Mandate period.[58] As I have argued elsewhere, the press provides a unique insight into the thinking of an important segment of the population, presenting the views of writers, teachers, businesspeople, union leaders, government officials, and others influential in society.[59] For these same reasons, a window into the political dilemmas of the day can often be offered by the press, and particularly by a distinctive journalistic voice.

The most influential Palestinian newspaper during the first half of the twentieth century was likely *Filastin* (Palestine),[60] launched by 'Isa al-'Isa together with his cousin Yusuf al-'Isa in January 1911 in the rapidly growing port city of Jaffa.[61] 'Isa al-'Isa ultimately produced some of the most scathing critiques of the leadership of the Palestinian national movement, in particular the approach taken by the mufti and his allies, although he was for a time less critical of the mufti's rival, Raghib Bey al-Nashashibi, and indeed was aligned with him at one stage. *Filastin* managed to hold its own throughout the Mandate period, although many rivals sprang up, and each political faction had its own supporters among the press, in a shifting picture that changed constantly.

Filastin was not only the Jaffa region's foremost journalistic opponent of Zionism; within a few months of its launch it had an avid readership in other parts of Palestine, and well beyond.[62] Launched as a biweekly, it shut down during World War I, and then returned in 1921, coming out three times a week until 1929, when it started to appear daily, thereafter becoming the country's foremost paper. It was not coincidental that Jaffa should have been a center for the Arab reaction to Zionism, or that Haifa should have been the venue for another newspaper that devoted extensive attention to the danger posed by Zionism, Najib Nassar's *al-Karmil* (named for Mount Carmel, which overlooks the port of Haifa), which first appeared in 1908. For in the initial decades of modern political Zionism, from the late 1880s until World War I, Zionist land purchase and colonization were mainly concentrated in two areas: the citrus-producing coastal region around Jaffa, where the new Jewish suburb of Tel Aviv (later to become a city larger than Jaffa) was founded in 1909, and in the fertile Galilean hinterland of Haifa. The modern Zionist movement thus first established its roots in Palestine along the coast, rather than in the rocky highlands of central and northern Palestine where the major cities of Jerusalem, Nablus, and Hebron were located and most of the prestigious Muslim notable families that dominated the country's politics originated.[63]

In population terms as well, the great majority of those who came in the first and second aliyahs, or waves of modern Jewish immigration to Palestine, arriving before 1914, were located in the coastal regions and in Galilee. During this period, these two regions were also the scenes of the most extensive Zionist land purchases, and of the greatest friction between the local population and the more aggressive, nationalist settlers of the post-1904 second aliyah.[64] Although Jerusalem included the largest concentration of Jews in Palestine before 1914, these were mainly members of the old yishuv, the traditional Jewish community of Palestine. They tended to be religious and anti- or non-Zionist, were mainly Mizrahis or Sephardis (Eastern and Mediterranean Jews) rather than Ashkenazis (European Jews), were mainly Ottoman citizens, usually spoke Arabic and were familiar with the Arab cultural milieu, and were generally on good terms with their Arab neighbors.[65]

At the same time as it was the venue of the most active Zionist colonization activity, the coastal region was also the scene of the most rapid urban, industrial, and social development among the Arabs of Palestine. Thus, the Jaffa and Haifa areas and the adjacent Galilee region were the sites of the most intensive and constant friction between Arab inhabitants of the country and Zionist newcomers from Europe. It was also in these rapidly growing cosmopolitan port cities, with their active economic, social, and political life (and which, as we have seen, by the end of the British Mandate in 1948 were the two largest Arab population centers in Palestine[66]), that the most prosperous, active, and respected Arabic-language newspapers developed. *Filastin* was soon the foremost among them, rivaled in popularity and circulation only by the Jaffa-based *al-Difaʿ*[67]: throughout the Mandate period, *Filastin* was Palestine's main Arabic-language daily, and probably the country's fiercest and most consistent critic of the Zionist enterprise.

In addition to Zionism, the central issues on which the newspaper focused included the encouragement of education, the struggle of the Arabic-speaking Greek Orthodox laity in Palestine to free their church (which was under the jurisdiction of the patriarch of Jerusalem) from domination by the Greek-speaking higher clergy,[68] Muslim-Christian relations, and rural conditions, in particular the poverty of the peasantry. In many cases, these issues also came to be connected to Zionism, whether in terms of the local patriotism that engendered much of ʿIsa al-ʿIsa's concern for education, or the questions of religious and national identity raised both by the struggle within the Greek Orthodox Church and by the conflict with the Zionist movement, or the problem of rural poverty with its inevitable linkage to land sales to the Zionist movement by absentee owners, with the consequent dispossession of the Arab peasantry, the fellahin.

The concern for the lot of the peasantry expressed in *Filastin* was manifested in its policy of sending a copy of each issue to every village in the Jaffa region. The paper stated that this was done as a public service in order to show the fellah "what is happening in the country, and to teach him his rights, in order to prevent those who do not fear God and his prophets from dominating him and stealing his goods."[69] This profound concern was at the root of al-ʿIsa's fears regarding Zionism. In time, the problem of peasant dispossession by Zionist land-purchase became acute. This raised the possibility that the Zionist newcomers might in time dispossess the entire Arab population of Palestine, a growing fear among Palestinians in the 1930s, as the Jewish population of the country expanded rapidly and from under 18 percent in the 1920s reached nearly a third of the total.[70]

In this and other ways, *Filastin* played a major role in shaping a sense of Palestinian identity, which clearly was one of its main aims, given that its title means "Palestine." Thus only three years after the newspaper was founded, its editors were talking, in a 1914 editorial, of the country of Palestine (*al-bilad al-filistiniyya*), and the "Palestinian nation" (*al-umma al-filistiniyya*) as being imperiled by Zionism. "We are a nation threatened with disappearance in the face of the Zionist tide in this Palestinian land," the editorial stated. This idea of a Palestinian nation was clearly complementary in the minds of Yusuf and 'Isa al-'Isa with the idea of the Arab nation, *al-umma al-'arabiyya*, whose existence they invoked in the same editorial.[71] This powerful overall nationalist orientation comes through in a speech 'Isa al-'Isa delivered many years later, stating that while he originally was drawn to journalism in order to champion the cause of the Arab Orthodox laity and lower clergy against the Greek hierarchy, he soon became involved in other national questions, between Arabs and Turks, and between Palestinians and Zionists.[72]

As time went on, moreover, *Filastin* came to be relied upon throughout the Arab world for news of Zionist policy initiatives and the progress of Zionist colonization in Palestine, thereby playing an important role in establishing Zionism as an issue that concerned all Arabs. Even before World War I, the paper's editorials and articles on Zionism were picked up and reproduced by other newspapers, not only in Palestine but in Beirut, Cairo, Damascus, and other centers throughout the Arabic-speaking world. *Filastin* became even more influential regionally after World War I, when readers in different parts of the Arab world showed an increasing interest in the Palestine question, and came to rely on articles reprinted from *Filastin* for news and opinion on this subject. This newspaper was thus a journalistic pioneer of an unwavering opposition to Zionism on both the Palestinian and Pan-Arab levels. It deserves the attention it has begun to receive as an important organ of opinion in pre-1948 Palestine, and one of the foremost Palestinian papers to have an impact on the rest of the Arab world, as does its editor, 'Isa al-'Isa.[73]

'Isa al-'Isa was born in Jaffa in 1878, studied at the Ecole des

Frères in Jaffa, and the Greek Orthodox school in Kiftin in North Lebanon,[74] and then graduated from the American University of Beirut (AUB), learning Arabic, Turkish, French, and English in the process.[75] He held a variety of jobs in Jerusalem and Jaffa, including working for the Iranian Consulate and the Coptic Monastery in Jerusalem, before traveling to Egypt soon after the turn of the century. He did his journalistic apprenticeship working for several Egyptian newspapers, which were universally recognized as the best Arabic-language papers of their day.[76] His family produced a number of writers, journalists, and intellectuals, including his uncle, Hanna al-ʿIsa, founder in 1908 of the Jerusalem bimonthly journal *al-Asmaʿi*, and his cousin Yusuf, with whom he founded *Filastin*, and who later founded the Damascus daily *Alif Ba*.

In the first four years of its existence its outspoken criticism of the Zionist movement led to *Filastin* being shut down repeatedly by the Ottoman authorities, who were concerned that intemperate criticisms of Zionism risked stirring up interreligious enmity. One of these shutdowns resulted in a court case brought against them by the Ottoman authorities in May 1914 which ʿIsa and Yusuf al-ʿIsa won, provoking a delirious reaction from their supporters (who were reported to have carried them from the courtroom on their shoulders).[77] This episode cemented both the newspaper's reputation, as well as the Ottoman government's enmity for the al-ʿIsa cousins. After World War I began, and with it an intensification of the censorship with which the newspaper struggled constantly under three different regimes—Ottoman, British, and Jordanian—*Filastin* was shut down once again. The newspaper was closed this time for six years. Its two editors were exiled to Anatolia, only to be released in 1918 with the collapse of the Ottoman Empire and the establishment of an Arab state in Damascus.[78]

Involved in Arab nationalist circles since before the war, ʿIsa al-ʿIsa thereafter became secretary, and later head, of King Faysal's Diwan, or private secretariat, in Damascus. He was appointed to this position during the first meeting between the two men toward the

end of the war in Dar'a in southern Syria in September 1918, where
the Arab army was halted during its march northward on Damascus. As described in al-'Isa's memoir, at this first meeting Faysal,
upon greeting al-'Isa, stated that he knew of him from reading *Filastin* before the war. The amir told al-'Isa that he and other Arab
deputies in Istanbul had much appreciated "your jihad," another
indication of the range and impact of *Filastin*'s campaign against
Zionism. Faysal instructed the young newspaper editor to join him
and the Arab army in their march on Damascus, which he did.[79]
This was the beginning of al-'Isa's complicated lifelong connection
with the Hashemites, the dynasty originally based in the West Arabian region of the Hejaz that ruled over Syria, Iraq, and Jordan at
different times from the 1920s until the present. Al-'Isa spent the
years from 1918 until 1920 in Damascus serving the independent
Arab regime during its short and tempestuous existence.

Within the inner councils of the fledgling Arab regime, al-'Isa
tried to balance his strong Pan-Arab sentiments and his loyalty toward Faysal with his profound concern regarding the growth of
Zionist influence in Palestine in the wake of the Balfour Declaration
of 1917, and Britain's establishment of its control over Palestine. Like
many other Arabs in Syria and Palestine, who had not earlier known
of the declaration's existence, he was shocked when he first heard of
it. This took place immediately after the British army occupied Damascus in 1918, and al-'Isa obtained a few Egyptian newspapers and
magazines that reported what was by that point old news.[80] Britain's
formal, explicit support of Zionism created a deep crisis for Faysal
and his supporters, who were heavily dependent on the British and
hoped (futilely, as it transpired) for British backing against French
ambitions in Syria. The resulting dilemma was even more troubling
for Palestinian Arabists in Damascus and elsewhere, who were profoundly wary of the newly revived aspirations of Zionism in their
country, which was now under British military occupation.

The immediate post–World War I period, and in particular the twenty-two months of Arab rule in Damascus, were thus crucial in the development of a separate Palestinian political identity.[81] The imperative of preserving the independence of the weak, new Arab state in Syria, and the concomitant need to retain British support against French encroachments, led Faysal and some in his entourage, notably a powerful faction of Damascene notables, to favor making major concessions over Palestine to the Zionist movement. The idea behind this tactic was that an alliance with Britain's Zionist protégés might enhance the standing of the Syrians in British eyes and thereby help them deal with the constant pressure from the French. This approach in turn produced a reaction from many Palestinians in Damascus, who saw it as a betrayal of the wider Arab cause, and of their own country, to benefit narrow Syrian interests.

In his autobiography, al-ʿIsa relates one of the critical moments in Damascus when the balance between his loyalty to Pan-Arabism and his Palestinian identity was most sorely tested. During a trip by King Faysal to Europe to attend a conference, al-ʿIsa was acting head of the Diwan, and it fell to him to decode a telegram from Faysal to his subordinates in Damascus to the effect that the press should be prevented from attacking the Zionists, who he said were supporting him during the conference. Earlier in his memoir, al-ʿIsa noted that he himself was responsible for paying subsidies to the press and thus influencing its political orientation, presumably including encouraging its outspoken opposition to Zionism. He then relates:

> I grew nervous and angry and told myself, 'they are compromising over Palestine, which the Zionists will cut off from the body of the Arab lands.' Amin ʿAbd al- Hadi was the Secretary of the Military Governor.... I called him and asked him to come immediately... and told him: 'I am a Palestinian and you are a Palestinian, and Palestine is dear to us. I serve this Arab government in order to work to save Palestine, and I think you feel the same way. Take this telegram and read it...'[82]

Loyal though al-'Isa was to the ideology of Arabism and to Faysal, his higher loyalty was clearly to Palestine. He resigned immediately after this episode, but Faysal reinstated him after his return from Europe, and he remained chief secretary of the Royal Diwan until the fall of Faysal's government in July 1920.[83] Placed thereafter on a British blacklist, it was only many months after the French had crushed the independent Arab regime in Damascus that al-'Isa was allowed to return to Jaffa.[84] He was finally permitted by the British to reopen *Filastin* in March 1921.[85]

As his journalistic reputation grew, 'Isa al-'Isa came to be renowned throughout the world of Arabic letters for his quick wit, his acid pen, his satirical poetry, and his excellent style. He had a sharp sense of humor, but also a sharp tongue, which in time earned him powerful enemies, eventually including the mufti, Hajj Amin al-Husayni. The relationship between the two men did not start badly. In his memoir, written after he had been forced to flee the country after threats from the mufti's henchmen, who later burned his home, al-'Isa dryly notes his first contact with al-Husayni in Cairo in May 1914. This took place when the future mufti was a student at al-Azhar in Cairo, and al-'Isa was visiting Egypt in order to gain support for his campaign against Zionism in the wake of the Ottoman authorities' second closing of *Filastin*. He reports without comment that a delegation of al-Azhar shaykhs and students headed by al-Husayni visited him to "express their appreciation for my struggle [*jihadi*] to defend Palestine, and for the oppression and losses I suffered because of it."[86] The two also seem to have collaborated during the two years of Faysal's government in Damascus, which both served faithfully until the end. Indeed, in his memoir, al-'Isa makes a point of noting that during this period al-Husayni often visited him in his office and at his home, where they discussed the Palestinian cause and the means of advancing it.[87]

However, their differences escalated dramatically in the 1930s, as al-'Isa became identified with a number of the mufti's rivals, including Raghib Bey al-Nashashibi, and his newspaper developed into a fierce critic of al-Husayni's policies and actions. After the widening of the Arab revolt and the flight of the mufti to Lebanon in 1937, inter-Palestinian differences were gravely exacerbated. As British repression intensified and the polarization of Palestinian politics grew, any criticism of the line taken by the Palestinian national movement dominated by the mufti was punished increasingly harshly. This reached the point that in November 1938, soon after he had been forced by repeated threats against his life to flee to Beirut, al-'Isa's house in al-Ramla was burned down by partisans of the mufti. All of his books and papers were lost.[88] 'Isa al-'Isa remained in exile in Beirut for most of World War II, and continued to write prolifically for *Filastin* and other newspapers. *Filastin* continued production in Jaffa under the editorship of 'Isa al-'Isa's son Raja until April 1948, just before the fall of the city—at the time the largest Arab urban agglomeration in Palestine—to Zionist forces.[89]

In his memoirs, written in Beirut between 1942 and 1947,[90] 'Isa al-'Isa noted: "[When] I launched the newspaper *Filastin*, my objective in publishing it was to serve the Orthodox cause in the first place," in the struggle with the Greek upper clergy.[91] Speaking after World War II, al-'Isa declared that thereafter, he found himself in the midst of a national conflict being fought on two fronts: one Arab-Turkish and the other Arab-Jewish. He said that he joined in both without hesitation, without ever abandoning the Orthodox cause.[92]

Why was what al-'Isa called "the Orthodox cause" so important at this time, and why did it have relevance beyond the large Greek Orthodox Arab community in the cities and towns of Palestine? What was at issue was control of the Greek Orthodox Church in Palestine, and the considerable assets in land and property that it owned, by the local communities and by priests who issued from the Arabic-speaking laity, rather than by the Greek-speaking upper clergy who previously had dominated the Orthodox Church throughout the Ottoman Empire. After a lengthy struggle, the upper hierarchy of the patriarchate of Antioch and the East (which was located in Damascus) was fully "Arabized."[93] Nevertheless, the patriarchate of Jerusalem, which was responsible for the Orthodox faithful and the material possessions of the Church throughout Palestine and Jordan, remained (and remains to this day) completely under the control of Greek-speaking clergy.[94]

Beyond the basic question of control over the patriarchate and its resources, at issue was the level of spending on education and other services for the laity, which the Arab Orthodox accused the Greek hierarchy of restricting. Equally controversial was the issue of the sale to Zionist interests of some of the Church's extensive landholdings, which became a sensitive political matter as Zionist land purchases increasingly provoked Arab concerns.[95] Like all matters involving language and ethnicity in this era, this rapidly became a "national" issue, with a heightened awareness of their Arabism among the Orthodox Arabs of Syria and Palestine as one of the primary consequences.

It can indeed be argued that the Arab consciousness of many Arab Christians (who numbered about 11 percent of the Arab population of Palestine) in this era was strongly intensified by this conflict between Greeks and Arabs within the Orthodox Church in Syria and Palestine.[96] Unquestionably, al-'Isa was an ardent Arabist: his love of the Arabic language, especially its poetry, was demonstrated in much that he wrote in *Filastin,* and in some of his verses, which became famous throughout the Arab world.[97] His connections with King Faysal and other leading Arab nationalist figures early in the century continued in later years, although al-'Isa grew increasingly bitter about the failure of the Arab regimes, including those headed by the Hashemites, to come to the succor of the Palestinians. His disillusionment reached its nadir after the loss of Palestine in 1948, when he wrote this bitter verse:

> Oh little kings of the Arabs, by the grace of God
> Enough feebleness and infighting
>
> Once upon a time our hopes were on you
> But all our hopes were dashed.[98]

Such a critique was particularly significant coming from a dedicated former supporter of the Hashemites such as 'Isa al-'Isa. Beyond his attachment to King Faysal, al-'Isa was also one of the earliest leaders of Hizb al-Difa'. This political party, organized by Raghib Bey al-Nashashibi in December 1934 after he lost an election for the position of mayor of Jerusalem, came to be aligned with the Hashemite Amir 'Abdullah of Transjordan.[99] In time it was also seen by many as being close to the British and the Zionists. In 1939 al-'Isa withdrew publicly from the party. Most likely he did this because of his dissatisfaction with either al-Nashashibi or 'Abdullah, or both. His relationship with al-Nashashibi dated to before World War I, and was cemented when the then-deputy in the Ottoman Parliament used his influence to moderate the harsh terms of al-'Isa's exile by the Ottoman authorities.[100] However, al-'Isa had nothing positive to say about al-Nashashibi during the part of his memoir devoted to the latter years of his life.

It is apparent, moreover, that al-'Isa never developed the same close relationship with 'Abdullah as he had had with the amir's younger brother Faysal, nor did he ever have the same degree of respect for 'Abdullah. This is evidenced by the uncomplimentary passages in his memoir where al-'Isa describes two unsatisfying encounters with the Jordanian ruler.[101] Having for much of his life advocated the interrelation of the Palestinian and Arab spheres, and the need for the Palestinians to rely on the other Arabs, near the end of his days, in exile from a Jaffa that was no longer an Arab city, 'Isa al-'Isa was forced to recognize that the Arab rulers could not be relied upon, just as he had long argued that the Palestinian leadership had failed. In November 1948, writing from Egypt at a time when the full dimensions of the catastrophe that had befallen the Palestinians were clear, al-'Isa wrote the following bitter words in a poem published in an Egyptian journal under a transparent pseudonym: "Between His Majesty ['Abdullah] and His Eminence [the mufti], my country was lost, without doubt."[102] It is worth mentioning that the weight of Palestinian opinion in the hard years that followed

1948 came to hold similar critical views about the leadership of both in the disaster that had befallen them.

Paramount for al-'Isa was his concern, bordering on an obsession, with Zionism. Very soon after he founded *Filastin,* Zionism became a central concern of the newspaper, which quickly came to devote constant and extensive attention to it. In the section of his autobiography immediately after that already cited relating to the Orthodox cause, al-'Isa wrote:

> There was the problem of Zionism.... There were those in the Committee of Union and Progress [the ruling party in the Ottoman constitutional period, 1908–18] in sympathy with [the Zionists], who tried to achieve their aims via political or financial pressure. So I adopted this cause as well, and exerted my efforts until the Jews saw me as their worst enemy, which they still do until this day.[103]

In fact, much more attention was devoted to Zionism than to any other matter in the pages of *Filastin,* almost from its inception in 1911 until its closure in 1967. In the pre–World War I period, it soon matched the intense focus on the subject of Zionism of the Haifa paper *al-Karmil,* founded three years earlier. A survey of the Arabic-language press coverage of Zionism during this period shows that these two papers were the leaders of opinion on Palestine and in much of the rest of the Arab world on the dangers of the Zionist movement to the population of the country and indeed of the region.[104]

In his autobiography, al-'Isa relates that after one of several closures of his paper by the Ottoman authorities, he traveled to Egypt to publicize the case in the press there. His first success was in getting a Palestinian friend who was editor in chief of the French-language paper *Journal du Caire* to publish a front-page interview with him on the subject of Zionism. This was followed by the publication of a number of articles and letters by al-'Isa in the Arabic-language press, including responses to articles in the prestigious pro-British *al-Muqattam*. The newspaper's correspondent in Palestine was Nisim Malul, who played an important role in the Zionist movement. Suddenly, however, Egyptian newspapers began to refuse to print his articles, with some of their editors claiming that "the Zionist question does not concern Egypt or the Egyptians." In spite of this setback, *Filastin* was reopened by the Ottoman authorities, and al-ʻIsa returned to Palestine triumphant.[105]

Related to this profound concern about the dangers inherent in the progress of Zionist colonization of Palestine was al-ʻIsa's strong sense of the salience of an independent Palestinian identity, which was an Arab identity to be sure but had a specificity of its own nevertheless. For al-ʻIsa and others of his generation, their Arabism was directly related to their sense of being Palestinian and their love of country. This in turn was related to an acute social consciousness, based on a belief that the struggle for Palestine would be decided at the level of the individual peasant and the individual Zionist settler. As a result, a large number of lead articles in *Filastin* were devoted to agricultural matters, and in particular to the state of the peasantry.[106]

In an editorial describing the success of Palestinian farmers at the Haifa agricultural fair of 1927, al-ʻIsa underlined one of the main reasons for his concern for the Palestinian peasant: the conflict on the land with the Zionist movement. Thus, he noted, "If a tenth of a tenth as much of the concern and efforts and wealth were spent on the local fellah as is spent on the Zionists, Palestinian agriculture would be in an enviable situation."[107] This concern for the peasantry was linked to a fear that social divisions weakened the Palestinians in the face of what al-ʻIsa perceived as a unified Zionist movement. Thus the subtitle of another editorial stated: "Whoever humiliates a worker, humiliates the nation."[108] Such sentiments were understandable coming from a resident of Jaffa, which together with Haifa had a large working-class population and was the natural destination of dispossessed peasants who had lost their land as a result of land purchases by the Zionists.

The sale of land to the Zionist movement by large absentee landowners, many of them non-Palestinian, was a major topic in *Filastin* and other newspapers during the prewar years,[109] and during the Mandate. The paper frequently carried articles about land sales on Page 1 with titles like "Selling Wholesale" and "The Party of the Brokers and the Party of the Government."[110] The anger of al-'Isa in the face of the apparent blindness of so many of his compatriots, especially the rich and powerful ones among them, to the danger that he perceived, was often expressed, sometimes intemperately, in the columns of his paper. A theme touched on before the war—that of the Arabs going from masters of the land to outsiders—recurred in later years. A typical title for an article warning against this danger was one published in 1929: "Strangers in Our Own Land: Our Negligence and Their Awakening."[111] As we have seen, by the end of the 1930s, the yishuv had grown to nearly a third of the population of the country, the exclusively Jewish economy that it controlled was larger than that owned by the Arabs, and land purchases, which amounted to a small fraction of the country's total area, nevertheless provided the strategic backbone for a Jewish state. Even at this stage, the warnings of al-'Isa and others like him had already been proven to be prescient indeed.

Like much of what he wrote, this editorial was implicitly a criticism of the leaders of the Palestinian community. Beyond furthering our understanding of the common themes and ideas that increasingly bound Palestinians together as a people over the decades after its founding in 1911, *Filastin* exposes us to a critique of the failures of Palestinian leadership from within Palestinian society. Unlike critiques sympathetic to the parties the Palestinians were struggling against, the British and the Zionists, it is animated by a deep Palestinian patriotism and an expert knowledge of the country. Subjective, partisan, and often acerbic, it remains one of the best sources for understanding the failure of Palestinian leadership in the years leading up to 1948.

4

The Revolt, 1948, and Afterward

General Strike and Revolt

Much has been written about the Palestinian revolt of 1936–39, which was sparked by the death of Shaykh 'Iz al-Din al-Qassam in 1935, began with a six-month general strike, and ended with the crushing by British forces of a nationwide armed insurrection. Even more has been written about the 1948 war, whose result for the Palestinians was what they called *al-nakba,* the catastrophe of their dispossession, and which for Israelis marks the independence of their national state. It is not possible to recapitulate in detail here these two sequences of events, nor will I attempt to do so. What has not been fully explained before, however, is how the crushing of the 1936–39 revolt largely determined the outcome of the 1948 war for the Palestinians; and how the failures of their leadership, and the absence of structures of state, contributed to their military and political defeat in both cases; and finally how this heavy legacy affected them thereafter.

I have already shown how Palestinian political efforts up until the mid-1930s were stymied by the inability of the leaders of the national movement to agree on appropriate strategies, to mobilize and organize the populace effectively, to create an accepted and recognized representative national quasi-state forum (given that access to the structures of the colonial state was denied the Palestinians by the British), and to break decisively with the structures of colonial control. My purpose in this chapter will be to explain how these same problems effectively both doomed the Palestinian revolt, and precluded a unified effort to resist the takeover of large parts of Palestine by Zionist forces in the first few months of 1948.

It may well have been the case that both of these efforts were doomed no matter what the Palestinians did: nowhere around the globe during the interwar years was an armed revolt of the colonized successful, nor did an anticolonial movement secure full national independence (Egypt and Iraq being partial exceptions, since both countries had achieved at least nominal independence by 1922 and 1932 respectively). This was particularly unlikely in a contest with the greatest imperial power of the age in a site that was as strategically vital as Palestine was to Great Britain on the eve of World War II. It was made all the less likely by the alliance until the end of the 1930s of Britain with a worldwide Zionist movement and a yishuv rooted in Palestine, both of which grew stronger and more determined as the situation of the Jews of Europe worsened dramatically year by year. Both in 1936–39, and again in 1947–48, the Palestinians undoubtedly faced overwhelmingly unfavorable odds, on the international, regional, and local levels. But these factors, decisive though they may have been, are not enough by themselves to explain the Palestinian failure to achieve self-determination and establish a state during these crucial twelve years between 1936 and 1948. Once again, it is necessary to come back to the fact that however bad all their options undoubtedly were in an exceedingly difficult situation, the Palestinians did have choices, and some of them may have been less bad than others. We have already examined how poor were some of the choices made by their leadership until the mid-1930s. Even more fateful ones awaited them.

The 1936 Palestinian general strike and the armed revolt that followed were momentous events for the Palestinians, the region, and the British Empire. The six-month general strike, which ran from April until October and involved work stoppages and boycotts of the British- and Zionist-controlled parts of the economy, was the longest anticolonial strike of its kind until that point in history, and perhaps the longest ever. At one stage during the armed revolt that erupted all over the country in September 1937, British forces lost control of much of the countryside to armed bands and were briefly forced to withdraw from several of the major cities, including the Old City of Jerusalem, Jaffa, Acre, Jericho, and Bir Sabe' (Beersheva). The less accessible and more rugged areas of the countryside escaped British control for a longer time. The British military commander in Palestine wrote in August 1938 that "the situation was such that civil administration of the country was, to all practical purposes, non-existent."[1] The spectacle of a few thousand poorly armed Palestinian peasants successfully resisting the might of the British Empire for such a lengthy time encouraged Britain's aggressive and ambitious regional rivals, Italy and Germany; had an impact on Arab and Islamic opinion and on the colonized world generally; discouraged and angered the Zionist movement; and infuriated British politicians, officials, and military officers.

In the end, the might of Britain, the lack of significant external support for the revolt, the absence of a unified Palestinian military or political structure combined with the reemergence of Palestinian disunity, and the failure of the revolt to enunciate an achievable political goal, led to its suppression. The cost to Palestinian society was great. Hundreds of homes were blown up (perhaps as many as two thousand),[2] crops were destroyed, and over one hundred rebels were summarily executed simply for the possession of firearms, or even ammunition.[3] Curfews, administrative detention, internal exile, and other punishments were liberally applied, and particularly cruel means were employed by the British, such as tying villagers to the front of locomotive engines to prevent rebels from blowing up trains. An entire quarter of the Old City of Jaffa was dynamited (under the rubric of "urban renewal") after the British failed to bring it under control. Total Arab casualties during the revolt were approximately 5,000 killed and 10,000 wounded, while those detained totaled 5,679 in 1939.[4] The number of those exiled or forced to flee is unknown, but is probably in the thousands. In an Arab population of about 1 million, these were considerable figures: they meant that over 10 percent of the adult male population was killed, wounded, imprisoned, or exiled.[5] Although some of the casualties were simply bystanders, these figures give some indication of the extent of popular participation in the revolt, and of its all-encompassing national nature.

The repression of the revolt had an impact not only on the populace, but also on the Palestinians' ability to fight thereafter, and on the already fractured capabilities of their national leadership. A high proportion of the Arab casualties included the most experienced military cadres and enterprising fighters.[6] By the end of the revolt, most of the top Arab political leaders and thousands of other cadres, militants, and fighters were imprisoned, interned by the British in the Seychelles, in exile, or dead. The British also confiscated large quantities of arms and ammunition from the Arabs during the revolt, and continued to do so during later years.[7] By the end of the revolt, existing political divisions within the Palestinian polity had become envenomed, leading to profound rifts between the majority supporting the revolt and a minority that had become alienated from the leadership: the consequence was assassinations, infighting, and further weakening of the Palestinian position. The impact of the revolt on the Palestinian economy was also severe, although some of that damage was self-inflicted, as a boycott of British and Jewish goods and of the mandatory government during the strike and the revolt simply opened up opportunities for the already larger Jewish-controlled sector of the economy of Palestine to expand further.

The revolt profoundly affected others besides the Arabs of Palestine. For the yishuv, it meant a sudden interruption in the growing wave of immigration to Palestine. This came at a time when it appeared that had there been a continuation of the trend in the annual level of immigration (which had topped sixty-one thousand in 1935), a Jewish majority in Palestine was within reach. Moreover, as Nazi persecution of Jews in Germany escalated, while most countries of the world callously refused to open their doors (at a time when European Jews able to find refuge could still escape), the prospect of the closing of the doors of Palestine to Jewish immigration was particularly chilling. Even as Zionism won new adherents the world over as Nazi Germany slid toward new depths of depravity in its treatment of Jews, the Zionist movement faced a grave crisis in Palestine. Meanwhile, the yishuv joined in the fight against the Palestinian revolt, extending its support to British repressive efforts. More Jewish policemen were recruited, trained, and armed, and existing Zionist military formations were expanded and strengthened, receiving British training and eventually acquiring valuable combat experience against the Palestinian rebels.

The British welcomed this support, even as they began to question their own long-standing commitment to Zionism. As the general strike and later the armed revolt ground on, the need to bring their vital Palestinian possession back under control had obliged the British to deploy over twenty thousand troops and considerable contingents of the Royal Air Force to Palestine by September 1936, and even more in the fall of 1938. This was a military burden that the empire could ill afford, with conflict looming in Europe: indeed, the revolt spread and took over several major cities in the summer and fall of 1938 because British forces had to be held in reserve during the Czechoslovak crisis over the Sudetenland between Britain, France, and Germany. It could only be crushed when the Munich accord freed up large numbers of British troops for service in Palestine. The need to spend large sums of money and deploy so many troops for such a long period to suppress the revolt in Palestine was clearly causing serious headaches for the British government and for imperial military planners. British leaders thus watched with dismay as a commitment to support the Zionist project that had initially been perceived as promising various advantages while involving limited liabilities gradually became an onerous burden. By the end of the 1930s Palestine had become an embarrassment to the British in a number of respects.

As if all this were not bad enough, newspaper and radio depictions of Britain's fierce repression of the Palestinian Arabs, amplified by Italian and German propaganda, caused anger and resentment in the Arab world from Cairo to Baghdad and beyond. The situation in Palestine thus gravely compromised already complicated British relations with Arab rulers and their nationalistic subjects. This was a crisis that the British Empire could ill afford at a time when this strategic region was all the more vital in view of the potential for a war with Germany and Italy in which it was feared (correctly, as it transpired) that the Mediterranean would once again be a central theater, as it was during World War I. From being a major asset to the defense of British interests in Egypt, the Suez Canal, and along the land route to the Gulf, Palestine was becoming a considerable liability. Finally, in 1939, after several years of costly and ugly repression had finally broken the back of the Arab revolt in Palestine at great harm to Britain's standing in the Arab and Muslim worlds, Britain would be obliged to reassess its weighty commitment to Zionism.

While sympathy for the Palestinians was widespread in the Arab countries, particularly in Lebanon and Syria, and increasingly in Egypt and Iraq, the revolt posed acute problems for the Arab elites who dominated their respective national governments. At just that moment in 1936, leaders in Syria and Egypt were involved in delicate negotiations over treaties with their colonial overlords that would have given these countries a greater measure of independence from France and Britain respectively. Neither the Syrian nationalist leaders, who hoped for British support in their dealings with the French, nor the ruling Wafd Party in Egypt, which had enough problems with the British as it was, could afford to alienate London over the Palestine question. In consequence, both were more subdued in condemning the British than they otherwise might have been. At the same time, public opinion in both countries was increasingly agitated by news of the revolt and its suppression by the British. There was intense popular pressure on Arab leaders to take a decisive stand on this emotional issue, and many

Syrians, Lebanese, and Egyptians volunteered to go to Palestine to fight, notably the Egyptian Muslim Brotherhood.[8] Similar considerations obtained in Iraq and Saudi Arabia, whose governments were in large measure dependent on British support, although as nominally independent countries they could be somewhat more open in disagreeing with Britain.

The initial result of these contradictory pressures was the intervention of the Arab rulers in the fall of 1936 to press the Palestinians to suspend their general strike. This *démarche*, combined with unrelenting British military pressure, and their dire economic situation, impelled the Palestinians to halt the strike, without the British making any significant concessions. This initiative had far-reaching implications, however: for the first time, the Arab countries had been brought into the Palestinian imbroglio. This was to be the beginning of a series of interventions that would eventually end with the subordination of the Palestinians to the Arab states, a situation that continued for many decades, until the mid-1960s. In the meantime, however, it appeared as if calm might be restored to Palestine. Once again, Britain's regionwide system of indirect colonial control had proven its worth, although it was to be sorely tested within months as the disturbances in Palestine erupted in open revolt in the fall of 1937, after a British commission headed by Lord Peel published its recommendation for the partition of Palestine and the creation of a Jewish state. The revolt rose to a crescendo in the following months.

A rebellion by the Palestinians against such a formidable foe could not have been sustained without widespread popular support. The heavy casualties suffered by the Palestinians give ample evidence of their willingness to make sacrifices in order to achieve their national goals of independence from Britain and an end to the process whereby they saw their country slipping under the control of foreigners. Nevertheless, deep cleavages eventually emerged in Palestinian society. These were in large measure rooted in the divisions that had been evident previously. Even though the entirety of the deeply fractured Palestinian political class had managed to pull together in April 1936 to create a new body grouping leaders of all major factions, headed by the mufti, the Arab Higher Committee, differences among the members of this class continued and were eventually exacerbated. These disagreements were partly over tactics, but also over the growing preeminence of the mufti as he became increasingly identified with militant resistance to the British. This stance was unacceptable to other Palestinian politicians, notably Raghib Bey al-Nashashibi, who was adamantly opposed to a final rupture with the mandatory power. As we shall see, some of these differences may not have been as absolute as they appeared, for even in exile in Lebanon on the eve of World War II, the mufti was apparently hoping to restore his links with the British.[9] Nevertheless, this dispute became so bitter that some supporters of al-Nashashibi and others were eventually stigmatized by the rebels as collaborators, and harassed or even assassinated, while others later joined the British in helping to suppress the revolt.

Other important cleavages included that between the senior political leadership, drawn mainly from the notable class, and both the militants who had initiated the general strike of 1936 and the guerrilla fighters in the hills who by late 1937 had launched a nationwide armed revolt that resulted in the British losing control over much of the country for a time. There was deep mistrust between the nominal Palestinian political leadership grouped together in the Arab Higher Committee and many of those who were actually involved in the armed resistance to the British.[10] The latter suspected the notables of being overwilling to compromise with the British, with whom the militants knew they had been on good terms for so long. The ending of the general strike in October 1936 without any achievements but a British promise to send out yet another royal commission, that headed by Lord Peel, was seen by these militants as substantiating their fears. Those fears were fully realized when that commission in July 1937 recommended the partition of Palestine and the creation of a Jewish state. One consequence of this deep mistrust was that when wholesale armed revolt erupted in October 1937, there was even less willingness on the part of those who animated it to accept the leadership and guidance of the notables, most of whom by then were under arrest or in flight. When the British government in 1939 finally came to realize that perhaps it had to place limits on its engagement to the Zionists embodied in the Balfour Declaration and the Mandate, and that it was finally obliged to compromise with the Palestinians, the latter were defeated, demoralized, and hopelessly divided along several divergent fault lines.

On top of all the cleavages already mentioned, by late 1937 the mufti had escaped to Lebanon ahead of a British dragnet that had swept up most of the other members of the Arab Higher Committee, depositing them in exile in the Seychelles. He remained in Lebanon until 1939, persona non grata with the British, and separated from most of the rest of the Palestinian leadership, but in touch with the leaders of some of the rebel bands.[11] In Beirut, the mufti was subject to severe restrictions, including house arrest by the French mandatory authorities, who kept him under close surveillance, as did the British and the Zionists.[12] He was nevertheless allowed to receive visitors, and managed to engage in a broad range of political activities with Palestinian, Lebanese, and other Arab political personalities, to the intense chagrin of the British and the Zionists.

Under these loose conditions of confinement, the mufti tried to play on the latent rivalry between Britain and France, as well as their concern to prevent their German and Italian regional rivals from turning the situation in Palestine to their advantage. Thus, in one conversation with French officials just before the outbreak of World War II, in August 1939, the mufti sought to win their favor by assuring them that he was advising his friends in the Pan-Arab movement to avoid an insurrection against the French in Syria.[13] Such tactical moves may have given the mufti a small margin of maneuver, and may have lulled him into thinking that he could play on such great-power rivalries with little cost to himself or to the cause of Palestine. The falsity of this notion was to be proved when he fled to Germany during World War II, becoming a pariah, and gravely harming the Palestinian cause with which he had become identified.[14]

Perhaps the most costly action of the mufti before he left the Middle East for Berlin in 1941 was his role in opposing Britain's 1939 White Paper. This episode reveals in full the deep divisions among the Palestinians, the weakness of their national institutions, and also the force of the mufti's personality and of the position that he had developed. Following the crushing of the 1936–39 revolt, the British sense that they were obliged to make a concession to Arab sentiment in order to bolster their position in the Middle East para-doxically created a small opening in the iron cage that had encircled the Palestinians since the beginning of the Mandate.

This opening was small indeed. It first became apparent at the St. James Palace Conference in March 1939, convened by the Chamberlain government to resolve the Palestine imbroglio, which brought together British cabinet ministers, the leaders of several Arab states, and a number of Palestinian leaders (with Zionist rep-resentatives meeting separately with the British). There and in the White Paper, issued two months later as a consequence of this con-ference, Britain for the first time promised to impose limitations on Jewish immigration and land purchase, both central Palestinian de-mands for two decades—indeed there had been demands for limits on Jewish immigration during the late Ottoman period. Britain also abandoned the 1937 Peel Commission plan to partition Pales-tine and to create a Jewish state, offered instead responsible govern-ment within five years, the opening of senior positions within the government to officials recruited in Palestine (at a ratio of two Arab to one Jewish official), and a promise of full independence within ten years. These offers were far less tantalizing to the Arabs than they may have appeared, for they were hedged around with condi-tions meant to rob them of some of their substance, including the necessity to secure the approval of the yishuv for the final steps envisaged, notably independence. There were many other hidden traps and reservations in the proposals contained in the White Paper, as we saw in Chapter 2.

In spite of these drawbacks, and in spite of the opposition of the leaders of the rebel forces, now dispersed and in disarray, many members of the Palestinian political leadership, including initially most of the Arab Higher Committee, were inclined to accept the White Paper, as were all the Arab governments. This was partly a result of weariness on the part of the Palestinian public with the crisis situation that had dragged on for years, and of the fact that the British initiative, which for the first time met some long-standing Arab demands, had been furiously opposed by the Jewish Agency in Palestine and its supporters abroad. Moreover, in the lead-up to the St. James Palace Conference, the British had acted to appease Arab feeling. After years of asking for tighter restrictions on the mufti's activity (indeed at one point demanding his exile to the distant Alawite region of Syria), the British in 1939 had asked the French authorities to loosen the conditions of surveillance over al-Husayni in Lebanon,[15] had released several members of the Arab Higher Committee from detention in the Seychelles to enable them to engage in consultations with the mufti and go to London to attend the St. James Palace Conference, and had taken a number of other conciliatory measures.

Initially, the mufti seemed favorable to this process of détente with the British, and at one stage it even appeared as if he might go along with the general thrust of the White Paper. After extensive consultations, he assented to members of the Arab Higher Committee, including his cousin Jamal al-Husayni, and the latter's brother-in-law, Musa al-'Alami's, attendance at the St. James Palace Conference in London as representatives of the Palestinians. Even after the breakdown of the conference, he attempted to keep a line open to the British. Speaking to intermediaries with the French authorities in Lebanon in March 1939, the mufti asked for French mediation between the Palestinians and the British, and asserted that the Arab world would not sympathize with Germany and Italy in case of a conflict between them and Britain and France.[16] But when in May the Arab Higher Committee finally had to take a position on the White Paper, the mufti imposed his views on his colleagues and secured a rejection of this ambiguous British initiative. It appears that a majority of the members of the Arab Higher Committee opposed the mufti and favored accepting the White Paper, and although there is some disagreement among historians about this, it is definitely the case that his opposition never wavered, and that he carried the day.[17]

Hajj Amin al-Husayni was acting in part out of fear of forces he did not fully control, but that his actions, and his earlier inaction, had helped to unleash: these were represented by the remaining scattered rebel bands in the hills of Palestine. Before the crucial May meeting of the Arab Higher Committee in Lebanon, a number of the remaining leaders of the disorganized guerilla groups had in April issued a strident statement rejecting the White Paper, calling for complete independence for Palestine and stating that the Palestinian people had not staged an uprising in order to get high positions for a few *effendis* (educated members of the upper classes). It concluded by saying ominously that the Palestinians were subject neither "to the Nashashibis or to the Husaynis, nor to the Arab kings, who were ruling by the grace of Britain."[18] The mufti could not have misunderstood this barely veiled warning to him not to accept the White Paper and thereby return to the path of cooperation with Britain, a path that he had previously followed for so long, and for which he had long been criticized by younger and more militant activists.

In fact, the mufti no longer had that option: the British had been categorical in excluding him from the St. James Palace Conference, although they were careful to allow his colleagues in the Arab Higher Committee to consult with him in his exile in Lebanon after their release from exile in the Seychelles.[19] The British would never reconcile with or forgive the mufti, whom they blamed for their embarrassment during the long Palestinian revolt of 1936–39. They felt for him an animosity that was partly explained by a sense of betrayal on the part of leading British officials by a figure who for many years had had their full confidence. The reaction of the mufti was equally personal: his jealousy of others in the Palestinian leadership was such that he would not allow them to compromise with the British if he were to be denied what he felt was his due as national leader of the Palestinian people. The Palestinians were to suffer again many decades later from this damaging conflation of the national cause with the personality of an overweening leader in the twilight era of Yasser 'Arafat's dominance of the Palestinian national movement.

In consequence of this bruising sequence of events over the preceding three years, by 1939 the situation had spun entirely out of the control of the nominal leaders of the Palestinians. Now they were so weak that they could be dictated to by defeated rebels who were barely able to stay in the field in the face of overwhelming British armed might. The mufti in effect chose to listen to this warning from those who clearly had profound suspicions of him and his class, rather than fellow members of the Arab Higher Committee like 'Auni 'Abd al-Hadi, who counseled acceptance of the British initiative. By the sheer force of his personality, backed up by his presumed links with the rebels in the field who had shown little hesitation in assassinating those who opposed them, he prevented his colleagues from accepting the White Paper. While it may be questioned whether acceptance of the White Paper would have had much positive effect on the Palestinians' fortunes in the long term, given its ambiguity on key provisions, and in view of the fact that a world war was about to begin, the Holocaust was on the doorstep, and British power in the region was about to wane, rejection was certainly not advantageous to them. Its effect was to hand such initiative as remained in Arab hands over to the British, the Zionists, and the Arab governments, which were at least as divided among themselves as were the Palestinians, and much more beholden to the British. This was perhaps the last important decision the Palestinians took by themselves for several decades.

But in fact, by this stage the Palestinians had already lost most of whatever autonomy that they had enjoyed during the first decades of British rule. The preparations for the St. James Palace Conference were largely made by British officials and leaders of the Arab states, between whom much of the important negotiation before, during, and after the conference took place. Nevertheless, the Arab states agreed beforehand to defer to the Palestinians on what positions to take at the conference, and were largely faithful to this commitment. The Palestinians, who were deeply divided, as we have seen, along many different fault lines of party, family, class, and region, were rapidly becoming wards of Arab states that themselves were barely independent, and that remained largely under the influence of the European powers. This process would reach its apogee during the 1948 war.

Before moving to a discussion of that war, it is worth asking whether, had the Palestinians taken a different course before World War II, they might have avoided the catastrophe that befell their society in 1948. Could they have compromised and accepted some form of Jewish national home within the context of an Arab state in Palestine before 1939? Had they done so, would this have had any effect on the powerful drive of the Zionist movement for a Jewish majority and an independent Jewish state in Palestine? Beyond this, should the Palestinians have accepted a variety of British proposals in the 1920s and early 1930s that might have given them some form of representative institutions, albeit based on acceptance of the Mandate and the principle of the Jewish national home, and without representation proportional to their majority status? Finally, would the Palestinians have been better off had they been more militant in dealing with the British much earlier? Or would they have benefited had they been able to rein in the revolt of 1936–39 and win some political gains from it?

It seems unlikely that at almost any time before World War II the Zionist movement would have accepted any formula that would have limited Jewish immigration, and therefore in time the possibility of a Jewish majority, and with it a Jewish state in Palestine. This was the clear objective of the Zionist movement from its very beginnings—indeed political Zionism made little sense otherwise —and it never really wavered from this objective. This determination was only reinforced by the rise of Nazism in the 1930s, which seemed to validate the essential premises of Zionism and make its proposed solution to the Jewish problem appear all the more prescient and all the more urgent. Nor does it seem likely that the British government would have accepted such a formula, unless it was forced to do so, as it was in 1939 by three years of turbulent unrest and the imminence of World War II.

Might it nevertheless have been advantageous for the Palestinians to try to come to terms with the idea that what they saw as their country, Palestine, might also be considered as a national home for what they saw as another people? Perhaps it might have been to their advantage, difficult though it is to imagine such an initiative in the circumstances of the time, and in view of the fact that Zionism, like most nationalist movements, saw that it alone had national rights in its homeland, and was fixated on achieving statehood and independence. Accepting such an idea in some form would certainly have removed or at least weakened the ludicrous but widely believed accusation that the Palestinians were motivated by no more than anti-Semitism in their opposition to Zionism, rather than just being a colonized people trying to defend their majority status and achieve independence in their own country. But it probably would have been difficult if not impossible to get most Palestinians to make such a distinction, and accept in principle a project that they feared in practice was intended to dispossess them. The reasons were many: they included deep-seated Palestinian attitudes about their national rights in what they saw as their country, the spread of Arab nationalism and the movement toward independence of other Arab states with which the Palestinians naturally compared themselves, and what the Palestinians knew of the Zionist movement's clear ultimate ambition of establishing a Jewish state in what they understandably believed was an Arab land.

It is important to understand in this regard that Palestinians did not see Jewish immigrants to Palestine primarily as refugees from persecution, as they were seen by most of the rest of the world. They saw them instead as arrogant European interlopers who did not accept that the Palestinians were a people or had national rights in their own country, believed that Palestine instead belonged to them, and were coldly determined to make that belief into a reality. There was further a stubborn insistence on the part of most Arabs on seeing Jews as members of a religious rather than a national group (this attitude was to linger on among Arabs generally for several decades). Thus while an attempt to come to some sort of accommodation with Zionism might have been diplomatically wise, it was most probably doomed to fail because of both the drive of the Zionist movement for supremacy in Palestine, and the natural resistance to this drive of the indigenous population.

Once the Nazis came to power in Germany in January 1933, it can be argued that there was in any case no longer any hope of avoiding a collision between the two national movements. If there was ever any slim possibility for compromise or coexistence between them when the Jewish population of Palestine as a proportion of the whole stagnated between 17 percent and 18 percent from 1928 until 1932, this possibility evaporated rapidly as the flood of Jewish refugees from Nazism brought this proportion to over 30 percent by 1938, and gave the Zionist leaders confidence in their ultimate triumph. By the end of the 1930s the die had been cast, and the ultimate conflict over control of the country between a determined minority and a disorganized majority was virtually inevitable.

Could the Palestinians have improved their situation by accepting some British proposals, whether for a legislative council or an Arab Agency?[20] Given the low ceiling that would have been imposed by the British in view of the terms of the Mandate, and that necessarily would have obliged the mandatory government to act in support of the Zionist project, any such body, irrespective of its makeup, would undoubtedly have had little impact on changing the nature of the pro-Zionist policies followed by the British in Palestine. Moreover, it would have given tacit Palestinian approbation to the idea of a Jewish national home in Palestine, and indeed of the subordination of their rights to those of a Jewish majority, both of which were naturally anathema to the Palestinians.

Nevertheless, any elected representation, no matter how hemmed in by restrictions, or how limited in proportion to the absolute Palestinian majority of the population, would have given the elected Palestinian representatives an uncontestable legitimacy, and an unparalleled platform from which to make their case. The Congress Party in India used state assemblies to just this end in the late 1930s. As with some limited form of acceptance of a Jewish national home, in the end this would probably have had at best only diplomatic or propaganda value. And there is no guarantee that the Palestinians would ever have been granted even sham representative institutions, given the ferocious opposition of the Zionist movement to anything that gave the Arabs a recognized, official, representative voice, and of British officials and politicians to anything that would have weakened the terms of the Mandate. But in view of the glaring weaknesses of the Palestinians in just these realms of diplomacy and public relations, acceptance of such proposals might conceivably have slowed the slide of their country into the hands of the Zionist movement.

As to whether the Palestinians would have benefited had they adopted entirely different and more militant tactics earlier on during the Mandate period, the answer to this seems to be an affirmative one. A Palestinian revolt against their colonial overlords much earlier than that which eventually transpired in 1936–39—like that of the Egyptians in 1919, the Iraqis in 1920, and the Syrians in 1925—would have made the British confront much earlier the dilemma inherent in their commitment to Zionism that they were only forced to come to grips with in 1939, when it was probably already too late for the Palestinians. The case of Palestine was of course not as straightforward as those of these other Arab countries, because of the Zionist project and the British commitment to it embodied in the terms of the Mandate. Nevertheless, the concession of a measure of independence by the British in 1939, analogous to similar concessions made by Britain and France with respect to these other cases, indicates what might have been possible for the Palestinians had they acted earlier. Similarly, a resolute and universally accepted Palestinian policy of noncooperation with the British in the 1920s or even in the early 1930s might have had an impact. We saw in earlier chapters why the shortsightedness of Palestinian elites prevented such a course from being adopted. Finally, as we have just seen, acceptance of the White Paper, while it probably would have come as too little too late, might have slightly improved the position of the Palestinians in view of the difficult odds facing them.

In the end, however, because things happened as they did, the Palestinians ended the 1930s in a particularly disadvantageous position. By 1939 the yishuv was larger, more prosperous and economically secure, better organized, and better armed than ever before. The horrors of Nazi persecution, well known to the entire world, only steeled the determination of Zionists and their supporters everywhere, while the far greater horrors of Hitler's Final Solution, only a few years in the future, were to have a decisive impact in convincing Jews and non-Jews alike of the merits of Zionism, and in greatly reinforcing and broadening its appeal.

More to the point, the White Paper, dead letter though it was in large measure because of the outbreak of World War II, convinced farsighted Zionist leaders like David Ben-Gurion, who would become the first prime minister of Israel, that the Zionist movement was obliged to acquire a new great-power sponsor. With the Zionist movement's Biltmore Program (pointedly enunciated in New York in 1942) calling for a Jewish Commonwealth in Palestine, Ben-Gurion began the process of setting more explicit and more ambitious goals and reorienting the movement toward the United States, which he correctly identified as the great power of the future. Although the landing of American troops in Iran and North Africa only took place the following year, it was already clear to him that Britain was a declining power and the United States a rising one, in the Middle East and in the world as a whole. Very few Middle Eastern, or for that matter world, leaders were as perspicacious in this regard as was Ben-Gurion.[21]

The Palestinians, meanwhile, had made a supreme effort in 1936–39, only to come up short. They had been resoundingly defeated on the battlefield, and their society would long suffer from the aftereffects of this defeat. Because their leadership failed to accept the White Paper, moreover, they had failed to take advantage of the momentary weakness of the British position or to win any political gains from the sacrifices that had been made by the rebels who had tenaciously but unsuccessfully fought superior forces of British troops, backed by air power, for many months in the hills of Palestine. We have seen that the mufti could in large measure be blamed for the tactical error of rejecting the White Paper. But the larger defeat of the Palestinians was certainly not solely his fault. It was a function of nearly two decades of leadership failure, the absence of national or representative institutions, and the inherent weaknesses of Palestinian society facing more powerful, more coherent, and better-organized foes.

In view of this background, the terrible events of 1947–49 for the Palestinians in an important sense were no more than a postlude, a tragic epilogue to the shattering defeat of 1936–39. With the events of these four years, the Palestinians entered a new and even more difficult era that persisted for many decades afterward. This was an era characterized by an even more divided leadership with diminished standing, much of it in exile and physically separated from its people, without the ability to provide a centralized national framework to confront the challenges to come. This era began with a Palestinian society under conflicting strains that ultimately shattered it, sapped by the debilitating struggle against years of British repression, and leaving it vulnerable to the expulsion in 1948–49 of more than half of the Arab population of Palestine from their homes and lands.

Finally, 1936–39 marked when the political initiative on the Arab side passed to the Arab states, all of which were deeply under British influence and thus unable to act with full independence. At the same time, these Arab states were riven by dynastic and national differences. They had first entered the Palestinian arena in 1936, at the behest of both the British and the Palestinian leadership, and also in pursuit of their own interests. They were to continue to dominate Palestinian politics for many decades. In the lead-up to the St. James Palace Conference, the leaders of the Arab states had said that they would follow the line set down by the Palestinians, and they were generally faithful to their word. This was the last time for many decades that the Arab states would cede any form of primacy in Palestinian affairs to Palestinian leaders. Thereafter, these states in effect took responsibility for the Palestinian cause, but each major Arab state came to follow its own line and to seek to serve its own interests, generally with disadvantageous consequences for the Palestinians.

After two decades in an iron cage largely defined for them under the Mandate by the British and the Zionist movement, in 1939 the Palestinians began a disorienting period of transition during which they lost control over their own fate. This period only ended a decade later in the wake of the 1948 war, when the Palestinians found themselves dispersed, divided, and caught between the new state of Israel and the Arab states, which between them controlled the entire territory of former mandatory Palestine. The name Palestine appeared to have disappeared from the map, and the Palestinians from the political arena. This new stage lasted for nearly two decades after 1948, until the rise of the PLO at the end of the 1960s returned the Palestinians, if not Palestine, to the map, and restored some measure of control over Palestinian affairs to Palestinians.

War, *al-Nakba,* and Arab Tutelage

The decade from 1939 until 1949 marks a new low point in the story of the Palestinians' effort to achieve their national objectives of independence and statehood, low even by comparison with what preceded it. Worse was still to come. For most of this ten-year period, the key actors in this story are not Palestinian, and many are not Arab. Its most important element is how the Palestinians themselves lost agency, whether to the nascent Israeli state, to the neighboring Arab states, or to international actors. It was here, in the bitter endgame of the Palestine Mandate, that the Palestinians suffered the most from their previous failure to establish a recognized representative national body. They were unable to defend their society in the civil war that erupted as soon as the United Nations General Assembly voted for the partition of Palestine into a Jewish and an Arab state in Resolution 181, passed on November 29, 1947. Even before that, they were either not consulted, or were effectively ignored by the various international efforts that culminated in this resolution. This was true of the actions of the British government at the end of World War II, when it still believed it could hang on to Palestine, of the Anglo-American Commission of Inquiry of 1946, created in response to increasing American involvement in the Palestine question in support of Zionism, and of the committee set up by the new United Nations organization in 1947 to make recommendations on the future of Palestine once the problem was thrown into its lap by Britain's abdication of its responsibilities in Palestine.

Even if the Palestinians were occasionally nominally represented in the post–World War II deliberations that sealed their fate as a people, in practice they were effectively ignored. Most frequently, if spoken for at all, they were spoken for by the Arab states, each of which had its own considerations and calculations, all of which were weak, and some of which, like Lebanon, Syria, and Transjordan, had only just won a precarious independence. Even such limited Palestinian efforts to speak for themselves internationally as took place were entirely dependent on the support of Arab states. These efforts ultimately foundered because of these states' inconsistency and because of divisions among them (as well as among the Palestinians themselves). It is clear that for most of the major actors dealing with Palestine at this stage, the Palestinians were considered a negligible factor if they were considered at all. British, American, and other international diplomats and statesmen paid them little heed, except for occasional efforts to exclude them. Even the Arab states, while generally hoping that the Palestinians would not be overwhelmed by the Zionists, were often most concerned about how the endgame of the Palestine Mandate would affect their relations with Britain and the other great powers, the other Arab states, and the Jewish state that was gradually emerging.

This was even true of the Palestinians' Zionist rivals for control of Palestine. For all the shifts in momentum of the civil war that erupted in Palestine at the end of 1947—at least in its earlier stages—the eyes of planners for the Israeli state about to be born were already firmly on the Arab armies across the frontiers of mandatory Palestine, even as they dealt with the Palestinians. It was of course vitally important to these planners that Zionist and later Israeli forces first overcome Palestinian resistance and then clear as much of the country as they could of its Palestinian population. They understood perfectly that otherwise the Jewish state called for by the partition plan would not have control of its internal lines of communication. Most importantly, they understood the well-established demographic calculus of Palestine, which meant that without such ethnic cleansing, the new state would have had nearly as many Arabs as Jews (the expanded territory eventually incorporated into Israel after the 1949 armistice agreements would have had many more Arabs). But at least as important as this objective was the driving forward and establishing of strategic lines on which the Arab armies could be confronted should they enter Palestine, as they did after May 15, 1948.

Thus the Palestinians began this phase of their tortured national history in a particularly disadvantageous position. Even when important elements of the Zionist movement turned against the British starting at the end of World War II, with attacks on British targets such as senior officers, the British headquarters in Jerusalem, trains, and barracks, by militia groups like the Irgun, founded by followers of Revisionist Zionist leader Ze'ev Jabotinsky, and its even more extreme offshoot Lehi (known to the British as the Stern Gang) led by Yitzhaq Shamir, the Palestinians did not benefit. Unlike the 1936–39 revolt, when the British allied themselves with the Zionist movement in confronting the Arab uprising, now the British ignored the Palestinians. The reasons for this were simple: the Palestinians were weak and not particularly favorably disposed toward Britain, and their leader, the mufti, was discredited because of his wartime alliance with the Nazis. The British preferred to rely entirely on their own resources to fight the Zionists, with support from reliable and trusted clients such as King 'Abdullah of Transjordan, with his small but battle-hardened British-commanded, -trained, -armed, and -financed army, the Arab Legion.[22]

In consequence, when Britain finally succumbed to a combination of American and international pressure in light of the awful revelations of the Nazis' Final Solution, relentless Zionist attacks, and their own weariness with the endless Palestine imbroglio, all of this coming on top of Britain's exhaustion in World War II, the Palestinians again did not benefit. The British threw the problem into the lap of the newly established United Nations, perhaps cynically hoping that the organization would fail to deal with this intractable problem, necessitating the maintenance of some form of British influence in Palestine.[23] Their chosen instrument for the maintenance of a British role in the region was no longer their sponsorship of the Zionist project, and certainly not the Palestinians, but rather their faithful Arab allies in Transjordan, Iraq, and other parts of the Arab world. In particular, the British agreed with 'Abdullah's prime minister Tawfiq Abu al-Huda on a visit to London in January 1948 that Transjordan would take over the areas allotted to the Arabs under the partition plan.[24] 'Abdullah had come to a similar understanding in November 1947 with emissaries of the Jewish Agency such as Moshe Sharret and Golda Meir.[25] Given the Palestinians' increasing dependence on the Arab states, this reinforced connection between Britain and several key Arab states, and in particular the collusion between 'Abdullah and the Zionist leadership, was to cause them many further problems.

By contrast with British policymakers, who had come to resent the Zionists bitterly for turning against them (a sentiment that was more than reciprocated), American and Soviet planners saw the nascent Jewish state as a possible asset in their efforts to diminish the overwhelming influence of Great Britain in the Middle East. Both appreciated the vital strategic importance of the region, both were in search of local allies and clients, and both saw Britain as an obstacle to the enhancement of their own influence. Although we naturally tend to see the United States and the Soviet Union as the primary powers in the Middle East (as elsewhere) in the wake of World War II, in fact this only became true in the mid- to late 1950s. Their ascendancy, and the eclipse of both of the formerly dominant great powers in the region, Britain and France, was only fully brought home during the Suez crisis of 1956, when the latter, acting in collusion with Israel, were humiliated by the United States and the Soviet Union, which turned back their tripartite invasion of Egypt.

In the meantime, what this meant for the Palestinians was that no great power was on their side. The United States and Soviet Union were overtly ranged against them, both voting for partition and for the establishment of a Jewish state in 1947, and immediately recognizing Israel on May 15, 1948. The reasons were simple: both looked with disfavor on the Palestinians because of the mufti's years in Berlin, and neither had developed any links with them. The Palestinians, meanwhile, had even less of a presence in, or understanding of, the Soviet Union or the United States than they had

had with regard to Britain. By contrast, the Zionist movement had made major inroads in the United States, developing a strong position within the American Jewish community, which became broadly supportive in the wake of the Holocaust, and building on relations with Congress and with American presidents that went back to the close links between American Zionist leader Louis Brandeis and President Wilson.[26] Even with the Soviet Union, which was generally unfriendly to Zionism, during and after World War II the Zionist movement had managed to build a relationship that served them in good stead in 1948 when a major Czech arms deal helped the young Israeli state.

The British, while not favorably disposed toward Israel because of the bitterness of the last years of the Mandate, were also not well disposed toward the Palestinians, against whom they still held the revolt of 1936–39 and what they perceived as the "betrayal" of the mufti. They rather looked toward their various local Arab clients and allies to advance their interests. The most important of these, King 'Abdullah of Transjordan, was no friend of the mufti's, and had coveted a role in Palestine at least since the 1937 Peel Commission, which recommended that the part of Palestine which was not to become a Jewish state or remain under British control be attached to his domain. Expansion of his power was 'Abdullah's idée fixe at this stage, and the idea of doing so westward across the Jordan animated his secret diplomacy with both Britain and the Jewish Agency, with whose leaders he met repeatedly.[27] This meant that 'Abdullah, Britain, the new state of Israel, and the United States and the Soviet Union, notwithstanding all the many differences between them, in effect shared one objective in Palestine: preventing the establishment of the Palestinian Arab state that had been called for by the partition plan.

The Palestinians had only a very thin reed to hang on to, those Arab states that opposed King 'Abdullah's ambitions in Palestine: Egypt, Saudi Arabia, and Syria. Through the newly established Arab League, founded in Alexandria in 1944, these states attempted to restrain 'Abdullah, albeit to little effect in the end. All were militarily weak (Saudi Arabia did not even have a modern army at this stage), their armies far less well-equipped and -trained and considerably less battle worthy than the Jordanian Arab Legion, which was also closest to the scene and had extensive familiarity with Palestine, having helped the British army to garrison the region until Britain's withdrawal in May 1948. During World War II, the Egyptian and Iraqi armies had been looked on with deep suspicion by the British (indeed the latter had fought the British in 1941), who had kept them on a very short leash, and little was done thereafter to build them up. Moreover, the Arab states had limited financial means, found great difficulty in coordinating strategy, and did not entirely trust the mufti, who by 1947 had returned to the Arab world, making Cairo his base, and with whom their experiences over more than a decade had been less than reassuring. Efforts to make the Palestinian case internationally were crippled by differences among the Arab states, as well as among Palestinian leaders. These efforts included Musa al-'Alami's Arab Office project, funded by Iraq but ultimately opposed by al-'Alami's erstwhile colleague the mufti, and later repudiated by the Egyptian-dominated Arab League.[28] This initiative provided the Palestinians, for the first time in their existence as a people, with diplomatic representation abroad, and they initially opened offices in London, New York, and Geneva. The Arab League eventually came to back the mufti as the best obstacle to King 'Abdullah's ambitions in Palestine and elsewhere in the region, and the Arab Office project eventually died and the offices were closed.

The results on the battlefield in Palestine reflected the same elements as had been in evidence for twelve years, since the 1936 general strike: the weaknesses of the Palestinians, the divisions among the Arab states, the determination, organization, and competence of the Jewish Agency (which on May 15, 1948, was to transform itself into the government of the new state of Israel), and the broad international support that the Zionist movement enjoyed. The Palestine war, which began with bloody skirmishes as soon as the partition resolution was passed on November 29, 1947, escalated rapidly. This war had two major phases. The first was a civil war between the forces of the contending parties within Palestine, the Jews and the Arabs. The second was a war between the armies of the newly established state of Israel and four Arab states. The first phase involved on one side the military forces of the embryonic Jewish state, primarily the Hagana, already a single quasi-regular military force that generally coordinated with military units of the dissident Zionist splinter groups, the Irgun and Lehi. On the other side, it involved disunited Palestinian irregular forces, organized locally and led mainly by veterans of the 1936–39 revolt, together with an Arab volunteer force sent into Palestine at the end of 1947 by the Arab League, Jaysh al-Inqadh al-'Arabi, the Arab Liberation Army (ALA).[29] The balance between the two parties was lopsided: Zionist forces, most of them under a central command and organized as a regular army, numbered well over fifty thousand, including reserves, while the Arab forces, nearly all of them irregulars with widely divergent levels of training (if any), armament, and organization, numbered a total of under ten thousand. Even more grave, from the very outset there were profound political divisions and no cooperation whatsoever in the field between the local Palestinian forces and those of the ALA commanded by Fawzi al-Qawuqji.[30]

This first phase of the conflict went on for about six months until the rout of the inferior forces of the Palestinians and the ALA in April and early May 1948, a defeat marked by the fall of several major Arab cities, scores of villages, and the expulsion or flight of between a quarter of a million and 350,000 Palestinians. This phase ended on May 15, the date of the simultaneous termination of the British Mandate, the proclamation of the state of Israel, and the entry of several Arab armies into Palestine. The entry of the Arab armies marked the beginning of the second phase of the 1948 war, an interstate war fought between regular armies: those of the new state of Israel and four of its Arab neighbors. Although there were seven independent Arab states at the time, the only Arab armies that actually entered Palestine were those of Egypt, Transjordan, Iraq, and Syria.[31] Moreover, by prior agreements between King 'Abdullah and the Jewish Agency, and between 'Abdullah and Britain, the most powerful and combat worthy of these armies, the Transjordanian Arab Legion (and the Iraqi forces that were under 'Abdullah's command and control), never crossed into the territory allotted to the Jewish state. These two armies fought Israeli troops only in the area originally assigned to the Arab state, or in the area of Jerusalem —which according to the partition plan was supposed to have been an international *corpus separatum*—and thus they never invaded the territory of the Jewish state.

Although it was not initially apparent, in the fighting during the first phase of the war between the Hagana and its Arab opponents, the former were considerably superior to the latter in weaponry, numbers, and organization. Their most important asset, besides these advantages, was unity of command. For the first few months of the fighting, until March 1948, the Palestinians nevertheless appeared to be holding their own. They maintained control over most Arab-inhabited regions of Palestine, and managed repeatedly to cut the roads linking major cities and some of the isolated Jewish settlements, including at the end of March the critically important road from the coast to Jerusalem. However, as soon as the Hagana and its allies went on a nationwide offensive early in April 1948, on the basis of a military plan for linking up most of the major Jewish-inhabited regions of the country, known as Plan *Dalet*, they rapidly showed their overwhelming superiority.[32] By the end of their offensive, they had overrun the major coastal cities with large Arab populations, Haifa, Acre, and Jaffa, as well as Tiberias, Beisan, and other cities and towns, and scores of villages, and set hundreds of thousands of Palestinians on the road to exile.[33]

In some of the heaviest combat, along the hilly, winding road leading up to Jerusalem from the coastal plain, the Zionist forces made their first significant progress on April 9, clinching a decisive victory after several days of seesaw fighting with the capture of the strategic hilltop village of al-Qastal. The charismatic Palestinian commander of the Jerusalem region, 'Abd al-Qadir al-Husayni, died in this crucial battle, and two of his key lieutenants were wounded. This defeat was triply devastating for the Palestinians. 'Abd al-Qadir al-Husayni was the most universally respected Palestinian military commander, a man of unquestioned courage, and the top figure in the high command of the Jerusalem area because of his combat experience going back to the 1936–39 revolt, and his lineage as the son of the celebrated Palestinian nationalist Musa Kazim al-Husayni and a relative of the mufti. His death deprived the Palestinians of their most gifted military leader and an important unifying figure. Secondly, following his death, a huge funeral cortege for him in Jerusalem several miles distant drew the attendance of most of the fighters who had succeeded in briefly retaking al-Qastal. In consequence, the village was now once more occupied, this time for good, by the Hagana, giving it firm control over this strategic high point on the vital road to the coast. Finally, even more devastating, on the same day, April 9, 1948, Irgun and Lehi forces, backed by Hagana artillery, took the neighboring village of Deir Yasin, and after several hours of fighting killed many of its surviving inhabitants, blowing up their homes. The figures given for the number of victims ranged from the contemporary Red Cross estimate of 254 to a high of 350, but the most detailed and careful study of the massacre gives the names of 100 persons killed, 75 of them children, women, and the elderly.[34] Some of the survivors were paraded through Jerusalem before being taken back to the village and shot.

The Palestinians did not recover from the impact of this triple blow. With the capture of al-Qastal, Deir Yasin, and a half dozen other Arab villages along the strategic road to Jerusalem, a major obstacle to supply of the city's large Jewish population had been removed and an enormous inroad had been made into the area allotted to the Arab state under partition. It was becoming increasingly clear that this Arab state would never be allowed to see the light of day. The flight of the Palestinian population from areas conquered by the Hagana and other Jewish forces increased under the impact of the shock of the Deir Yasin massacre, growing to a flood with the fall of Tiberias, Haifa, Jaffa, and other towns later in April and into May. Arab Palestine was crumbling, and the implications of the absence of a single Palestinian national authority that could have raised and organized forces to defend it were now acutely clear: as individual cities, towns, and villages, most often defended by their own inhabitants with scarce help from outside, fell to the well-organized, centralized forces of a state that had not yet been declared.

Before his death, 'Abd al-Qadir al-Husayni had rushed back to join in the al-Qastal battle from Damascus, where he had been unsuccessfully begging for more arms from the Arab League's Military Committee. His appeals for weapons from the well-supplied ALA were also rejected by al-Qawuqji, who by now had come under the influence of the archrival of the Palestinians, King 'Abdullah. These two failures spoke volumes about the parlous state of the military formations at the disposition of the Palestinians on the supremely important Jerusalem front, and the lack of unity on the Arab side. Things were even worse in Haifa, Jaffa, and elsewhere. But beyond this, these incidents reveal both how devastating were the inability of the Palestinians to recover from their defeats of 1936–39, and their failure over a much longer time to create a quasi-state structure matching that possessed by the Zionists, which could unify them politically and allow them to organize and supply a single nationwide military force in a battle both sides had long known was coming.

The results for the Palestinians of the fighting in April and the first half of May between the forces of the nascent Jewish state and the disorganized Palestinian local forces and the units of the ALA were devastating. They included seizure by the Hagana of extensive Arab-owned and -inhabited areas, and a growing exodus of the

Palestinian population. These results marked the end for many decades of Palestine as a predominantly Arab country, as well as of the ability of the Palestinians to operate as independent actors. They marked as well the beginning of decades in the wilderness for the Palestinians. Far from being able to dream of a state of their own, they were now faced with an existential test of whether they would be able to remain together as a people. Paradoxically, later events showed that the traumatic impact of the shared experience of 1948 on the entirety of Palestinian society helped to weld it together even more strongly, obliterating much that had transpired before 1948, rendering many earlier divisions irrelevant, and creating a sort of tabula rasa on which Palestinian identity could be reestablished.

This new post-1948 world first manifested itself in the struggle over who would "represent" the Palestinians. King 'Abdullah immediately acted to further his own dynastic and nation-state interests, his army having retained the largest part of Palestine that had not been incorporated into the new state of Israel. He organized a conference at Jericho in the Jordan River Valley in December 1948, inviting pro-Hashemite notables from across the West Bank, who made a "demand" for the unification of the region with Transjordan. In 1950 the Transjordanian parliament ratified the unification of the two banks of the Jordan into what now was called the Hashemite Kingdom of Jordan. 'Abdullah was doing more than annexing the largest remaining Arab piece of Palestine. He was also laying claim to representation of the Palestinians. His only challengers for this role, the discredited mufti and an Arab League–supported All Palestine Government established in Gaza, were both further undermined by the defeat of Egyptian forces in southern Palestine in one of the last phases of the 1948 war, obliging this government to withdraw to Cairo.[35] Neither it nor the mufti was to play a major role thereafter in Palestine or Palestinian politics, although the mufti remained alive until 1974, and through a shadow Arab Higher Committee under his control continued to claim to represent the

Palestinians until the bitter end. By this time, of course, the mufti had long since been eclipsed by younger men of a much different stamp.

From this point onward and for many decades, most Palestinian political activity would take place outside Palestine rather than inside it. The reasons for this had to do with the policies of the three states that controlled the territory of the former Mandate for Palestine. The state of Israel kept a tight rein on the 150,000 Palestinians in the 78 percent of Palestine that had been brought under its control by the time of the 1949 armistice, maintaining a military government and oppressive movement and political restrictions on them until 1966. The Jordanian authorities saw virtually any independent Palestinian organization as subversive and as a threat to the unity of the kingdom, and ruthlessly combated political activity of most kinds, making the West and East Banks of Jordan highly inhospitable for independent Palestinian political action. The Egyptian military authorities, in control of the Gaza Strip at the end of the war, allowed only limited Palestinian activity, and none that could jeopardize Egypt's armistice agreement with Israel.[36] Among the now dispersed Palestinians, scattered in tents in refugee camps or in rented accommodations, living among relatives or precariously scratching out a living in their new places of exile, a new generation of political activists took the stage, and soon found themselves forced to operate farther afield because of controls on their activities by these three states.

This new generation of Palestinian activists was rooted in a major change in the social basis of political power, which deeply influenced the politics of the subsequent decades. The entire stratum of leaders drawn from the notable class who had dominated Palestinian politics until 1948 had been swept away by the tidal wave of the *nakba* that had engulfed Palestinian society. Beyond being discredited for their failures in the years up to 1948, beyond many of them being demoralized and dispirited, they now were frequently deprived of the social basis of their political power, as many of the wealthiest lost their lands and homes, and all lost their social status in a society that no longer felt deference for what was seen as an outmoded, *depassé* class that had failed its own people. It is striking how few members of the major families of Palestine played a political role after 1948, whether the old notable families of Jerusalem and Nablus, other landholding families, or those that had risen to wealth through trade and commercial agriculture in the coastal cities. In this respect, the Palestinians anticipated similar processes that affected Syria, Egypt, and Iraq after each country went through revolutionary social upheavals in the 1950s and 1960s. In the Palestinian case, it meant the eclipse of the old political class and the rise of an entirely new generation of activists from new social strata, and with a different educational background, a different worldview, and entirely different solutions to the problems of Palestine and the Palestinian people.

This new generation operated in the conditions of extreme dispersion and fragmentation that characterized Palestinian society after 1948. Divided between Israel, the West and East Banks of Jordan, and the Gaza Strip, and with others in camps in Lebanon and Syria, or even farther afield in Iraq and Egypt, a segment of the Palestinian population lived in refugee camps, while some inside Israel, in the West Bank and the Gaza Strip, remained in their homes. The class and social divisions that had plagued Palestinian society before 1948 seemed to abate for a time thereafter. Certainly the loss of much of the material basis for the wealth of the upper classes in consequence of their losing much of their property had an impact, as did the fact that now in a certain sense all Palestinians appeared to face the same fate. Of course this was not entirely the case. Some of the old notables gravitated to the Hashemite regime in Amman, which was pleased to accept them as clients and offer them positions. And many of the upper classes retained human and real capital accumulated over generations. Nevertheless, there was more of an even playing field in this brave new world, where education and skills were vital, and where a newly educated generation, trained in the newly established schools of the UN Relief and Works Agency (UNRWA), created to minister to the needs of the Palestinian refugees, were able to find jobs all over the Arab world. It was Palestinians of this new diaspora, in Cairo, Beirut, and Kuwait, who in the subsequent decades were to revive Palestinian identity and a Palestinian national movement on a new basis. These educated young men, and a few women, worked in different ways through Pan-Arab and transnational groups like the Ba'th Party, the Muslim Brotherhood, the Syrian Socialist Nationalist Party, and the Arab Nationalist Movement (ANM), and through bodies like the Union of Palestinian Students in Cairo. In time, they came up against the constraints placed on Palestinian activism by the Arab regimes, and had to decide how they related to the Arab governments that, since their first intervention in Palestinian politics in 1936, had played an ambiguous role at best, and often a negative one as far as the Palestinians were concerned.

By the time the Arab League founded the Palestine Liberation Organization (PLO) in 1964, in an attempt to keep control of the Palestinian arena and head off burgeoning Palestinian activism, it was already too late to stop such independent development. Fateh, a reverse acronym for Harakat al-Tahrir al-Filastini, the Palestinian Liberation Movement, and its archrival, the ANM, later the progenitor of the Popular Front for the Liberation of Palestine (PFLP) and other groups, were already rapidly winning adherents in universities, schools, and refugee camps. Within a few years, they came to dominate the PLO and to impart to it a new impetus, and a purely Palestinian tenor, replacing the heavy hand of Arab government control that the Egyptian-dominated Arab League had exercised.

Palestinians involved in these nascent national organizations were not unmindful of the bitter experiences of the past. Among the heroes singled out in their publications by the new Palestinian organizations that took over the PLO in 1968 were Shaykh 'Iz al-Din al-Qassam, and 'Abd al-Qadir al-Husayni, both of whom had died in battle, in 1935 and 1948 respectively. They became symbols of mil-

itancy for the next generation. Conspicuously absent in these publications was any reference to the failed notable leadership of the
Mandate period, which had disappeared, apparently unmourned,
from the arena of Palestinian politics. It remained to be seen how
much better their successors would do in meeting the new challenges that faced the Palestinian people.

5

Fateh, the PLO, and the PA: The Palestinian Para-State

The Palestinians after 'Arafat

In November 2004, the Autumn of the Patriarch finally ended. Yasser 'Arafat's death closed a lengthy era in modern Palestinian politics during which his larger-than-life figure towered over the resuscitated post-1948 Palestinian national movement. 'Arafat dominated Palestinian politics in multiple capacities during most of his lifetime of seventy-five years. He was elected president of the Union of Palestinian Students in Cairo in 1952 when he was in his early twenties, was preeminent among the founding leaders of the Fateh movement in Kuwait in the late 1950s, became chairman of the Executive Committee of the PLO in 1969, and finally in 1996 was elected president of the Palestinian Authority (PA).

In any national movement, whether successful or not, such a founding (or refounding) figure plays a unique role. This was certainly the case with 'Arafat, as it was with Nehru, Sukarno, Nyerere, Bourguiba, 'Abd al-Nasir, and others before him. They seemed the stuff of myth, and their successors often appeared lackluster in comparison. After such a long period during which he sometimes seemed omnipresent, 'Arafat departed from the scene at a time when the Palestinians faced a reinforced occupation and decades-long dispersal, while confronting a cohesive American-Israeli alliance, and still suffered from a nearly century-old tradition of weak self-governance and disunity. These are long-standing problems that could not have been resolved by any single individual. Nevertheless, there has often been a tendency to personalize Palestinian politics, such that every decision, every vagary, every flaw, has been described as being the work of one man: Yasser 'Arafat.

It is true that to 'Arafat (and to his fellow founders of Fateh) goes much of the credit for reviving the Palestinian cause in the two decades immediately after the debacle of 1948. In the 1950s and 1960s, the young leaders of Fateh, including Salah Khalaf (Abu Iyyad) and Khalil al-Wazir (Abu Jihad),[1] among whom 'Arafat for his entire life was first among equals, galvanized Palestinian politics with their fiery militant rhetoric, their air of mystery, and their vague ideology, which had the potential to embrace virtually all political tendencies. Also extremely attractive to many Palestinians in the 1950s and 1960s was Fateh's insistent preaching of direct, armed action against Israel, combined with its independence from Arab governments. This struck a chord among those seeking redress for their recent dispossession, particularly at a time when the governments of the Arab countries bordering Israel (with the exception of the short-lived Syrian neo-Ba'th regime, in power from 1966 until 1970) were generally quite careful to avoid any provocation of the powerful Jewish state.

The ascendancy in the 1950s and 1960s of the leaders of Fateh, along with the rise of other competing militant groups, represented a thoroughgoing generational change and a striking alteration in the image presented by those who represented the Palestinians. It involved a shift from the domination of Palestinian politics by sober men in their fifties and sixties wearing suits and red tarbushes (and in the case of Hajj Amin al-Husayni, in the traditional robes of the ulema) to the leadership of militants in their twenties and thirties wearing short-sleeved shirts and military fatigues. 'Arafat's trademark checked kaffiyeh headdress harked back to the dress of the rural Palestinian rebels of the late 1930s. More importantly, these sartorial changes also represented a shift from the failed elitist politics of the notables of the Mandate era, disastrously dominated as they had been by the old urban aristocratic families, to modern mass-based politics.

At the same time, an important social change in Palestinian leadership took place: the leading elements of Fateh and the other major political movements of the period were drawn from individuals of diverse class, social, and regional backgrounds, with very few, if any, coming from among the urban notables, and many having lower-middle-class, rural, and refugee-camp origins. Because the rise of Fateh and the other militant groups ushered in an era of true mass politics, involving many more people in political activity than had been the case in the 1920s through the 1940s, the leadership stratum became far larger and broader. At the same time, the educational level of the new generation of leaders and cadres was in many cases higher than those of the 1930s and 1940s. This reflected the increasing prevalence of education in Palestine during the mandatory period, when these new militant leaders were born, as compared with the late Ottoman period, when those who dominated Palestinian politics during the Mandate period came to maturity. Over time, the remarkable efforts in the field of education of the United Nations Relief and Works Agency (UNRWA), the agency responsible for providing services to the Palestinian refugees, bore fruit as well, and the Palestinians came to have the highest literacy rate in the Arab world after Lebanon. This, too, eventually affected Palestinian politics.

Yasser 'Arafat dominated the Palestinian political scene for over two generations. However, if he deserved much of the credit for returning to center stage a people who momentarily appeared to have disappeared from the Middle Eastern scene after 1948, to him also belonged a share of the blame for the problems with which his people were saddled at his death. This is particularly true of the flaws in the political structures that developed during 'Arafat's era of dominance of Palestinian politics. Yasser 'Arafat, an easily caricatured figure who did not arouse sympathy in most Western, and many Arab, observers, readily lent himself to the personification of everything relating to Palestine. Indeed, in some measure he encouraged it. He was egocentric, reveled in attention, and was jealous of rivals. He worked tirelessly to keep all the strings controlling Palestinian politics, particularly the financial ones, in his hands alone. He lived single-mindedly for his political work, and he worked incessantly, putting in longer hours than his colleagues in the Palestinian leadership. He had few distractions, took little recreation, and never vacationed. In everything he did, he exploited to the full his capacious memory, his relentless drive, and his powerful, domineering personality.

The political structures 'Arafat was largely responsible for creating, while they mirrored aspects of other patriarchal regimes and political movements in the modern Arab world, also closely reflected his personal characteristics, notably in terms of his indomitable desire to be in charge. As the preeminent founding leader of the major Palestinian political formation, Fateh, as the chairman beginning in 1969 of the PLO Executive Committee, and as the first elected president of the PA, 'Arafat left his mark on styles of authority, forms of organization, and structures that have endured after his passing.

While 'Arafat deserves credit for some of the successes, and can be blamed for some of the failings, of Fateh, the PLO, and the PA, he cannot be considered as solely responsible for either. Some of these failings were a result of problems that were manifestly structural and deeply seated, notably the failure of the Palestinian polity during the Mandate period to develop the attributes of stateness, or even to appreciate the importance of developing quasi-state structures as a paramount national goal. 'Arafat's preference for the personal over the organizational, his notorious tendency to create duplicate lines of authority (and often duplicate structures, notably within the security services), his systematic undermining of administrative routine, and his general preference for controlled chaos over order, can be faulted in part, but in part only, for the Palestinians' failure to move much further than they had during the Mandate period toward a stable, unified quasi-state structure.

Against this background must be set the undeniable fact that Fateh was remarkably successful in dominating Palestinian politics from soon after its establishment in the late 1950s until 'Arafat's death, a period of great fluidity and difficulty for an independent Palestinian political movement. Moreover, there is little question that the recognition of the PLO as the sole legitimate representative of the Palestinian people, by the Palestinians themselves, by the Arab states, and by most of the world, was a considerable achievement, for which 'Arafat deserved much of the credit. The Arab Higher Committee and other earlier Palestinian national bodies had never known such a level of unrivaled, universal recognition. At the same time, it must be acknowledged that this was an achievement undermined by the hollowness of the structures of the PLO itself, which in turn can in part be blamed on the deeply ingrained habits of Yasser 'Arafat.

Beyond the lack of a strong, unified central body dominating and organizing Palestinian politics, an absence that long anteceded 'Arafat's emergence, new complications arose for the Palestinians after 1948. A particular problem was their physical dispersal and the consequent fragmentation of the Palestinian polity after 1948, which in many ways has come to define the Palestinian condition. Today some 5 million Palestinians live in former mandatory Palestine west of the Jordan River, divided into four distinct groups. Over 1.2 million are citizens of Israel, as they or their families have been since 1948. They constitute nearly 20 percent of that country's population, a large non-Jewish minority in the self-proclaimed state of the Jewish people, where they have negligible political influence. In 2006 the over 3.6 million Palestinians in the West Bank, Gaza Strip (which remains under effective Israeli control even after the disengagement of 2005), and East Jerusalem were enduring their fortieth year of Israeli military occupation (two generations in their lives, and two-thirds of the lifetime of the state of Israel). Those in the three areas under occupation are hermetically sealed off from one another by Israel. Each of these four groups—those with Israeli citizenship; a quarter million Arab Jerusalemites who since the 1967 annexation of East Jerusalem are "permanent residents," but not citizens, of Israel; 2 million plus West Bankers; and over 1.3 million Gazans—is subject to a different legal framework; the West Bankers and the Gazans face stringent movement restrictions.

Outside Palestine, meanwhile, live between 4 and 6 million Palestinians (reliable figures are not available). They exist in situations ranging from the utter misery (since 1982) of those in refugee camps in Lebanon,[2] to a wide diversity of conditions, some of them quite comfortable, in various other Arab countries, Europe, and the United States. These Palestinians "of the diaspora" (al-shatat in Arabic) possess a variety of passports, laissez-passers, and refugee documents, some of which are looked upon with great suspicion by certain states, and some of them face harsh restrictions on their movement in consequence. The largest single group of Palestinians of the diaspora, between 2 and 3 million, carry Jordanian passports, and most of them live in Jordan. What unites the overwhelming majority of these 4 to 6 million people is that they or their parents or grandparents were obliged to leave their homes and became refugees in 1948 or afterward, and that they are barred from living in any part of their ancestral homeland, Palestine.

While Palestinians coped with this inhospitable environment, Palestinian political structures suffered from the efforts of several Arab governments to dominate them, even as they continued to be the object of the hostility of Israel and the Western powers. And while the PLO struggled to resist Arab pressures, under the slogan of "preserving the independent Palestinian decision," its weakness and dependence on different Arab states for diplomatic support, bases, and money often drew it into a delicate and exceedingly dangerous balancing act. 'Arafat was a past master at this, and indeed it may have been his greatest skill. One consequence of decades of this constant leaping from one ice floe to another, however, was that by the end 'Arafat had exhausted the patience of many of the leaders, Arab and others, with whom he dealt over the decades.

But 'Arafat alone cannot be blamed for all of the many strategic errors made by the PLO after it came under the control of independent Palestinian groups in 1968. Among them were the multiple mistakes made in Jordan before 1970 and in Lebanon until 1982, involving the PLO in bloody and ultimately disastrous conflicts in both countries. Claiming to be a movement of resistance to the Israeli occupation that did not interfere in the politics of its host countries, the PLO was inexorably drawn into Jordanian and Lebanese internal affairs, and became embroiled in costly wars, leading to its expulsion from both countries.[3] Equally harmful was the PLO's equivocation about a two-state solution and an end to armed violence long after that course had supposedly been conclusively decided upon. This was shown in the failure to impose internal discipline on a pro-Iraqi splinter faction, the Palestine Liberation Front (PLF), headed by Muhammad 'Abbas (Abu al-'Abbas), after the 1985 *Achille Lauro* hijacking and the murder of a U.S. citizen,[4] and after another PLF seaborne attack on a beach near Tel Aviv in March 1990 jeopardized ongoing negotiations with the United States.[5] A blunder of a different sort was the PLO's disastrous alignment with Saddam Hussein after Iraq's invasion of Kuwait in 1990. In spite of the enthusiasm of many Palestinians for the reckless action of the Iraqi dictator, it should have been obvious that this adventure was doomed to fail and would drag the PLO down with it. Finally, there was the lamentable error of accepting a series of flawed accords with the Israelis, beginning with the 1993 Oslo agreement.

It cannot be stressed strongly enough that many of these strategic blunders grew out of collective decision-making by the entire Fateh-PLO-PA leadership. In the end, all of them were the responsibility of the entire leadership, not of one man alone. There was, however, dissent over several of these decisions, notably Abu Iyyad's strong disagreement with the PLO's support for the Iraqi invasion of Kuwait, for which he may well have paid with his life. Abu Iyyad fully recognized the many dangers for the PLO inherent in aligning with Iraq in 1990–91. He understood, as 'Arafat and some other

Arab leaders apparently did not, that the United States was without rivals or constraints in the new post–Cold War world after the collapse of the Soviet Union, and that it could and would easily drive Iraqi forces from Kuwait, completely changing the Middle Eastern strategic map. He understood further the disastrous impact of such an alignment for the PLO's vitally important relations with Saudi Arabia and the other Gulf countries, which stood squarely in opposition to Hussein's invasion of Kuwait. Finally, Abu Iyyad understood that this ill-considered decision spelled doom for the well-to-do Palestinian community of a quarter of a million people in Kuwait, a crucial pillar of the PLO's prosperity and independence. He did not live to see his forebodings realized: he was assassinated in Tunis with two other PLO leaders on January 14, 1991, the day before the U.S.-led offensive against Iraqi forces in Kuwait began, by a double agent whom the Palestinian intelligence services, headed by Abu Iyyad, had utilized to penetrate and destroy the Abu Nidal group, a terrorist organization sponsored by the Iraqi regime.

However, if 'Arafat dominated Palestinian politics for most of his adult life, over the years since the early 1970s much changed in the internal balance of Fateh and the PLO, notably with the assassinations by agents either of Israel or of Arab regimes, in particular those of Iraq and Syria, of many of the most important leaders of Fateh and the PFLP. Especially after the assassinations in Tunis of Abu Jihad in 1988 and Abu Iyyad in 1991 (by Israel and the Abu Nidal group respectively), there remained virtually no one within the Palestinian leadership who could stand up to al-khityar, the "old man," as 'Arafat was respectfully referred to privately. Before this, although he was always first among equals, 'Arafat had at times been obliged to defer to his comrades, particularly on those rare occasions when they succeeded in banding together to oppose him. Moreover, several of the founding leaders of Fateh had their own organizational bases and sources of support. They could afford to defy 'Arafat (although given his temper and autocratic tendencies they were generally loath to do so).

In consequence of the balance of power within the leadership of Fateh, and of the variety of political tendencies in the Palestinian political arena, there were serious internal and public deliberations about strategy within Fateh and the PLO from the 1950s until the mid-1980s. There was also a degree of freedom of expression among Palestinians generally that was rare in the Arab world at that time. One example of these contentious strategy deliberations was the wide-ranging debate in the late 1970s and early 1980s over whether to end the pretence of using bases in Lebanon to wage "armed struggle" against Israel (which already had become desultory) and instead follow a "Jordanian option" (*al-khiyar al-urduni* in Arabic) of reconciling with the Hashemite regime in order to develop closer political ties with the occupied territories. This debate took place over several years in newspapers, at public meetings and seminars, and in open and closed conclaves of the Palestinian leadership. By contrast with this robust contention over strategy until the mid-1980s, for the decade and a half until his death, Yasser 'Arafat increasingly made most decisions himself, surrounded by a coterie of deferential yes-men.

Paradoxically, the man whose longevity, luck, and skill enabled him to dominate Palestinian politics more and more completely as time went on became less and less personally impressive over the same period. After a close brush with death in an air crash in the Libyan Desert in April 1992, 'Arafat seemed diminished to those who had known him before. His memory, always one of his most potent weapons, was no longer what it had once been. Thereafter, his alertness would appear to vary from day to day. In his two or three final years, the once vigorous 'Arafat seemed increasingly frail as his health visibly declined. In his late seventies, mortality was revealing itself in a man who had once seemed unchanged by the passing years, but who had lived a hard, dangerous life for five decades. This increasing feebleness was most apparent after the Israeli army immured 'Arafat in the spring of 2002 in the wreckage of his headquarters,[6] creating a situation where the elected and universally recognized leader of the Palestinian people (though his term as elected president of the PA ran out in 2000) was immobilized and virtually imprisoned. Increasingly isolated from reality, largely cut off from his own people, receiving only a few visitors compared with the many who had flocked to see him in Beirut, in Tunis, and in Gaza and Ramallah before 2002, 'Arafat was even more dependent on a close circle of trusted aides, chosen more for their absolute loyalty than for their competence.

Even in infirmity, however, 'Arafat was a more formidable politician than his colleagues in the Fateh, PLO, and PA leaderships, Abu al-'Ala (Ahmad Quray') and Abu Mazin (Mahmoud Abbas). Both these men failed miserably in 2003 to impose themselves against 'Arafat's will in the newly created post of prime minister. 'Arafat thereafter decisively showed himself more able than men half his age, rapidly crushing an open challenge to his authority in the summer of 2004 by Muhammad Dahlan, former chief of Preventive Security in Gaza (one of more than a dozen competing PA security services created by 'Arafat). But 'Arafat's isolation, and his increasing loss of focus, left the Palestinian polity drifting like a rudderless ship, without any recognizable strategy at a time of supreme crisis, as the intifada ground on with devastating effects for the Palestinians. The Oslo period (1991–2000), adjudged in retrospect to have been disastrous by most Palestinians, was fully identified with 'Arafat. It was followed by four years of the second intifada, which 'Arafat had ambiguously embraced, and which exhausted and debilitated Palestinian society.

Not surprisingly, the passing of this figure, who had inspired strong positive and negative feelings among his people, elicited both intense mourning and veiled relief among Palestinians. There was a sense of anxiety at the disappearance of the only leader most of them had ever known, combined with a sense that change was imperative after a long period of aimlessness and lack of direction. Resentment at a father figure who had clung to power for too long was joined with deep insecurity after the disappearance of the icon whose person had come to symbolize the Palestinian cause. There was, in consequence, a strange mixture of wrenching sadness and mild elation at the funeral and in the days after 'Arafat's burial, when the meaning of his absence began to sink in among Palestinians everywhere. Strangely, very soon after his passing Yasser 'Arafat seemed to have disappeared without a trace, his picture hanging in PA offices and his name invoked in a perfunctory fashion on occasion, but otherwise seemingly forgotten.

The PLO: Appearance and Reality

It was long commonly believed that the PLO had finally provided the Palestinians with the responsible, mature, state-like framework that they had lacked throughout their modern history. Operating as the almost universally accepted representative of the Palestinian people (once organizations led by Fateh had ended the Arab League's tutelage over Palestinian politics), and described as carrying out many of the functions of a state, the PLO under the leadership of Fateh was broadly seen in terms of a teleology of evolution from a liberation movement to a para-state that would eventually lead the Palestinians to full-fledged statehood and independence.[7]

Perhaps the high point in this narrative was the signing of the Oslo Accords between the PLO, represented by Yasser 'Arafat, and the Israeli government, represented by Prime Minister Yitzhaq Rabin, on the White House lawn on September 13, 1993. As part of the so-called "Oslo process" that followed, after the founding of the Palestinian Authority (PA) in the West Bank and Gaza Strip under the aegis of the PLO leadership that returned to Palestine from Tunis in the mid-1990s, it appeared to many that the PLO had crossed an important threshold toward the final goal of statehood. This view was nearly universally held, with the notable exception of those animated by an inveterate hostility to the Palestinian national movement,[8] and a few critical Palestinian voices.[9] Notwithstanding these criticisms, in the mid-1990s most observers were in agreement that the PLO and the PA, both dominated by Fateh, were on the point of becoming the Palestinian state whose establishment many at that stage saw as virtually inevitable.

In 2006, over a dozen years after the signing of the Oslo Accords, it was abundantly clear that this transformation had not taken place, and indeed did not seem at all likely in the near term. Outside of Palestine, the hollow shell of the PLO currently exists in a nearly moribund state; in certain crucially important respects it barely continues to function. It has failed to provide many needed services to refugee camp residents in Lebanon and elsewhere, often lacks the funds to pay its employees their salaries, and has done a poor job (with the exception of the efforts of a few able ambassadors) of representing Palestinian diplomatic interests abroad. The PLO, and with it the problems of the over 4 million Palestinians of the diaspora, a majority of the entire Palestinian people, are largely neglected by most of the senior Fateh leadership, who returned to Palestine in the mid-1990s to take up the top positions in the PA.

Meanwhile, inside the occupied West Bank and the recently evacuated (but still Israeli-controlled[10]) Gaza Strip, a weak and badly fractured Fateh-dominated PA was certainly not thriving. This was true even before the January 2006 elections for the Palestinian Legislative Council (PLC) were won by Fateh's main rivals in Hamas, throwing Palestinian politics into turmoil. The PA had been hammered and humiliated by the armed might of Israel for most of the four years of the second intifada, from late 2000 until the end of 2004, as the areas Israel had evacuated in the mid-1990s were reoccupied. The founding core of both the PLO and the PA, the Fateh movement has been riven by conflicts between its old and new guard, and between returnees from exile and local West Bankers and Gazans. It was also plagued by rivalries between the widely loathed warlords who emerged from the competing security services created by Yasser 'Arafat, first in the PLO and then later in the PA. The result is that Fateh, the political movement that has dominated Palestinian politics for nearly four decades, has for the past few years often seemed to be paralyzed, never more so than during the 2006 PLC elections, in which this paralysis was a major cause of its defeat. The PA itself, thoroughly dominated by Fateh, was widely accused of corruption, featherbedding, and nepotism, accusations that have much substance in fact, although it has been cogently argued recently that some of these criticisms miss their mark.[11]

Beyond these damaging criticisms, the effective monopolization of power in the PA by Fateh never brought unity and discipline to the Palestinian political scene. This reprised a pattern that dated back to the old days of the PLO in Beirut. Fateh had effectively dominated Palestinian politics since the late 1960s, and had never really practiced power-sharing, except when obliged to do so for reasons of national unity in the face of an overwhelming external threat. Yet this near-monopoly over decision-making did not translate into a truly unified national movement, with the PLO remaining notorious for the indiscipline of its various constituent factions. Later, during the late 1980s and through the 1990s, Fateh's political hegemony inside the occupied territories was severely undermined by the inability of the PLO and later the PA, to co-opt or incorporate Hamas and its smaller Islamist rival, Islamic Jihad, which proved more resistant to its blandishments than had its secular rivals like the PFLP. The independence of these Islamic groups was to prove a constant source of ambivalence as to where the center of gravity in Palestinian politics lay, which confused and angered Palestinians.

Most importantly, Fateh lost much of its legitimacy and credibility due to its failure to negotiate more effectively with the Israelis, to provide protection, security, or proper governance for the 3.6 million Palestinians under its sway, and to deliver effective leadership for the struggle of the entire Palestinian people for the recovery of their national rights. In consequence, armed groups and major opposition factions like Hamas were increasingly able to operate with impunity and nearly complete freedom during the intifada, there was no unified focus of Palestinian political action, and the

Palestinian political situation remained highly fragmented and sometimes chaotic. The defeat of Fateh in the 2006 elections was a resounding repudiation of what the Palestinian public in the occupied West Bank and Gaza Strip perceived to be these and other failures on its part.

Moreover, from the grim perspective of at least the past six years of Palestinian history of intifada and crushing Israeli repression, of consolidated occupation and constantly expanding Israeli settlements, it is clear that this entire teleology, and the narrative about the PLO that is based on it, is very much open to question. Whatever may happen in the West Bank, Gaza Strip, and East Jerusalem, independent, sovereign Palestinian statehood there seems as far off as ever. Some sober analysts now feel that an irreversible situation has been created by nearly four decades of Israeli occupation and settlement, and that Palestinian statehood, and with it a two-state solution, are now in fact completely impossible.[12]

Whether or not this is the case, this new situation provokes a number of difficult questions. What was the old narrative about the PLO and Palestinian statehood based on? To what extent did the PLO actually correspond to the perceptions that many had of it? To the extent that these perceptions were incorrect, what role did the PLO actually play? Finally, what were the PLO's real achievements, and what do its failures tell us about the enduring problems of the Palestinians in establishing structures of state, problems that I have explored in earlier chapters? In the remainder of this chapter I will focus on these questions.[13] In answering them, I begin with an attempt to explain why so many people believed for so long that the PLO would achieve its aims, in spite of clear evidence that it was not seriously preparing to build the Palestinian state that had been its formal objective for several decades.

It may have been the case that the exaggerated expectations about the PLO on the part of outsiders were rooted in sympathy for the Palestinian people, in the general positive aura that once surrounded national liberation movements, and especially in approval of the PLO's revised goal of a Palestinian state alongside Israel. The new PLO program embodying this proposal was adopted tentatively beginning in the mid-1970s, was made more concrete in the intervening years, and was finally and formally consecrated in the 1988 Palestinian Declaration of Independence. The declaration, based on resolutions of the Palestine National Council, the PLO's "parliament in exile," from the late 1970s and the 1980s, called for a Palestinian state in the West Bank, Gaza Strip, and East Jerusalem within the pre–June 5, 1967, frontiers that had been delimited by the 1949 armistice lines, to coexist with the state of Israel.

This new objective, replacing the PLO's original 1964 goal of the elimination of Israel, which in 1969 was amended to the establishment of a secular democratic state in Palestine for Muslims, Christians, and Jews, replacing Israel, appeared fair to many, particularly Westerners. It seemed to put an end to questioning of the legitimacy of Israel and of the entire process of its creation at the expense of the Palestinian people. Once the PLO had finally adopted this aim, which appeared to satisfy most Palestinians, it was possible for outsiders to be pro-Palestinian, while not being seen as in any way anti-Israeli or anti-Zionist, or worse, being accused of being anti-Semitic. This seems to have assuaged the consciences of some in the West. Many Western observers wanted to be assured that the PLO was effectively working toward a two-state solution, and that such a solution was viable, because it was convenient for them, rather than because such a conclusion had necessarily been fully thought through or was the result of rigorous or informed analysis. Although this shift in objectives was entirely genuine for most Palestinians (notwithstanding uninformed arguments that it was not[14]), there should have been some question as to how competently the PLO was working toward this goal, or whether it was in fact a realizable one.

It could thus be argued that many felt that the PLO was a body effectively representing the Palestinian people and furthering their cause, and that it was moving them inexorably toward statehood, not because the PLO was in fact necessarily doing these things but because they wanted to believe this. This self-deception affected Palestinians and non-Palestinians alike. As we shall see, the strategy of the PLO was in many respects largely ineffective, if not incoherent, and was often counterproductive. This strategy was characterized by profound internal flaws, some of which only became fully manifest when the PLO emerged from its largely clandestine incarnation as a national liberation movement and established the PA in the mid-1990s. In spite of some notable successes over the past four decades, the PLO has failed to tilt the balance of power that overwhelmingly favors Israel. By some calculations, quite the contrary has happened: in many respects, the situation is worse for the Palestinians today than it was in 1964 when the PLO was founded. By contrast, others would argue cogently that given the daunting odds against them, the Palestinians could hardly have done much better than they did.[15]

In view of the experience of numerous other colonized countries and their national liberation movements from the 1940s until the 1970s, the idea that the Palestinians would achieve statehood and independence, and that the PLO constituted the core of that state-in-becoming, was not in fact so far-fetched. Statehood and independence seemed to be the natural culmination for such national movements, and indeed that was the outcome for the overwhelming majority of them in this period. It may have seemed all the more likely that this would take place once the PLO gradually accepted a two-state solution starting in the 1970s, and dropped its previous strategic aim of replacing Israel with a secular, democratic state in which Palestinians and Israelis would have equal rights of citizenship.[16] At the same time, and partly in consequence of this fundamental reorientation, the PLO received unanimous Arab and increasing international recognition as the sole legitimate representative of the Palestinian people, starting with the Rabat Arab summit and Yasser 'Arafat's address to the UN General Assembly, both in the fall of 1974.

Given the PLO's shift to advocacy of a Palestinian state alongside Israel, Palestinian liberation and statehood would not now have to be at the expense of maintaining the state of Israel in its present form, as would necessarily have been the case had it held fast to the aim of a secular, democratic state in place of Israel. But this gradual change in the PLO's objectives did not initially produce acceptance by either Israel or the United States of the idea of an independent Palestinian state in the West Bank and Gaza Strip. In spite of this major evolution in the PLO position, the Palestine cause in the late 1970s and 1980s appeared to be marking time or even going backward. This was partly because of the incoherence of the Palestinian position and the internal contradictions in Palestinian strategy (still ostensibly wedded to the continuation of armed struggle while moving toward a negotiated, political solution). However, it was also a consequence of the rejectionist stand of the United States and Israel. Neither power would negotiate with the PLO in the 1970s or 1980s, nor did they support the idea of the establishment of an independent Palestinian state alongside Israel.[17] This stand was linked to their joint demand that the Palestinians cease all violence against Israel and against Israeli troops and settlers in the occupied Palestinian territories. Palestinians, in other words, were required by the United States and Israel to cease their resistance to an illegal occupation as a precondition for being allowed to negotiate for an end to that occupation.

There was a particularly noticeable lack of progress in achieving Palestinian goals during the decade after the expulsion of the PLO from Beirut in 1982 following the Israeli invasion of Lebanon. Not even a sequence of events that initially appeared positive could stop the slow decline in the PLO's fortunes. These events included the boost to Palestinian hopes and a striking change in the image of the Palestinians provided by the first intifada of 1987–91, and the beginning of an American dialogue with the PLO after the 1988 Palestinian Declaration of Independence, and after the PLO thereafter renounced terrorism. The PLO-U.S. dialogue was soon broken off following the failure of the PLO to discipline one of its factions, the

Iraqi-backed PLF, for perpetrating an attack on a Tel Aviv beach in 1990 after the PLO had formally renounced terrorism. This dialogue had not, in any case, changed official American opposition to Palestinian self-determination and the creation of an independent Palestinian state. The PLO's fortunes thereafter declined even further when Yasser 'Arafat, supported by most of the PLO leadership, took the disastrous decision to align the PLO with Iraq during the 1990 crisis over Iraq's invasion of Kuwait. The support of Arab and Western governments for the PLO thereupon declined, and a Palestinian state appeared an even more distant mirage.

The Palestinian-Israeli negotiations at Madrid, Washington, D.C., and Oslo, starting in 1991, appeared to put the process toward statehood back on track, and seemed to justify the highest hopes of, and for, the PLO. In fact, however, a careful examination reveals that what came to be known as the Oslo process brought the Palestinians no closer to their goals of liberation, independence, and statehood (some of the details will be explored in Chapter 6). Few bothered to undertake such an examination at the time.[18] Instead, most allowed themselves to be swept away by the euphoria of the heady first few years after this apparent turning point in the fortunes of the Palestinians, as an interim Palestinian Authority was established, Israel appeared to hand over to it control of most Palestinian population centers, a select number of lucky Palestinian exiles returned to their homeland, and negotiations for a permanent settlement continued.

By virtue of the Oslo Accords and the subsequent Israeli-Palestinian agreements based on them, the PLO leadership entered into a multistage process seemingly designed by its Israeli and American architects to make progress toward fully independent and sovereign Palestinian statehood, while encouraging rapid movement toward ending Israel's occupation and its colonization of Palestinian lands. In fact, quite the opposite happened. Crucially, during the decade of negotiations running from the spring of 1991, when secretary of state James Baker began shuttle diplomacy to organize the Madrid conference, until January 2001, when the Taba talks between Palestinian and Israeli negotiators, the last gasp of the Oslo process, ended, the number of Israeli settlers in the occupied Palestinian territories doubled. Additionally, the occupation was reinforced in myriad significant ways, making it stronger and more all-encompassing than ever before. Over more than a decade and a half, what was deceptively described as a "peace process" certainly did not produced Israeli-Palestinian peace.

From the mid-1970s onward, PLO rhetoric had been increasingly focused on the establishment of a Palestinian state: many simply assumed that since the rhetoric was sincere (it was), there was necessarily commensurate activity going on to turn it into reality (there wasn't). That this was not the case was difficult for outsiders to verify during the lengthy Lebanon war, when much of what the PLO did in terms of providing quasi-state functions was a necessarily ad hoc response to wartime conditions. It was equally difficult after the evacuation from Beirut, when the PLO was confined to distant places of exile like Tunis and Yemen, and when it was working clandestinely to build institutional ties to the population of the West Bank and Gaza Strip via the so-called "Jordanian option," and then after the first intifada broke out at the end of 1987. Such highly charged situations necessarily led to opacity in the behavior of the PLO. But with the return of the PLO leadership to Palestine and the formation of the PA in consequence of the Oslo Accords in the mid-1990s, it began to become apparent, first to those in occupied Palestine living under its rule and eventually to others, that over the preceding decades the PLO had done precious little to prepare for independent statehood. As time went on, the "interim phase" laid down by the Oslo Accords, and which according to the PLO's own rhetoric was an antechamber to statehood, appeared to be more and more of a dead end.

The first decade of the existence of the PA has been testimony to the unpreparedness of the PLO leadership for the duties attendant on creating a real state. It is true that the PLO leaders who dominated the PA were severely inhibited by Israel's overwhelming power (and by restrictions written into the Oslo Accords to which they themselves had consented) from obtaining sovereignty, statehood, or even jurisdiction and real control in most of the occupied territories. Nevertheless, there was much that they could have done in spite of these crippling disabilities that they did not do. Notably, when they established the PA they failed to create a solid framework for the rule of law, a constitutional system, a balance of powers, and many of the other building blocks of a modern state to organize the governance of the 3.6 million Palestinians whose welfare they were now responsible for. It is not entirely surprising that this should have been the case: most of the leaders of the PLO, from 'Arafat on down, had spent their entire careers in the atmosphere of a clandestine, underground liberation movement, and proved to be poorly suited for the task of state building, for transparent governance, or for a stable structure of governance based on law.

It is nevertheless a testament to the intensity of the aspirations of the Palestinian people for democracy, and also to the efforts of the PLO/PA leadership, that over the span of a decade the PA has managed to hold two presidential and two legislative elections, as well as municipal elections, in spite of the suffocating conditions of occupation. Palestine, not a state, not sovereign, and under occupation, has thus been one of the first Arab countries with the exception of Lebanon to witness a democratic change of government in the wake of the January 2006 elections. Whether those external powers, led by the United States, that proclaim their support for democracy in the Middle East will allow that democracy to continue to exist looks questionable at the time of writing.

The many successful efforts in the direction of effective statebuilding, not the least of them the creation of a functioning democracy in nearly impossible circumstances, rather than being mainly the work of returned PLO exiles, tended to be produced by members of three sometimes overlapping groups. These were Palestinians from the occupied territories who had worked in education, health services, and other aspects of governance before the PA was established, or various institutions of civil society like universities, cooperatives, and unions, or in the remarkably resilient Palestinian private sector, based both inside and outside of Palestine. Things in Palestine that worked, or worked well, after the PA was established, such as some public services (telephones and cell phones, for example), and several sectors of the economy, were largely the work of the private sector, or of those who had worked to provide services to the Palestinian people for many years under the shadow of the occupation.

A few Palestinians sensed the unpreparedness of the PLO for its state-building responsibilities even before the PA was established. These were the individuals from the occupied territories and the diaspora, few of them with any prior diplomatic or negotiating experience, who were brought together (in an arrangement brokered by Secretary Baker in the teeth of the opposition of the Shamir government) as members of, or advisors to, the Palestinian delegation to the 1991 Madrid peace conference and the subsequent ten sessions of bilateral negotiations with Israel that continued in Washington, D.C., until June 1993. I was invited to participate as an advisor.[19] What became immediately apparent to members of the group was that what little advanced planning the PLO had done for the eventuality of negotiations with Israel and statehood thereafter was virtually worthless, and that it covered hardly any eventualities.[20] Nearly twenty years after the PLO had begun moving toward a two-state solution, and nearly four years after the 1988 Palestinian declaration of statehood and independence, it transpired that almost nothing had been done to prepare for the moment when independence actually had to be negotiated, and statehood prepared. The contrast with the diplomatic efforts of the Jewish Agency, the para-state that paved the way for the creation of Israel, could not have been more striking—nor could the similarity to the poorly coordinated diplomatic efforts of the Palestinians before 1948.

The Palestinian delegation in Madrid and Washington therefore found itself obliged to begin its preparations from scratch, and in extremely difficult circumstances, including Israeli preconditions supported by the United States that dictated that it be subsumed within a Jordanian-Palestinian joint delegation, as well as who could and could not be a member of the official delegation that participated in negotiations with Israel. The circumstances also included the inexperience and radically different backgrounds of most of its members, many of whom had never worked together before. Through twenty months of hard-won experience, this delegation eventually acquired a reasonable degree of negotiating expertise as a result of its on-the-job training, and developed a high level of cohesion between leading figures from the West Bank and Gaza, academics from the diaspora, and senior PLO cadres. All of this experience and this expertise were completely, and deliberately, ignored by the PLO leadership and the entirely separate, and underqualified, team that it assigned to negotiate the secret Oslo Accords midway through the negotiations in Washington.[21] Not surprisingly, the Israeli delegation at Oslo, which we now know was assiduously aided and abetted by the Norwegian hosts (for reasons that can only be speculated at),[22] out-negotiated the PLO team at every turn, as is amply evidenced by the end product, the Oslo Accords. While this outcome was doubtless largely determined by the imbalance of power between the two sides, and by the Norwegian hosts systematically tipping the scales in favor of the already heavily advantaged Israelis, it also reflected the inexperience and lack of preparation of those who negotiated it on the Palestinian side, as well as the sometimes skewed priorities of the PLO leadership.

The Oslo Accords were a foretaste of what was to come in every Palestinian-Israeli negotiation over the following few years. During the 1990s, one unsatisfactory and unbalanced partial accord governing relatively minor matters succeeded another. All the while, the truly weighty matters, the so-called final status issues (Palestinian sovereignty and statehood, the status of Jerusalem, the refugee issue, Israeli settlements, and water) were kept off the table by the negotiating framework imposed by the United States at the insistence of Israel at the beginning of the process. The supposed logic of this procedure, that partial, interim accords would "build confidence" between the two sides, was proven false by subsequent events. The result of the entire Oslo process was a steep decline in mutual confidence, particularly when one considers the expansive possibilities that beckoned in the euphoria affecting both sides that was attendant on the Madrid Peace Conference and the signing of the Oslo Accords. In fact, the real logic of the partial interim approach was that it was intended by its Israeli and American architects to relieve Israel of having to make any hard decisions on ending the occupation and settlement of the West Bank, Gaza Strip, and East Jerusalem. Instead, Israeli occupation and settlement were massively reinforced during the period of negotiations.

It was only in July 2000 that the Palestinian leaders were finally allowed even to begin negotiating on final status issues at the hastily arranged Camp David summit, during the last few months of U.S. president Bill Clinton's eight years in office. There they found not real negotiations, but a meager take-it-or-leave-it proposal from Israeli prime minister Ehud Barak, fully backed by Clinton. Though Yasser 'Arafat and his colleagues showed themselves remarkably inept in their public handling of this unacceptable proposal, they were by no means solely responsible for the failure at Camp David, for which there is more than enough blame to go around.[23] What is important to note here is the high degree of unpreparedness of the Palestinian side for what they found at Camp David. This was a problem that has plagued the Palestinians in their international negotiations since the very beginning in the 1920s. It became particularly acute at the moment when the PLO leadership in 1992–93 in effect took negotiations with Israel out of the hands of the relatively competent delegation of generally respected figures from the occupied territories (such as Dr. Haidar 'Abd al-Shafi, Faysal Husayni, and Dr. Hanan 'Ashrawi), and others from the Palestinian diaspora and the PLO, that they had chosen and sent to Washington, and placed it instead in the hands of the team of loyal PLO officials that they appointed to negotiate the Oslo Accords, while calling all the shots from Tunis.[24]

There had been efforts by PLO leaders in Tunis, especially 'Arafat, to micromanage the work of the Madrid-Washington delegation in 1991–93 as well, sometimes to the detriment of the Palestinian cause, but this delegation was much better prepared to generate its own position papers and negotiating documents, and to resist such pressures from Tunis with well-founded arguments. One can see how this might have caused the PLO leaders, grown autocratic over many years of undisputed power, to be suspicious of the delegation they had sent to Madrid and Washington. In one instance, much of the delegation, myself included, was present when Faysal Husayni had a long, angry phone dispute with Yasser 'Arafat over the negotiating position to be taken in Washington.

A final problem with the PLO negotiating position may simply have been the steady decline in the competence of its leadership, and indeed of the effectiveness of the organization itself, in the years after it was forced to leave Beirut in 1982. Many of the most dynamic individuals who had founded Fateh, and who had dominated the PLO for the first decade and more after the mid-1960s, as well as other competent PLO leaders, had disappeared by the mid-1990s. Most of them were eliminated as a result of assassination by Israeli or Arab intelligence services or by others acting for them, like the Abu Nidal organization, while a few of them died of natural causes or were otherwise disabled. PLO leaders who were assassinated between 1968 and 1991 included Abu 'Ali Iyyad, Ghassan Kanafani, Sa'id Hamami, Abu Yusuf al-Najjar, Kamal Nasser, Kamal 'Adwan, Majid Abu Sharar, Abu Hassan Salameh, Brig. Gen. Sa'd Sayil (Abu al-Walid), 'Isam Sirtawi, Abu Jihad, Abu al-Hol, and Abu Iyyad.[25] However well or badly it had performed in Beirut or before, the PLO itself, fragmented and spinning its wheels in a variety of widely scattered locations in its post-1982 exile—most of them far from any concentration of Palestinian population—was not what it had once been. And, as we have seen, in his last years, Yasser 'Arafat was not the leader he had once been.

Many Palestinians were privately highly critical of the PLO in the post-Beirut phase, but generally preferred not to talk about its failings in front of outsiders, Arab or foreign, in effect muzzling themselves and helping to retard any process of self-criticism or renewal. Moreover, the lively political debates that characterized Palestinian politics when Beirut was its center, fed by a plethora of newspapers and magazines, research centers, a lively publishing industry, and a vigorous public sphere, and including Lebanese and other Arabs as well as Palestinians, gradually died out after 1982. Nothing arose to take their place in Tunis, where the bulk of the PLO leadership found itself, completely isolated from the Palestinian people. Meanwhile, inside the West Bank and Gaza Strip, the omnipresent Israeli occupation severely inhibited freedom of expression, as did suffocating governmental repression in the various Arab countries where most of the rest of the Palestinian population was located. Nevertheless, the PLO continued to be represented in over one hundred countries, where its offices generally had the status of embassies, and it could still credibly claim to represent the Palestinian people. To some, looking from afar, all seemed to be as it had been before 1982. Few outsiders, and not all Palestinians, noticed just how hollow this edifice had become.

The PLO's Achievements

When the PLO was founded in 1964, the existence of the Palestinian people as a coherent entity, indeed the very idea of "Palestine," appeared to be in a grave, and perhaps in a terminal, state. It was so grave that even five years later, a serious politician like Golda Meir could say with a straight face to a reputable publication that the Palestinian people did not exist, and that paper could publish her words without the slightest qualm.[26] The Palestinian people truly appeared in the mid-1960s to be facing an existential crisis of daunting proportions, and to be in serious danger of disappearing from the political sphere, just as their country had disappeared from the map, and indeed from public discourse. At this stage, nearly the only exception to this slow disappearing act could be found at the United Nations, where "the Question of Palestine" stubbornly kept appearing on the annual agenda of the General Assembly.

Today, over forty years later, although their existential crisis is in some respects as acute as ever, it is apparent to most observers not only that the Palestinians are a people with clear national rights, but that for all their material weaknesses and their lack of a state, they are nevertheless a significant factor in the Middle East. This is apparent if only from the inordinate amount of attention devoted to this relatively small people by the United Nations and the governments of the United States, Israel, and other countries over many years. One can debate precisely who deserves the credit for putting the Palestinians back on the political map, and bringing them back from the brink of oblivion, or if it could or should have been done differently. Certainly, acts of terrorism directed against civilians played a part in bringing the Palestinians to the attention of the world in the 1960s and afterward, acts that had and have an enormous cost, both moral and political. However, some would say that the revival in the salience of the Palestinians was mainly the result of the cohesiveness, persistence, and perseverance of Palestinian society and the Palestinian people, their steadfastness and their stubborn refusal to cease to exist in the face of the extraordinary pressures on them to disappear. Others would ascribe it entirely to the actions of the PLO and its leadership. Although this is an exaggeration, there can be little question that the PLO deserves at least some of the credit, and that this was a major, if not the most important, attainment of its leadership.

The PLO certainly deserves credit in whole or in part for at least three major achievements related to this revival of the Palestinian national movement over the past four decades. The first was to create a vehicle for the achievement of their national aims that was universally accepted among the entirety of the Palestinian people—at least by most of them for several decades—and that was broadly understood to constitute this people's sole central political address. The creation of an accepted forum grouping all major Palestinian political forces was something that no earlier Palestinian political leadership had been able to achieve during the mandatory period until 1948. Although the Palestinian Arab congresses, the Arab Executive, and later the Arab Higher Committee, could with at least some credibility claim to represent the Palestinians, as we have seen in earlier chapters, that claim was constantly contested, both overtly and implicitly, by various important Palestinian leaders and political forces (not to speak of the League of Nations, the British, and the Zionists, who never formally recognized any of them).

In effect, there was never an unchallenged, universally accepted structure within which Palestinian politics functioned before 1948. Thus Hajj Amin al-Husayni and the Supreme Muslim Council were for years a counterweight to the Arab Executive headed by his relative and rival Muza Kazim al-Husayni, while later Raghib Bey al-Nashashibi headed a coalition that bitterly contested the tactics and the primacy of the mufti and the groupings he led. This was simply not the case regarding the PLO: at least until the emergence of Hamas as a serious challenger to its legitimacy starting in the late 1990s, as a result of the political fallout of the disastrous 1991–2000 Oslo period and the subsequent second intifada, the PLO was for decades the largely uncontested face of the Palestinian national movement, and provided the central locus for Palestinian politics. Since the mid-1990s this has become increasingly true of the PLO's creation, the PA. The participation, and then the victory, of Hamas in the PLC elections in January 2006 underlines the extent to which the structures originally created by Fateh and its allies in the PLO remain the uncontested forum for Palestinian politics. This is now true even for Hamas, which never before accepted the legitimacy of the PLO or the PA, and now dominates the legislative arm and part of the executive branch of the latter.

A second related achievement was to parlay this acceptance and recognition by the Palestinian people of the PLO as their representative into recognition by the Arab states, and later recognition by the international community. In some ways this was an even more impressive achievement than the first, at least when it is compared with prior periods in Palestinian history. Starting in the early 1970s, the PLO was recognized by the Arab League, the United Nations, and eventually, after decades of foot-dragging, even by Israel and the United States, as the sole, legitimate representative of the Palestinian people. Indeed, for many years, more states have recognized the PLO than have recognized Israel, and the PLO has come to play a major role at the United Nations and in other international forums.

A comparison with the pre-1948 period is illustrative here. On the one hand, as we have seen, the Zionist movement, represented by the Jewish Agency, had an acknowledged international status enshrined from the outset in the League of Nations Mandate for Palestine. In consequence, although it did not have formal sovereignty, the Jewish Agency could and did intervene effectively as a recognized international actor at the League of Nations, or London, Paris, and other world capitals.[27] By contrast, no body representative of the Palestinians, whether the Arab Executive that emerged in the early 1920s from the Palestinian Congresses, nor the Arab Higher Committee formed by the leaders of all Palestinian parties in 1936, was ever formally recognized by the British, the League of Nations, or the international community, or for that matter by the Arab countries. The interwar period was of course a different era: no colonized people succeeded in liberating itself from colonial bondage before World War II; afterward, all eventually succeeded in doing so except for a very few, the Palestinians included.

Although the PLO was operating in an era more favorable to national liberation movements than had earlier incarnations of the Palestinian national movement, it was not easy to achieve Arab recognition of the representative nature and independence of the PLO in the teeth of furious opposition at different stages from major Arab states, including Egypt, Jordan, Syria, Iraq, Libya, and Saudi Arabia. All of these Arab powers at one time or another strongly opposed the PLO, or worked assiduously to limit its independence and freedom of action, if not to subordinate it entirely to their foreign policy objectives. Indeed, we have seen that the PLO was originally created in 1964 as part of an effort by the Arab League, led by Egypt, its dominant member-state, to contain and control the burgeoning manifestations of independent Palestinian nationalism. Perhaps the most consistent and single-minded efforts of Yasser 'Arafat and his colleagues in the Fateh leadership from the 1950s through the 1990s were dedicated to ensuring what they called "the independence of the Palestinian decision," meaning freedom from the interference of the Arab states. They eventually succeeded to a very large degree in achieving this, albeit at a cost in terms of the alienation of key Arab regimes, and of influential elements of the Arab public, who came to see the PLO as playing inter-Arab politics, rather than representing a noble cause with which they were largely in sympathy.

International recognition for the PLO as representative of the Palestinian people—indeed recognition that there was such a thing as a Palestinian people with national rights—was in some ways even harder to achieve, given fierce American opposition, and the not inconsiderable diplomatic and propaganda capabilities of an equally resistant Israel. Israel's international moral status as a state founded by and as a refuge for victims of the Nazis made this task all the harder. Insofar as what was in essence a national/colonial conflict in the Middle East could be framed solely in terms of the need for atonement for centuries of European anti-Semitism culminating in the Nazi Holocaust against the Jews, the Palestinians lost all agency, and indeed disappeared from the picture. Worse, a people that had been dispossessed and dispersed as a necessary part of the process of establishment of a Jewish national home were made to appear as no more than the latest in a long line of tormentors of the Jewish people, the most recent victimizers of the greatest victims of the greatest crime of the twentieth century. It was in these general terms that the conflict had been successfully framed by the Zionist movement even before the Nazi Holocaust, both before British and European public opinion, and in international forums like the League of Nations and later the United Nations. The Palestinians' original post-1948 objective of obtaining redress for their dispossession via eliminating Israel and replacing it with a Palestinian state could be and was fitted perfectly into this highly unfavorable framing of the conflict.

Though the shift in PLO objectives to a negotiated two-state solution starting in the mid-1970s and the gradual abandonment of armed struggle (both of which constituted pragmatic adjustments to circumstances, and marked a certain maturity of Palestinian political discourse) was an effective response to this narrative and greatly facilitated the winning of international recognition, it was nonetheless necessary to make extensive efforts to win over reluctant international actors. This was especially true in the West, where a richly justified sense of guilt about centuries of persecution of the Jews gave this narrative great lasting power. The PLO, and in particular Yasser 'Arafat himself, was nevertheless tireless in making efforts to garner recognition from countries the world over, eventually with remarkable success. This too was an undoubted achievement of the PLO, although there is good reason to be doubtful whether many PLO leaders had much understanding of the weight of that latent narrative in Western countries, and its continuing potential danger to the Palestinian cause.

The third major success of the PLO was to recognize the ultimate futility of exile politics, and to make the difficult decision to shift its center of gravity from the countries bordering Israel to the occupied territories. This shift, linked to advocacy of a negotiated two-state solution to the conflict with Israel, began in the late 1970s. It was finally put into practical execution with the implementation of the Oslo Accords, whereby most of the PLO's leadership and cadres were allowed by Israel to return to the West Bank and Gaza

Strip starting in the mid-1990s. For an organization founded in the Palestinian diaspora by exiles, this decision involved a major leap of faith. It ultimately necessitated a repudiation of the PLO's entire stated strategy of armed struggle from bases in countries surrounding Israel. It necessitated as well a risky shift from depending primarily on the support of the Palestinian communities in exile to those living inside Palestine under Israeli occupation. In time, all of these shifts led to the alienation of part of the PLO's own base, and contributed to the success of radical Islamist groups like Hamas.

The interim strategy adopted until the PLO could actually move to Palestine itself, was the so-called "Jordanian option" of the mid-1970s, whereby the center of gravity of the organization's efforts became the occupied territories, to be accessed through Jordan. This meant reconciling with the Hashemite regime in Jordan, with which the Palestinian national movement had been in conflict for many years (since before 1948). It also meant abandoning the illusion that military pressure on Israel from bases in Lebanon could effect any positive change in the unfavorable strategic balance, an illusion that could be given up more readily now that a two-state solution was increasingly seen by Palestinians as their best option. These conclusions were all fiercely resisted by dissidents within the organization, leading eventually to the creation of the "Rejection Front" by the PFLP and other radical PLO groups, and later to a scission in Fateh after the 1982 Israeli expulsion of the PLO from Lebanon. But with the eruption of the first intifada of 1987–91, and the fixing of international attention on Israel's occupation of the West Bank, Gaza Strip, and Arab East Jerusalem, all of these important shifts in PLO positions proved to be wise ones. They made it possible for the organization to take advantage of the leverage provided by the intifada against two decades of Israeli occupation, and to propel the Palestine question back onto the international agenda after years of a gradual decline in its salience.

Only a few years later, after Madrid and Oslo, most leaders and cadres of the PLO found themselves in the West Bank and Gaza

Strip, thanks largely to the impact on Israeli society and political thinking of the first intifada, which made the idea of continuation of the occupation unappealing to most Israelis, but also in part because of the choices the PLO had made in the late 1970s and 1980s in terms of focusing on the occupied territories and advocating a two-state solution to the conflict. These individuals only gradually realized that the PA that they now dominated was a sort of poisoned chalice, and that they had entered into a devil's bargain with the Israeli government, which had made the weighty decision to allow those who had long been sworn enemies of Israel to return to their homeland only in exchange for what it expected would be a hefty quid pro quo, in terms of serving Israel's interests.[28]

Nevertheless, there can be no question that moving the center of gravity of Palestinian politics, and the focus of the Palestine question, to the occupied territories from diasporic exile was a correct move for the Palestinian national movement, even if its execution was flawed in various ways. And for several tens of thousands of Palestinians, this move led to their own return to the homeland after decades in exile. Admittedly, only a few thousand leaders and cadres and their immediate families were allowed to return to the West Bank and Gaza Strip by Israel, after careful security vetting. Left outside of Palestine were millions of ordinary Palestinians still living in exile in Lebanon, Syria, Jordan, and elsewhere. Many of them understandably felt left behind, and even abandoned. This feeling was caused in part by the move to the occupied territories of most Fateh and PLO leaders, and leaders from the other factions, and their involvement since then in the affairs of the PA, which is supposed to be an interim authority without the attributes of sovereignty, concerned only with the affairs of the 3.6 million Palestinians living under occupation. Beyond this, some of the much larger number of Palestinians in the diaspora came to believe that in practice the possibility of their return to their homeland had become even more distant as a result of the Oslo deal. Little that has occurred since Oslo has been reassuring on this score, as the most that Israel has suggested that it might accept in the sole round of Israeli-Palestinian final status negotiations that ever took place on this matter, in 2000–2001 (an offer thereafter withdrawn by the Sharon government), was some return of unspecified numbers of Palestinians to a Palestinian state after its establishment.

Leaving aside this question of crucial importance for the majority of Palestinians who live outside their ancestral homeland, returning the locus of the Palestine question, the arena of Palestinian politics, and the center of gravity of the Palestinian national movement to Palestine, where a democratic system has been set up that has endured for over a decade, may be seen as the major achievement of the PLO leadership. It had particular salience since many of their other achievements now pale in light of what many regard as their numerous failures.

The PLO's Failures

Failure, like beauty, may be in the eye of the beholder. Each analyst of Palestinian politics probably would cite a different set of shortcomings in listing the PLO's failures, and any such assessment must perforce be in some measure subjective.

In assessing Palestinian failures, whether those of the PLO, those of earlier incarnations of Palestinian nationalism in the 1930s or 1940s, or those of later ones, such as the PA and Hamas, it is necessary to do so in terms of what was feasible for each at the time. As has emerged from the analysis in earlier chapters, one is obliged to weigh what the Palestinians could or could not have expected realistically to achieve in the late 1930s in the wake of the rise to power of the Nazis, and in the face of a determined Zionist movement and the power of an imperial Britain girding itself with grim determination for a major European conflict. Similarly, it is necessary to understand the constellation of power, both Arab and international, within which the PLO operated, and similarly to assess what it could and could not have done in those circumstances.

While this should not lead to the generation of counterfactual scenarios, a fruitless endeavor at best, it does mean that one must not hold actors in history to standards that would have been unrealizable at the time. For the Palestinian national movement during the Mandate period, this means that it is thoroughly unfair to expect them to have triumphed absolutely, as the Zionist movement ultimately did. We have seen some of the reasons for the failures of the former and the successes of the latter. That is not to say that the Palestinians could not in any circumstances have contributed to producing better outcomes for themselves. In order to have done so, for example, perhaps the Palestinians could have opposed the British more resolutely and systematically much earlier than they ultimately did in 1936–39, or alternatively, they might have tried to initiate some kind of binational historic compromise with the Zionist movement when it was at its lowest ebb in the late 1920s and early 1930s. Neither of these things happened, of course, and there are good historical reasons, many of them adduced in earlier chapters, for that, and for why things came out as they did. Some would argue that the historian's job is to explain how things came out, and leave it for others to draw conclusions. But even mulling over these might-have-beens of history reveals some of the rigid constraints within which the Palestinians operated during the Mandate, and why the results were as they were.

The Palestinians from the 1950s onward operated under a different set of constraints than those that had characterized the Mandate period. These most notably included the physical dispersal of the Palestinian people, and their subjection to a variety of political jurisdictions in several newly independent states, each one highly jealous of its sovereignty and prerogatives. These constraints became more severe as the originally relatively weak states that controlled the territory of the former mandatory Palestine, or hosted Palestinian refugees—Israel and the surrounding Arab states— grew stronger. Re-creating the Palestinian national movement, or creating an entirely new incarnation of this movement, was a difficult task in such circumstances. These circumstances remained in place over time, even as the PLO grew stronger and obtained a larger measure of recognition and legitimacy. They defined the universe within which it operated, until the mid-1990s move of the center of gravity of the PLO, together with most of its leaders and cadres, from outside of Palestine to the occupied territories, where they set up the PA. Constraints rooted in these circumstances still operate with regard to the political (and often the economic and social) life of the majority of Palestinians who continue to live in the diaspora.

Thus to fail to take into account the shark-filled waters, especially those in the Arab world, within which the Palestinian national movement in exile had to operate after 1948 is to ignore the fundamental conditions that shaped Palestinian existence in this period. And although navigating masterfully in these waters was one of the greatest accomplishments of the PLO leadership, and notably of Yasser 'Arafat, the undisputed captain of the ship until his death, the characteristics that made possible this feat were often less than optimal ones for other areas of endeavor. To put it more bluntly, the deviousness and subterfuge that were indispensable for a weak PLO in dealing with the predatory mores of the states that dominated Arab politics were much less well adapted to, or completely unsuitable for, other arenas. These characteristics ultimately severely restricted what could be achieved by the generation of PLO leaders who had grown up under these circumstances, most notably 'Arafat himself.

The often criticized approach of the PLO to its inter-Arab dealings, balancing one powerful state off against another and resisting their attempts to penetrate the Palestinian political arena, was in large measure necessitated by the PLO's weakness, the absence of reliable external sources of support, and its lack of a nearby secure base of operations. It came to be much caricatured in the Arab (and later the Western) press, with 'Arafat in particular depicted as shifty and untrustworthy. Given the backstabbing and double-dealing characteristic of much of inter-Arab politics, it was not surprising that one of the weakest of Arab actors should adopt an approach that might be depicted in such an unflattering way. The PLO in fact had little choice in this regard. Whatever its origins and the justifications for it, however, this approach was ill suited to dealing with non-Arab powers, especially Western ones. Most importantly from the perspective from which this book has been written, that of the Palestinians' failure to develop structures of state through most of their modern history, this same approach was also often dysfunctional. For example, it required sharply honed skills to balance the main pro-Syrian and pro-Iraqi factions of the PLO, Sa'iqa and the Arab Liberation Front (which were no more than Trojan horses for these two states, or worse, vehicles for their murderous intelligence apparatuses), and their overbearing and powerful patrons in Damascus and Baghdad. These skills included bluster, bluff, compromise, and sometimes deceit. These same skills proved to be a liability in dealing with non-Arab powers, and in building Palestinian state institutions. This was a major contributing factor to what can be described as the first of the main failures of the PLO: the failure to develop the organs of the PLO into the framework for a full-fledged Palestinian state. The PLO under 'Arafat's leadership did grow into a quasi- or para-state structure, with departments that were the functional equivalent of ministries carrying out a variety of financial, educational, medical, and social tasks. The PLO was hampered by having to do these things in difficult conditions of exile, where it often clashed with the regimes of Arab host countries, in Jordan, Lebanon, Syria, Egypt, and elsewhere. The Palestinians suffered, moreover, from the manifold inadequacies of the para-state institutions the PLO created. They were neither very well run nor efficient, nor were they particularly democratic. Operating mainly in conditions of war and civil war in Lebanon, the structures of the PLO's para-state had nevertheless functioned in an adequate fashion for fifteen years, until the expulsion of the organization and thousands of its fighters and cadres after the Israeli invasion of 1982. During this period, it succeeded in providing some basic services to the country's three to four hundred thousand Palestinians as well as to many Lebanese.[29] Nevertheless, cronyism, the arbitrary exercise of power, corruption, and the absence of discipline over its various factions always seriously marred the PLO's performance in Lebanon. These many defects, together with the heavy-handed interference of the PLO and its many constituent groups in Lebanese politics and in the everyday lives of Lebanese citizens, led to the alienation of the great majority of Lebanese from the PLO. This alienation was to cost the Palestinians dearly in 1982 and afterward.[30]

Between the evacuation of the PLO from Beirut late in the summer of 1982 and the mid-1990s, the organization's institutions in exile became ossified and lost most of whatever vitality they once had. Many PLO cadres who had worked within these structures in exile for more than a decade were allowed by Israel to return to the occupied territories after the 1993 Oslo Accords. There they provided the bulk of the Palestinian Authority's senior governmental officials and security officers (most lower-ranking employees and security personnel came from within the occupied territories). But the cadres who had previously run the PLO's institutions in Lebanon had spent the ensuing dozen or so years after leaving Beirut in enforced idleness in various Arab countries. Most of whatever good qualities they may have had in the 1970s and early 1980s had been eroded by the time they returned to Palestine after long years of enforced exile. When they did so in the mid-1990s, they were older, grayer, and thicker as they took up the reins of power in the PA, to finally enjoy its perquisites. Beyond this, given the backgrounds of most of them in clandestine, underground, and military activity, few had the requisite training, experience, or disposition for the routine tasks of governance and administration that awaited them in Palestine. It was little wonder that the PA exhibited in magnified form the flaws of the PLO's para-state in Lebanon.

One criticism that has been made of the PLO and the PA is that they shifted from being a national liberation movement to something else in the 1990s after the establishment of the PA, but well before the process of liberation—in terms of ending Israeli occupation and settlement and justly resolving the issue of the refugees—had been completed. Whatever the validity of this criticism, it is worth noting that long before Oslo, indeed as early as the 1970s in Lebanon, the PLO had become bureaucratized, and in this process became more and more of a quasi-state and less and less of a national liberation movement. From the moment that the main PLO military forces were moved up to Beirut and Sidon from South Lebanon in the 1975–76 phase of the Lebanese war, the pretense that their purpose was to liberate Palestine through armed struggle began to disappear. As these forces became more of a self-defense force for the Palestinian population in Lebanon (as well as a strike force against the PLO's enemies—Lebanese and Syrian—during the war there), as the PLO's strategy changed in the direction of diplomacy, and as its aim became a two-state solution, this pretense evaporated completely.

But none of this movement away from a "liberation" strategy and in the direction of a quasi state ever led to the next stage: the regularization and organization on a legal basis of the organs of the PLO, their democratization, and their preparation for a move into the occupied territories. Little that the PLO did in its Lebanese phase, and even less of what it did during the decade in the wilderness that followed, seemed to involve serious preparation for statehood. Given the harsh realities of the Palestinian position in a Lebanon wracked by internal conflict, external intervention, and war for the last decade of the PLO's presence there, from 1973 until 1982, perhaps this was in part understandable.[31] But it was not only the need to deal with constant emergencies that inhibited the PLO leadership from undertaking such a transformation. In Lebanon, and even more so after 1982, it was more the fact that having grown up as students and later as militants in an underground clandestine environment, having been raised in an atmosphere of distaste for the weak democracies in the Arab world, and of admiration for the strong regimes established by the likes of Jamal 'Abd al-Nasir in

Egypt and the autocratic Pan-Arabist Baʻth Party in Syria and Iraq, having never lived in a system where the rule of law prevailed, these leaders were ill-prepared to lead such a transformation. Not surprisingly, they failed to do so.

A linked failure was the inability of the PLO leadership to understand the limits of violence. This produced the strategic incoherence that resulted from, on the one hand, accepting a two-state solution and renouncing violence in 1988, but not, on the other, drawing the logical conclusion that what was necessary was the reeducation of the Palestinians away from armed struggle and toward a whole new approach of unarmed mass popular struggle. This would have meant following the path that was successfully and spontaneously blazed by the 1987 intifada inside the occupied territories, which depended on mass demonstrations that, while they were sometimes violent, generally refrained from the use of firearms and explosives, even in the face of brutal Israeli repression. Given their age, their background, and their experiences, the PLO leadership was manifestly incapable of undertaking such a transformation. This incapacity was most clearly revealed during the second intifada starting at the end of September 2000, when the militarization of what started as a popular struggle—whether in consequence of the encouragement of ʻArafat and his colleagues, or because of their inability to resist this trend, or both[32]—ultimately led to disaster for the Palestinians.

The incoherence that resulted from trying to be all things to all people was repeatedly brought home over the decades starting in the mid-1970s, when the shift to a diplomatic, negotiated solution began, and continuing until the second intifada wound down after the death of ʻArafat at the end of 2004. If the Palestinians had adopted diplomacy as their main means of struggle by the late 1970s, why were they still apparently attached to the rhetoric of armed struggle over a decade later? Even after the PLO abjured violence in 1988, against the dubious quid pro quo of the United States agreeing to direct contacts with the PLO, there still appeared to be some reticence on its part on this score, raising questions about Palestinian good faith. Such reticence may have derived from the fact that this commitment came in the humiliating form of a formal renunciation of "terrorism" by 'Arafat, which made no distinction between actual terrorist acts of random violence against innocent civilians and resistance against continued military occupation, and cast into retrospective doubt much of what the PLO had done in the intervening fourteen years.[33]

Although the PA showed its commitment to abjuring violence as its security services brutally repressed Hamas and Islamic Jihad in the mid-1990s when they carried out suicide and other attacks on Israelis,[34] the same ambiguity thereafter appeared even more strikingly during the second intifada, starting in 2001. For then the Palestinians engaged in suicide bombings against Israeli civilians were affiliated not only with Hamas or other factions that had never accepted the two-state solution and the concomitant renunciation of violence. They included as well members of the Fateh armed organization, under the transparent cover of the "al-Aqsa Martyrs Brigade." There were even claims that at the outset the "militarization" of the second intifada was initially the work not of Hamas but of Fateh, with the assent, explicit or implicit, of 'Arafat.[35] This was asserted regularly by the Israelis as well, although such assertions normally had to be regarded with some skepticism. It was, however, incontrovertibly the case that the suicide bombings against civilians that later became the hallmark of the second intifada were above all the work of Hamas.

Whatever the case, there was at the very least a lack of clarity in the Fateh/PLO/PA camp about the limits of violence, and in consequence a strategic incoherence in the Palestinian position: if the Palestinians wanted to make peace with Israel within its 1967 frontiers, why were militant Palestinian groups killing Israeli civilians within these borders? If the problem was the occupation (and not the existence of Israel itself) why was the occupation itself not the sole target of Palestinian attacks? One did not have to be aiming at discrediting the Palestinians to ask such questions, and indeed they were increasingly asked by Palestinians as the intifada wore on and produced significantly more devastating results for Palestinian society than for Israel. This popular dissatisfaction played a considerable role in persuading all the Palestinian militant groups to radically scale down their attacks inside Israel proper from late 2004 onward, and in pushing Hamas, ever sensitive to the popular mood, to accept joining in the PA electoral process that it had always spurned. The question remained: why was it that it took popular disapproval in the wake of ferocious repression to convince those leading the armed struggle to desist? Where were Palestinian leaders when they were most needed? These are questions that have recurred in modern Palestinian history, in the late 1930s, the 1970s and 1980s, and now at the beginning of the twenty-first century. They bespeak serious structural problems in the Palestinian national movement that clearly are still unresolved.

A final failure of the PLO began with the departure from Beirut, was accentuated during the Tunis period from 1982 to 1991, and was exacerbated during the Oslo negotiations and consecrated with the establishment of the PA. This was the effective abandonment of the majority of Palestinians who live outside of Palestine. It was caused by the inability of the Palestinian leadership to act on the principle that the Palestinians are a single people all of whom suffered from their collective dispossession, and that consequently the amelioration of the lot of those under occupation was only part of the resolution of the Palestine problem.

The PLO leadership fell into this trap through accepting the negotiating formula imposed at Madrid in 1991 by James Baker at the behest of the Israelis. This provided for the issue of the refugees (and all matters of substance) to be dealt with subsequently to the negotiation of interim arrangements for the occupied West Bank and Gaza Strip, in final status negotiations that, in the event, were delayed for nearly a decade, until the abortive Camp David conference in 2000, and now have been delayed sine die. This delay created the unmistakable impression that the PLO leadership, which fulfilled its own "right of return" to Palestine under the Oslo Accords, had feathered its nest, and had come to care only for the interests of those under occupation, while forgetting those languishing in the refugee camps of Lebanon and others in the diaspora. For a PLO leadership that had risen to prominence in exile, borne on the shoulders of refugees, and buoyed especially by the sacrifices of those in Lebanon, this appeared cruel indeed. It contributed further to the delegitimation of this leadership, and helped to burnish the credentials of Hamas in particular, which, since it had never had any formal responsibility for the fate of the Palestinians, could uphold refugee rights in an absolute and uncompromising fashion. All of these and other failures came together in the elections for the PLC in January 2006, when Fateh paid for the perceived sins of the PLO it had dominated for nearly forty years.

6

Stateless in Palestine

Competing Forms of State

For most of the ninety years since the end of Ottoman rule in 1917, the inhabitants of Palestine have been sharply divided about the most appropriate state structure, or structures, for governing the country. Today, despite the near-universal international legitimacy accorded to the Israeli nation-state, and apparent international unanimity as to the desirability of creating a Palestinian state alongside Israel, the question of what state structure or structures are appropriate for this small country is still undecided. Indeed, this is a deeply fraught issue, a source of existential anxieties among both the Palestinian and Israeli peoples, although those anxieties have entirely different roots, whatever their superficial similarities.

As I have discussed here and elsewhere, like most peoples in the Arab world, the Palestinians gradually developed a sense of modern national identity rooted in a defined nation-state in the first few decades of the twentieth century.[1] This sense of common identity of the Arab inhabitants of Palestine was then cemented by the shared mass trauma of the destruction of Arab Palestine in 1948, which profoundly affected virtually all Palestinians in one way or another, and affects them still. In spite of their vigorous sense of collective national identity, the Palestinians have never succeeded in creating an independent state of their own, and have no sure prospect in the future of ever having a truly sovereign state, or of possessing a contiguous, clearly demarcated territory on which to establish it. Beyond this, for their entire modern history—since 1917—they have suffered from a series of traumatic impositions. These included the denial of their very existence and of their legitimacy as a national entity by Great Britain, the Zionist movement, and much of the rest of the world; domination and repression by a range of foreign powers; repeated expulsions from their homes, including the expulsion of over half their number in 1948; and over two generations of harsh, alien military occupation for many of them. In consequence of the lived experience of their own recent past over several generations, the Palestinians are thus understandably prey to profound, justified, and realistic fears of being destroyed and dispersed as a people.

By contrast, the Israeli people today have a very powerful state, one that has been in existence for over fifty-eight years. They nevertheless harbor intense fears of their own, for their state's continued survival and their survival as a people. These are born mainly of a recent history of discrimination, persecution, expulsion, and genocide against Jews that took place primarily in Europe, culminating in the Nazi Holocaust, all of this against the background of a two-thousand-year-old history of expulsion and persecution. Secondarily, these fears grow out of the anxiety attendant on the creation of a Jewish state in 1948 in a land two-thirds of whose inhabitants were at that time Arab, a land furthermore that was and is surrounded by "a sea of Arabs." This anxiety is perpetuated by the Zionist imperative of having to maintain the "Jewish nature" of an Israeli state, in the face of a constantly growing minority of Arab citizens that now constitutes nearly 20 percent of the population. Moreover, this is a state that fully and completely controls a territory—Israel together with the West Bank and the Gaza Strip—that today has a bare and rapidly shrinking overall Jewish majority.[2] These fears are powerfully reinforced by a peculiar Israeli narrative of their recent experience in Palestine, whose subtext is a specific reading of millennia of Jewish history.[3] This narrative sees the Israelis as the continuing victims of those they have decisively defeated, dispossessed, and dispersed, although they have been victorious in every military conflict they have engaged in over the nearly sixty years of existence of their state.

Clearly, for both peoples in Palestine, the Palestinians and the Israelis, this sense of victimhood (a sense that almost by definition involves a claim of exclusive victimhood) is underpinned by existential fears that in turn produce enormous anxiety about establishing a state, or for preservation of an existing state, in both cases as a shield against further misfortune. There is nevertheless an extraordinary contrast between the two national narratives, and between the degree to which the respective fears of the two sides are grounded in reality. There has also been a great gulf between the perceptions of the Palestinians and the Israelis as to the forms of state they have believed were appropriate for Palestine/Israel over the nearly ninety years since Ottoman sovereignty over Palestine ended.

During the hundreds of years of Ottoman rule over Palestine, the question of what forms of state were appropriate did not arise, at least not for most of the country's inhabitants. It is true that over nearly the last hundred years of the existence of the Ottoman Empire, the form and structure of the Ottoman state itself was a subject of constant contention among its subjects and citizens, and among interested foreign powers. However, until nearly the very end of its four centuries of control over Palestine, the Ottoman Empire was the unchallenged state framework within which nearly all of the country's Muslim and Christian inhabitants operated.

Importantly, until virtually the end of the Ottoman period, a majority of Palestine's Jewish population was of non-European origin, and most of them were Ottoman citizens.[4] Neither among the country's majority population of Ottoman Arab Muslims and Christians, nor among Ottoman Jews in Palestine, was there much serious thought about an alternative to the Ottoman state as a framework for their respective collective aspirations before 1914. Most members of both groups remained loyal Ottoman subjects until then. Even among non-Ottoman European Jews in Palestine in this period, a majority were deeply religious and unworldly, and for the most part had little interest in what state ruled over them.

The Zionist movement at this stage had not fully developed its view of what form of state was appropriate for Palestine, and in any case before 1914 its adherents were still very probably a minority among Jews in Palestine.[5]

The situation changed dramatically and rapidly in every respect after Great Britain occupied Palestine in 1917. In that year, Britain issued the Balfour Declaration pledging its support for the establishment of a national home for the Jewish people in Palestine. In later years it sought to carry out this pledge under a League of Nations mandate, while opening the country's doors to Jewish immigration, mainly from Europe. This changed the makeup of the yishuv, the Jewish community in Palestine, which every year grew more European, more secular, and more Zionist. Thereafter, two entities that increasingly came to see themselves as separate national groups in Palestine, the Arabs and the Jews, developed quite different views about the question of how Palestine should be governed, and under what form of state.

After a brief period of hope among some Palestinian Arabs that Palestine might be part of a larger independent Arab state, in particular the state established by King Faysal in Damascus in 1918–20, most Palestinians for the three decades until 1948 rather unimaginatively, but understandably, called simply for the establishment of an independent Arab state of Palestine. Like other peoples under foreign rule in the immediate post–World War I period—the Koreans, the Indians, the Egyptians, and others—many Palestinians had initially naively believed in the liberal promises about national self-determination included in Woodrow Wilson's Fourteen Points. (As we saw in Chapter 2, these ideas were later embodied in part in the Covenant of the League of Nations with specific reference to former Arab provinces of the Ottoman Empire, including Palestine.[6]) The Palestinians moreover considered themselves to be among the Arab peoples to whom Britain had promised independence in the Husayn-McMahon correspondence of 1915–16 and subsequent pledges.[7] They assumed that at the very least they should be treated as were the populations of other League of Nations Class A mandates, such as Iraq, Syria, Lebanon, and Transjordan, with governments drawn from the majority population, and a promise of eventual self-determination and independence.[8]

Palestinian Arabs consequently assumed that when they finally and inevitably came into their rightful inheritance as a sovereign people, the state they would dominate because of their majority status—as we have seen, in 1918 Arabs constituted over 90 percent of the population, while 98 percent of the country's land was either Arab-owned or public land—would naturally and necessarily reflect their ethnicity and national aspirations. They and their leaders gave little detailed thought to the nature of the constitutional and political relations that should obtain between the initially huge indigenous Arab majority and the powerful and growing Jewish minority. Moreover, they failed to pay sufficient attention to the fact that this minority was made up increasingly as the years went by of recent European immigrants who had strong national aspirations —indeed, most of them had come to Palestine solely to fulfill these aspirations. At this stage and for long afterward, Palestinian leaders made no significant proposals to address these aspirations in the context of the Arab state they envisaged: both the notable leadership in the Mandate period and subsequent Palestinian leaderships starting in the 1970s argued in the main that Jews should be treated as citizens like all others in a democratic state that would by force of demography be predominantly Arab, and that Judaism in any case was a religion, not a nationality.

By contrast, encouraged by the unstinting support extended to the Zionist enterprise for the first two decades of its rule over the country by Great Britain, the greatest imperial power of the age, most Zionist thinkers argued, publicly at first, that Palestine should be a Jewish national home as laid out in the Balfour Declaration and the League of Nations Mandate for Palestine. We have seen that in 1937 most Zionist leaders accepted the recommendation of the Peel Commission that the country be partitioned to make possible the creation of a Jewish state (although they felt it should be much larger than that proposed by Peel). They thereupon argued, starting with the Biltmore Program in 1942, that "Palestine should be established as a Jewish Commonwealth" with control over immigration in the hands of the Jewish Agency,[9] and finally in the mid-1940s that as much as possible of it should become a Jewish state. However, much earlier, indeed from soon after the outset of British rule, in the 1920s, Zionist leaders expected, and were given to believe confidentially by many of their official British interlocutors, that the entire country of Palestine would and should eventually become a Jewish state, even though they generally confined themselves in public to the ambiguous term "Jewish national home."[10] In their public statements these leaders gave little attention to the formal place to be given to the Arabs in the Palestine/Israel of the future, except perhaps as a tolerated minority after Jews had eventually become a majority in the country as a result of unrestricted immigration.

An influential minority of Zionist leaders, led by Ze'ev Jabotinsky (whose followers included two later prime ministers of Israel, Menachem Begin and Yitzhaq Shamir), were coldly realistic and much more forthright. Jabotinsky eschewed such circumlocution and diplomatic double-talk, and argued explicitly and publicly from the beginning that overwhelming force would be necessary to impose the Zionist program of making Palestine a Jewish state in the face of what he expected would be fierce and understandable Arab opposition. Jabotinsky wrote: "There is no choice: the Arabs must make room for the Jews in Eretz Israel. If it was possible to transfer the Baltic peoples, it is also possible to move the Palestinian Arabs."[11] At the other end of the political spectrum, a few leading Jewish thinkers, such as Judah Magnes and Martin Buber, advocated a binational state, because they saw the inherent injustice, and the ultimately tragic consequences for both peoples, of trying to carry out the full-scale Zionist program of creating a Jewish state in an overwhelmingly Arab country. Nevertheless, they did not flesh out what that formula might mean in practice, nor did they convince large numbers of Jews in Palestine of the force of their arguments.

In time it became clear to most mainstream Zionist leaders that it was not going to be possible to establish a state with a Jewish majority in predominantly Arab Palestine simply through Jewish immigration and Palestinian acquiescence, even with the application of compulsion by the British. Jabotinsky was therefore right about the need to use force.[12] Nevertheless, most Zionist leaders gave as little public attention as possible to their private and internal reflections about these matters. They knew full well that as late as 1948, Jewish-owned land in Palestine amounted to only about 7 percent of the country's total land area (and only 10.6 percent of its privately owned land, including much of the country's best arable land), that the vast bulk of the country's privately owned land and much of its urban property was in Arab hands, and that Arabs constituted a 65 percent majority of the country's population.[13]

As discussed in Chapter 4, most leaders of the Zionist movement eventually came to understand that the only means to create a state in Palestine with institutions whose nature would be determined, and fully controlled, by a Jewish majority, was to engage in what today is called ethnic cleansing. The neutral, bland term "transfer" was the Orwellian euphemism employed at that time to describe what amounted to an act of politicide.[14] The idea of transfer, which is still employed in Israeli political discourse, was discussed only privately in Zionist circles until 1937, when it became more respectable after being suggested in the report of the Peel Commission.[15] It was quietly acknowledged by most of these leaders that this process would necessarily have to be carried out by force, against the will of the majority of the population. If the British were not going to do this for the Zionist movement, as had become clear by 1939, the Zionists would have to do it themselves. The leaders of the movement could not have envisioned at the time the exact circumstances in which this process would eventually take place, which means that the much debated questions of "intentionality" and prior planning in regard to the expulsion of the Palestinian refugees is in fact largely irrelevant.[16] In any event, ethnic cleansing, however it transpired, was achieved through the terrorization and subsequent flight of about 750,000 Palestinians from 1947 until 1949.[17]

For well over a decade thereafter, Palestinians remained traumatized by these events. Preoccupied by the need to make new lives for themselves or to adjust to drastically changed realities, most of them paid scant attention to the problem of what form of state was appropriate for Palestine. If they gave the matter any attention, they generally did little more than project the imagined past into the future. Some of them unreflectively talked of "liberating" Palestine. This meant restoring an Arab Palestine that had never been a sovereign state, and whose social basis was irrevocably gone with the flight of over half the Palestinian people and the expropriation of most of their land.

In thus attempting to turn back the clock, Palestinians once again appear to have given little serious thought to the nature of the relationship between them and Israeli Jews who would remain in such a projected Palestinian Arab state, just as during the Mandate period, there was no appreciation of Zionism as anything more than a colonial movement that had dispossessed the Palestinians. Clearly, the fact that Zionism had also functioned as a national movement, and had founded a national state, Israel, was still not something that the traumatized Palestinians could bring themselves to accept, since these things had happened at their expense. The founding of the Palestine Liberation Organization (PLO) in 1964 consecrated this simplistic approach. The Palestinian National Charter adopted in 1964 by the newly formed Palestine National Council (PNC) specified that after the liberation of Palestine, only those "Jews who normally lived in Palestine until the beginning of the Zionist invasion," presumably meaning before 1917, would be entitled to remain in a future Palestinian Arab state that would replace Israel and encompass the entire country.[18] This was less generous than what leaders of the Arab Higher Committee including the mufti had been prepared to accept in negotiations with British envoy Col. S. F. Newcombe in Baghdad in 1940 based on the 1939 White Paper, which envisaged a self-governing unitary state encompassing all Arabs and the nearly five hundred thousand Jews then living in Palestine.[19]

The Palestinian National Charter thus represented both a step backward and a flight from the bitter reality that had encompassed the Palestinians. It would serve them poorly in subsequent years, as its rhetoric could easily, and not unfairly, be cited as evidence that the Palestinians did not accept the existence of the state of Israel or the presence in Palestine of the Israeli people. It was the basis for the charge that the Palestinians' political aim was "the destruction of Israel." The fact that it was amended at different times, that as time went on most Palestinians paid it less and less heed, and that the political programs adopted by successive PNCs progressively contradicted it, was rarely considered by those who had an interest in showing that there had never been any evolution in the Palestinian position. For them, this *mithaq*, a word normally translated as "charter," was invariably rendered as "covenant," in a transparent effort to make it seem more authoritative and solemn than in fact it was.

For their part, during the same period, most Israelis and Zionists presumably simply wanted the disappearance of the Palestinians, a majority of whom had just been successfully ethnically cleansed from what in consequence had now become the predominantly Jewish state of Israel, and most of whom were now outside the 1949 armistice lines that constituted its de facto borders. The Palestinians would ideally do Israel this favor by forgetting their lost homes and property, their homeland, and what had been done to them, and simply melting into the surrounding Arab countries, where many of them now resided as exiles. Jordan's annexation of the West Bank and its extension of Jordanian citizenship to all Palestinians on its territory—who thereby became the largest single community of Palestinians after 1948—facilitated the illusion that the Palestinians might somehow disappear.

Most Israelis and their supporters had already cleared their consciences in any case by accepting the standard canards produced by the Israeli state that in effect blamed the victims for their own dispossession, or denied their very existence: "Their leaders told them to leave"; "They intended to drive us into the sea"; "We were attacked by seven Arab armies"; "There are no Palestinians"; and so forth.[20] Moreover, after 1949, following the influx of massive numbers of new Jewish immigrants, a majority of Israelis had no memory of Palestine before 1948 and could not have known, except through such state-produced myths, what had actually happened to the Palestinians.[21] Israel became a polity described as the state of the Jewish people, where the small minority of remaining Arabs were "legally" despoiled of most of their land in the north, center, and south of the country, were kept under martial law and police state controls for the first eighteen years after 1948, and thereafter got third-class political, human, social, and economic rights[22] (second-class status was reserved for the wave of newly arrived Oriental Jewish refugees from the Arab countries, the Mizrahis[23]). Suspect because of their ethnicity, Palestinians inside Israel were non-Jews in a Jewish state whose legal system in principle provided for equal rights for all, but whose laws and political system in practice discriminated heavily in favor of Jews and against non-Jews.

The first fresh thinking among Palestinians about the form to be taken by a new polity in Palestine was the proposal put forward at the end of the 1960s, following the June 1967 war, during which Israel occupied the West Bank, Gaza Strip, and East Jerusalem, as well as the Golan Heights and Sinai Peninsula. This proposal originated with the Democratic Front for the Liberation of Palestine (DFLP). It was discreetly but effectively backed by leaders of the dominant, mainstream Fateh movement, who by now had wrested control of the PLO away from Egypt and the other Arab states that had originally sponsored its formation. This proposal called for a single, secular, democratic state in Palestine, in which citizens of all faiths would be equal. The democratic secular state model eventually became the official position of the PLO, although the nature of this projected state was never fully fleshed out. Fateh leaders like Yasser 'Arafat and Abu Iyyad were astute in using the DFLP to float the proposal, testing the reactions to it, and then adopting it as their own (this was to happen again when the PLO further modified its objectives and gradually adopted a two-state solution beginning in the mid-1970s).[24]

While addressing Palestinian aspirations for the "restoration" of Arab Palestine, this new approach also postulated the equal citizenship rights of Israeli Jews and Palestinian Arabs. In this it marked a significant change from the provisions of the Palestinian National Charter of 1964, and the first acceptance by Palestinians after 1948 that Israelis had full and equal political rights in Palestine alongside Palestinian Arabs. By contrast, most Israelis, and the Israeli government, were at this stage still not prepared to recognize full and equal political rights for the Palestinians: thus while the 1950 "Law of Return," one of the "Basic Laws" of Israel, allowed Jews anywhere the right to come to Israel and obtain Israeli citizenship immediately, the idea of the return of Palestinian refugees has been rigorously excluded by every Israeli government since 1948.[25] Nor did Israel at this stage accept the idea of a Palestinian state in the West Bank and Gaza Strip, which after 1967 were under Israeli occupation.

However, although the secular democratic state idea explicitly took into account Palestinian national aspirations, it did not address either implicitly or explicitly the issue of the collective or national rights of Israeli Jews, rights that official Palestinian political rhetoric still did not recognize. In this rhetoric, Israeli Jews in Palestine were still described as members of a religious, not a national, group, and thus were seen as having full civil, religious, and now political, rights as individuals, but *not* collective national rights. This idea, although it represented a clear advance on the backward-looking rhetoric of the original language of the Palestinian National Charter, nevertheless represented a continued Palestinian rejection of national rights for Jews in Palestine, and of the state of Israel itself. In consequence, this approach ran counter to the international consensus based on UN General Assembly Resolution 181 of November 29, 1947, which had called for the establishment of both a Jewish and an Arab state in Palestine, and which was the international basis for the legitimacy of Israel.

At least equally important in pragmatic political terms, it also ran counter to the implicit acceptance of the state of Israel within its pre-1967 war frontiers of June 4, 1967, by increasing numbers of Arab states. This recognition of the reality of Israel was embodied in the subsequent acceptance by the most powerful and important of these states, notably Egypt, Syria, and Jordan, of United Nations Security Council Resolutions 242, adopted on November 22, 1967, and 338, passed in October 1973. Resolution 242, which thereafter became the bedrock of efforts to make peace in the Middle East, explicitly called for acceptance of the right of all states in the region, including Israel, to live in peace with one another "within secure and recognized boundaries free from threats or acts of force." At the same time, it restricted Israel essentially to its territory before the June 1967 war through stress in the resolution's preamble on a core principle of the United Nations Charter, "the inadmissibility of the acquisition of territory by war," and by calling for Israeli withdrawal "from territories occupied" during the 1967 war.[26]

The Two-State Solution

By the mid-1970s it had become clear—at least to most perceptive Arab analysts—that no major country in the world, including the most influential Arab states and important backers of the Arabs like the Soviet Union, would countenance a solution to the question of Palestine not based on the recognition of the state of Israel within its 1967 frontiers. Most Palestinians, under the leadership of Fateh, eventually came to terms with this reality. This constituted a major, and still not fully appreciated, step. Starting in 1974 with the twelfth session of the PNC, the PLO's "parliament in exile," over a period of a decade and a half the organization haltingly and by stages abandoned the proposal for a single democratic Palestinian state in favor of a two-state approach to the problem of governance in Palestine.[27] This new departure, driven by the Fateh leadership in alliance with the DFLP, and opposed by the PFLP and other smaller groups (which later concretized their opposition by forming the "Rejection Front"), involved calling for creation of a sovereign, independent Palestinian state alongside Israel in an area restricted to the 22 percent of former mandatory Palestine, and composed of the occupied West Bank, the Gaza Strip, and Arab East Jerusalem, which had been controlled by Jordan and Egypt from 1948 until 1967. The key figures in the new "pragmatic" thrust of the PLO were Fateh leaders 'Arafat, Abu Iyyad, and Khalid al-Hassan, and DFLP leader Nayif Hawatmeh. In many ways, Abu Iyyad was the most important in winning over the several-hundred-member PNC in open session, since he was the most eloquent and charismatic member of the Fateh leadership. Behind the scenes, where most decisions were made, 'Arafat and the others played their role.[28]

The new approach was first put forward in embryonic form at the June 1974 PNC held in Cairo as a proposal for a "national authority" (ironically, the same term used for the entity created by the Madrid/Oslo process two decades later) on any area of Palestine that might be liberated. In subsequent meetings of the PNC, this two-state solution was further refined and clarified. It was formally and explicitly adopted by a meeting of the PNC held in Algiers in 1988, in the form of the Palestinian Declaration of Independence. This document was drafted in its Arabic version by the preeminent Palestinian poet Mahmud Darwish, and in its English version by the distinguished Palestinian literary and cultural critic Edward Said. The declaration rhetorically proclaimed the establishment of an independent Palestinian state alongside Israel on the basis of UN

General Assembly Resolution 181 of 1947, which had called for the partition of Palestine into an Arab and Jewish state. This was the first official Palestinian recognition of the legitimacy of the existence of a Jewish state, and the first unequivocal, explicit PLO endorsement of a two-state solution to the conflict.

Although this major evolution of the Palestinian position met several long-standing conditions for a settlement as put forward by Israel and the United States, it did not lead to any change in either country's stand on the basic issues at stake in the conflict, nor did it prompt peace negotiations. The only immediate effect of the shift in the Palestinian position was that the United States agreed to open contacts with the PLO, once the latter had renounced terrorism. However, in the wake of the 1988 Palestinian Declaration of Independence, neither the United States nor Israel, the two most powerful actors in the Middle East, explicitly accepted that the Palestinians were a people, with inalienable rights to self-determination and independent statehood.[29]

Nevertheless, after formal U.S. contacts with the PLO had been under way for three years (interrupted by the PLO's failure to deal decisively with a 1990 terrorist attack by the Iraqi-backed PLF, led by Abu al-ʿAbbas, described in Chapter 5), in the wake of the 1991 Gulf War, President George H. W. Bush and his secretary of state, James Baker, changed course. They obliged the reluctant Israeli government headed by Yitzhaq Shamir to begin negotiations with the representatives of the Palestinians under occupation, initially as part of a Jordanian-Palestinian joint delegation, starting at the Madrid Peace Conference in October and November 1991. This conference was meant to make possible "a just, lasting and comprehensive peace settlement through direct negotiations," with the aim of achieving "real peace and reconciliation among the Arab states, Israel, and the Palestinians."[30] But from the outset of these negotiations, the two-state solution to the Israeli-Palestinian conflict faced grave problems, problems that could ultimately prove fatal to the establishment of a Palestinian state. The most pressing among them has been the continuous building and expansion, whether during negotiations or in periods when talks were in abeyance, of a network of Israeli settlements throughout the occupied West Bank and Arab East Jerusalem, settlements whose strategic locations may well make impossible the creation of a contiguous, viable Palestinian state.[31] Thus the map that was ostensibly the subject of Israeli and Palestinian negotiation was all the while being drastically transformed by one party to the discussion.

The Palestinians' absurd situation, being restrained from negotiating for an end to Israel's occupation while Israel reinforced it, was strikingly revealed over nearly a decade of intensive negotiations. These negotiations started with the shuttle diplomacy of secretary of state James Baker in the spring of 1991 in preparation for the convening of the Madrid conference, and went on until the Camp David summit in July 2000, with no significant progress made on the core issues that separated the two sides. This impasse was inevitable because of the nature of the ground rules that were adopted for these negotiations. These were originally imposed on the Palestinians by the United States at the insistence of the Shamir government. They indefinitely froze dealing with any of the issues of substance between the two sides (the final status issues: occupation, settlements, Jerusalem, refugees, water, and permanent borders), while there was no concomitant freeze on the building of Israeli settlements in the West Bank and East Jerusalem. During this decade their population rose from about two hundred thousand to over four hundred thousand. Instead of focusing on resolving final status issues, Palestinian-Israeli negotiations until the Camp David summit in the summer of 2000 (and the Washington and Taba talks that followed) were limited by these restrictive rules to dealing with transitional administrative arrangements. This left untouched the expansion of settlements and the matrix of control of the Israeli occupation.

The practical effect of these Israeli-inspired and American-imposed ground rules was to lighten the moral, political, and security burden for Israel of its military occupation of the West Bank, Gaza Strip, and East Jerusalem for a decade, while allowing it not only to maintain, but indeed to reinforce, its presence in most of the occupied territories. Israel, which appeared to the world as if it was negotiating peace with the Palestinians, was simultaneously expanding not only its settlements but also the extensive infrastructure of roads, electricity, water, and phone lines needed to sustain them. Thus it has been argued by some observers that the lasting fruit of this nearly ten-year "peace process," which resulted in the Oslo Accords and subsequent Palestinian-Israeli accords that produced the Palestinian Authority (PA), has been the hardening of Israel's occupation regime, and a considerable expansion of its illegal settlements.

This happened in part because the United States failed to respect its own commitments in the joint U.S.-Soviet letter of invitation to the Madrid Peace Conference, and particularly in the U.S. letter of assurance to the Palestinians, both dated October 18, 1991.[32] The latter set out the U.S. position regarding actions by either side that would prejudge, preempt, or predetermine the outcome of the deferred final status negotiations. Described as "U.S. understandings and intentions" regarding the negotiating process, which it said was aimed, among other things, to provide "an end to the Israeli occupation," the letter stressed that nothing done in this phase should "be prejudicial or precedential to the outcome of the negotiations." It affirmed: "We encourage all sides to avoid unilateral acts that would exacerbate local tensions or make negotiations more difficult or preempt their final outcome." The letter further stated: "The United States has long believed that no party should take unilateral actions that seek to predetermine issues that can only be resolved through negotiations. In this regard the United States has opposed and will continue to oppose settlement activity in the territories occupied in 1967, which remains an obstacle to peace."[33]

If these statements meant anything, they meant that Israel could not unilaterally decide the fate of the territory that was subject to negotiations, which in fact Israel was engaged in doing by the continued building of settlements and the infrastructure to support them. The United States did nothing about these developments, its letter of assurance to the Palestinians notwithstanding. The Palestinians were unable to find the means through diplomacy, public advocacy, peaceful protest, or coalition building in Israel, the United States, Europe, and elsewhere to show the dangers of what Israel was doing, or to obstruct it effectively. This was not for want of efforts: Dr. Haidar 'Abd al-Shafi, the head of the Palestinian delegation at the Madrid and Washington negotiations, conveyed to the PLO leadership in Tunis the unanimous recommendation of the entire delegation that they be authorized to break off these talks once it became clear that the United States would not do anything to halt Israeli actions that predetermined the outcome of the negotiations, notably settlement expansion.[34] This recommendation was ignored, and prime responsibility for negotiations with Israel was eventually surreptitiously moved by the PLO from the hard-nosed Palestinian delegation in Washington to the more "flexible" group that negotiated the Oslo Accords, with ultimately disastrous consequences for the Palestinians.

Over time, a sort of resigned passivity fell over the previously highly mobilized Palestinians in the occupied territories and abroad. It is worth recalling that the Madrid Peace Conference and the Palestinian-Israel negotiations that followed were in a sense the fruit of the first intifada, which had galvanized Palestinian society and revealed to many Israelis after two decades that the occupation was untenable. After Madrid, most Palestinians assumed that securing a state through negotiations was only a matter of time. In effect, however, nothing of the kind was happening, as Israel was allowed by the United States, in spite of solemn pledges to the Palestinians by the first Bush administration, to help itself to huge bites of the pie that the two sides were supposed to be negotiating about.

During the over nine years of negotiations from the lengthy lead-up to the 1991 Madrid conference, until President Clinton belatedly convened the Camp David conference in late 2000,[35] while the Palestinians were barred from discussing any of the real problems between them and Israel, these problems grew worse. Occupation continued, as did seizures of Palestinian land for new settlements and the expansion of old ones, and the concomitant growth of the settler population. As a result of Israeli policies and the peculiar arrangements for Palestinian self-government that defined the prerogatives of the PA, there was no contiguous body of territory under PA jurisdiction, indeed there was no territory under its full and absolute control and jurisdiction, even the 17 percent of the West Bank that it nominally controlled. New bypass roads were constructed to enable settlers to travel between settlements without passing through Palestinian-populated areas. The building of this network of roads—designed exclusively for the use of Israelis and from which Palestinians were barred—involved the seizure of yet more Palestinian land. These roads helped encircle the Palestinian population ever more tightly in small cantons within the West Bank, isolated from one another and subject to "closures" (meaning in effect imprisonment within each canton) as and when Israel desired. The most rigorous closures blocked off access to Israel proper and to occupied Arab East Jerusalem. There, limitations on building by Palestinians combined with Israel's settlements in the eastern sector of the city dimmed hopes that it could ever become the Palestinian capital. Meanwhile, nothing was done to address the plight of those Palestinians who lived in exile or the critical issue of Israel's control of West Bank aquifers. All of these changes on the ground—occurring while peace negotiations were supposedly taking place—made the idea of a sovereign Palestinian state with defined borders grow ever more distant.

Each of these gradually worsening chronic problems undermined the legitimacy of the Palestinian leadership engaged in negotiations with Israel, and stoked Palestinian popular frustration. Over time, the leadership's popularity declined precipitously in consequence. This affected the image of the PLO and the PA generally, and even that of the preeminent symbol of Palestinian nationalism, Yasser 'Arafat, who according to one set of opinion polls went from being "trusted" by as much as 46.4 percent of those polled in the mid-1990s (several times more than his closest competitor) to numbers in the low- to mid-20s from December 2000 onward.[36]

As seemingly fruitless negotiations dragged on for a decade, many Palestinians came to perceive that vital segments of the 22 percent of historic mandatory Palestine composed of the West Bank, Gaza Strip, and East Jerusalem on which they had hoped to establish a sovereign state were being inexorably absorbed into Israel by this creeping process of settlement and de facto annexation. They thus came to feel that any peace based on a two-state solution was impossible to achieve. The situation continues to deteriorate: while by 2000 the settler population in these two areas had more than doubled to over 400,000, five years later it stood at nearly 450,000, in spite of the dismantling of the small settlements in the Gaza Strip.

Israel's Matrix of Control

Equally seriously in terms of Palestinian perceptions, over this decade of negotiations (and later during the four-plus years of the intifada that followed), Israel came to exercise a far greater measure of control than ever before over the Palestinian population and over the 83 percent of the territory of the West Bank wherein, by the Oslo and subsequent accords, it had full or partial jurisdiction. While settlements were immediately apparent to even casual visitors, much less visible was the way in which the Israeli occupation in fact came to increase its domination over the Palestinian people during this period. This occurred through the creation of a web of procedures, amounting to a new regime of control, including suffocating movement restrictions and an all-encompassing permit system, hundreds of permanent and temporary checkpoints, increasingly tight closures of the expanded Greater Jerusalem metropolitan area to most Palestinians, construction of Israeli-only bypass roads linking the ever-expanding archipelago of settlements in occupied territory and cutting off Palestinian communities from one another, the establishment of areas closed to Palestinians and of "nature preserves" also closed to Palestinian development, and more seizures of land for expanding the area of existing Israeli settlements and the building of new ones.[37]

The most important index of this process was the drastic reduction over time in the freedom of Palestinians to move from place to place, within the occupied territories including East Jerusalem, into Israel, or between the West Bank and Gaza. Until the end of the 1980s, movement in these areas was highly restricted only for certain limited categories of Palestinians (essentially those convicted of security offenses). Most others moved around more or less freely, indications of this being the more than one hundred thousand Palestinians who commuted to work daily in Israel, and the possibility of Palestinians traveling into Israel in cars with West Bank license plates with little hindrance. Thereafter, starting during the Oslo period, Palestinian movement was increasingly restricted, until it was allowed only with hard to obtain permits, for which certain very limited categories of persons were eligible (essentially high officials of the PA, who received special VIP permits); all other Palestinians were highly restricted in their movements. The Palestinians under occupation thus went from a situation in which most could move relatively freely throughout the occupied territories and Israel, with only a small category suffering severe movement restrictions, to one in which almost all Palestinians suffered severe movement restrictions, and only a very small category had any freedom of movement at all.[38]

As a result of these procedures and the new regime of control Israel gradually put into place over a decade and a half, by 2006 the 3.6 million Palestinians of the occupied territories, who formerly could move relatively freely to Israel, to Jerusalem, and between the West Bank and Gaza Strip, were in a fundamentally different situation.

Those in the West Bank had been confined to a patchwork of isolated cantons in the 17 percent of its territory administered by the PA set up under the provisions of the Oslo and subsequent "self-government" arrangements. They could barely move from one of these tiny cantons to another. These restrictions, while sometimes imposed on the pretext of security, were not relaxed in any fundamental way even when the security situation improved, until they became a suffocating blanket of permanent restrictions.[39] It remained only to build walls and electrified barriers to fence in the Palestinians of the West Bank, as had already happened around the Gaza Strip, for these cantons to come to resemble open-air prison camps. Once the intifada started, this was not long in coming, in the form of the so-called "security fence," which for that part of its length that passes through cities, towns, and heavily populated areas is a thirty-foot-high concrete wall with watchtowers, and elsewhere is a broad system of barriers, fences, and security roads. After Israel's 2005 withdrawal from the Gaza Strip, that region's inhabitants, while for the first time in decades free to move about within its limited confines, and to travel to Egypt, could not travel to Israel, where most had previously worked. Israel also maintained tight controls on all imports and exports to the Gaza Strip, which it controlled completely, cutting them off sometimes for weeks at a time, as happened in the spring of 2006, and restricting them at others.

The Israeli military occupation's imposition of this regime of control progressively suffocated the Palestinians by restricting their movement and their living space inside the occupied territories. Needless to say, all these measures cumulatively had a massive social impact and severely undermined their fragile economy. This impact was all the greater psychologically since this process started and began to take effect during a period when peace negotiations were ostensibly taking place. The degradation of the situation of the average Palestinian citizen accompanied stagnation in individual income even in the years before the second intifada began: thus GDP per capita hardly increased over the period of negotiations, from

$1,380 in 1995 to $1,386 in 2000. The lack of an improvement in the well-being of ordinary Palestinians had a strong negative effect on popular support for a peace process that many of them saw as progressively demoralizing and restricting them. Worse was to come economically after the intifada broke out: Palestinian GDP per capita declined from $1,386 in 2000 to $1,146 in 2004.[40] It has declined further since.

The impact of all this was exacerbated by the fact that the PA leadership failed to do much of what it could have done on its own, even in such impossibly restrictive circumstances. These included establishing a corruption-free system of governance based on a rule of law, establishing a balance between the executive and the legislative branches, attracting massive investment, and creating jobs. The elected Palestinian Legislative Council (PLC), which might have taken on a pioneering role as a separate branch of government, taking the lead in setting an agenda for the PA, instead was dominated by the elected president of the PA, the increasingly autocratic Yasser 'Arafat. 'Arafat brooked no opposition from the PLC, refused for years to sign a Basic Law (meant to serve as a transitional constitution) that it had passed, bullied the legislators, and generally established the unfortunate precedent of a serious imbalance between the powers of the executive and the legislative branches. The absence of a fully elaborated rule of law, on top of the uncertain state of the PA generally in terms of the lack of sovereignty, full jurisdiction, and real control over territory, created a poor environment for private investment. Some wealthy Palestinian expatriates did invest in the West Bank and Gaza Strip, but many of them came to rue their decision to do so as the economy failed to grow sufficiently in the 1990s, and then contracted after 2000. Pervasive governmental corruption also discouraged investment.

Instead of a new para-state structure emerging that might have marshaled and organized the energies of the Palestinian people to deal with the even greater challenges that the Oslo period produced, the new PA was essentially a copy of the post-Beirut PLO as that organization was described in the previous chapter: a patronage-laden and largely ineffective system rife with cronyism. This system conspicuously benefited PLO leaders and cadres who had staffed the Palestinian quasi state in Lebanon, and then had sat in enforced idleness in different sites of exile for over a decade after the expulsion of the PLO from Beirut in 1982. These individuals were chosen for most of the top positions in the PA essentially because of their loyalty and their revolutionary past rather than on the basis of merit. The senior figures among them enjoyed privileges and perquisites ranging from education abroad for their children to VIP status shrewdly granted by Israel that gave them relative freedom of movement and insulated them from the lot of the common people.

These leaders, many of whom came to be loathed by the population of the West Bank, Gaza Strip, and East Jerusalem, dominated a Palestinian Authority that failed to provide many of the services, or the leadership, that the population of these areas so badly needed. Although in the fields of education, health care, and infrastructure progress was made, as was shown in the last chapter, these improvements were achieved largely by officials originating in the West Bank and Gaza Strip rather than by the returnees from Tunis and elsewhere. Together with the hardships attendant on the imposition of Israel's new system of control and the expansion of Israeli settlements, increasing Palestinian loss of faith in the negotiating approach of the PLO and disgust with the PA's incompetence and corruption were among the root causes for the eruption of the second intifada at the end of September 2000. They contributed mightily as well to Fateh's defeat in the Palestinian Legislative Council elections of 2006.

The outbreak of the second intifada opened a period of over four years of sharply increased Palestinian-Israeli violence, at a level unparalleled since the Israeli invasion of Lebanon in 1982, and marked by horrific scenes of suicide bombing, aerial bombardment, and the employment of tanks and artillery in heavily built-up urban areas. Over this time, nearly five thousand people were killed in

Palestine/Israel and about thirty-five thousand were wounded (almost 80 percent of those killed, and an even higher proportion of those wounded, were Palestinians, with majorities on both sides being civilians). Thousands of Palestinians were imprisoned, and Palestinian cities, towns, and villages evacuated by Israel in the wake of the Oslo Accords were reoccupied. Meanwhile, as the intifada dragged on, Israel accelerated the imposition of its new regime of control that had already started taking shape during the Oslo era. This culminated in the annexation of another 10 percent of the West Bank under cover of the building of a "security barrier." Whatever this barrier may have done for Israeli security, it would have done even more had it been erected within Israel, along the Green Line marking the 1949 armistice boundary. Instead, it has been built virtually in its entirety within the West Bank, in many cases deep within it, thereby making possible the seizure of thousands of hectares of additional Palestinian land, along with their valuable water resources, separating Palestinian farmers from their livelihood, and sowing more resentment and anger for the future.

In apparent response to the intifada, the Israeli government under Ariel Sharon and his successor Ehud Olmert began a series of actions, among them the building of the barrier/wall, and including the 2005 withdrawal from the Gaza Strip, that were undertaken unilaterally and without negotiations with the Palestinians. Further actions, including ongoing extensions of the barrier/wall, withdrawing settlements (but not necessarily the Israeli army) from some parts of the West Bank while annexing other areas of the West Bank and East Jerusalem where major Israeli settlement blocs are located, are planned by the newly elected Israeli government, with or without negotiations with the Palestinians. While these actions appear directed at separating Israel from the Palestinians, and this is how they are presented to the Israeli public, they would in fact intensify Israel's domination over the occupied West Bank and Arab East Jerusalem. This is not only because large areas of Palestinian land and hundreds of thousands of Palestinians will be on the "Israeli" side of the barrier/wall when it is completed and becomes Israel's permanent frontier, as Israeli leaders increasingly proclaim it will. It is also because the annexation to Israel of the major "settlement blocs" located at strategic and central locations in the West Bank and around Jerusalem, and of the Jordan River Valley, will mean that Israel permanently controls the West Bank, even if its forces eventually do evacuate the areas left to the Palestinians. The implications of these projected actions for the creation of a viable Palestinian state, and therefore of the two-state solution, are ominous, and very possibly fatal.

A One-State Solution

The question of what state structure or structures are appropriate for Palestine and Israel has been profoundly influenced by the actions over many years of Palestinian leaders and different Israeli governments, as just described. It has been affected as well by important transformations in U.S. policy by the administration of George W. Bush since it came into office in January 2001. Until the Madrid Peace Conference in 1991, and for many years afterward, certainly until the failed Camp David/Taba talks of 2000–2001, the conventional wisdom was that the crafting of some form of two-state solution to the conflict over Palestine and Israel was just a matter of time. It appeared to many that such a resolution depended on little more than a hard round of Palestinian-Israeli bargaining over borders, and over just how restricted would be the sovereignty of a putative Palestinian state to arise alongside Israel, with issues like Jerusalem and refugees ultimately resolved by the stronger party imposing its will on the weaker one, with the help of its overbearing superpower ally.

Among some observers, however, a realization has been growing for years that this outcome is increasingly unlikely. This realization has taken shape irrespective of the merits or demerits in principle of the two-state solution, in spite of the long-standing desire of majorities of Palestinians and Israelis for their own state, and notwithstanding the (often grudging and hedged) acceptance by each people of a state for the other. Starting with Meron Benvenisti, a former deputy-mayor of Jerusalem, who from 1982 to 1990 ran the West Bank Data Base Project,[41] a variety of analysts have argued that the policies carried out consistently over four decades by Israel's military-security establishment and a succession of Israeli governments have changed everything.[42] In this view, the inexorable cementing of Israel's hold over the occupied West Bank and East Jerusalem have rendered moot the possibility of establishing what could legitimately be called a Palestinian state, and consequently have called into question whether a two-state solution is still possible. This is the case if a "Palestinian state" is taken to mean a viable, contiguous, sovereign, independent state on the entirety of the 22 percent of mandatory Palestine constituted by the Palestinian territories occupied by Israel in June 1967.

This realization has in turn instigated renewed consideration of the old idea of a one-state solution, as either the ideal outcome or as the most likely default outcome, for Palestine/Israel.[43] There are significant differences among those who have put forward this idea. Some argue that whether such a solution is desirable or not to the peoples concerned (and majorities of both Palestinians and Israelis appear to prefer to live in separate national states), it is the inevitable outcome of the extension into the immediate future of current trends. Those who hold this view, which might be termed the de facto one-state solution, see that it will come about (notwithstanding Israel's recent withdrawal from the Gaza Strip and possible further West Bank withdrawals) when the inexorable creeping de facto annexation of the West Bank and East Jerusalem at some point finally makes the creation of a contiguous Palestinian state physically impossible. This process is taking place against a background of continued Palestinian population growth, combined with the realization among most Israelis that further successful ethnic cleansing of the Arabs is impossible. Those holding this view see that eventu-

ally this process will produce what is in effect a single sovereign
Israeli-dominated polity throughout Palestine, with either rough
Arab-Jewish demographic parity or, more likely, an eventual Arab
majority. In this scenario, some feel, in time it will prove impossible
to keep the two peoples in one tiny land segregated, or to keep that
polity Jewish-dominated, as it eventually became impossible to
keep South Africa white-dominated.[44]

Those who foresee some kind of one-state solution emerging as
a default outcome of what is perceived as the current reality of only
one real state, one real sovereignty, and one people enjoying full
national, political, civil, and human rights between the Mediterranean Sea and the Jordan River, render no value judgments about
it. They do not advocate such a result; rather they perceive it as inevitable if present trends continue. There is little reflection among
those who hold this conception about the future constitutional
structure or other political arrangements between the two peoples.
The unspoken assumption is that these are likely to be highly unequal. Similarly, there is little consideration of how it would be possible in such a single state to overcome either the apparent desire of
both peoples for independent statehood, or the deep and abiding
distrust of each collectivity toward the other. This is therefore not a
normative position, nor does it involve advocacy: it purports rather
to be an empirical reading of current trends and their likely projec-
tion into the immediate to intermediate future. It does not address
the likelihood that because it is at odds with the aspirations of both
people, especially the Palestinians, such an outcome would be in-
herently unstable, and indeed might well be no more than a way sta-
tion on the way toward some other outcome.

Another strand of thinking about a one-state solution represents a throwback to the old Palestinian idea of a single unitary state
in Palestine with two variations. Some see this in terms of the
previous PLO conception of a secular, democratic state in all of
Palestine with equal rights for all its inhabitants, Israelis and Palestinians, whatever their faith, but no separate national rights for Is-

raelis. Others, notably leaders of Hamas, see this outcome in terms of an Islamic state in which non-Muslims would be tolerated minorities. Both of these groups actively advocate such an outcome as the ideal one, and many of the Palestinians among them make little effort to make it appealing to Israelis; indeed the violent actions, including suicide attacks on Israeli civilians, of groups like Hamas that advocate the one-state solution, make such an option even more detestable to Israelis. Others, whose views may overlap with these, and who ostensibly limit themselves to advocating the unlimited implementation of the right of Palestinians to return to their homes in Israel,[45] often do so without specifying explicitly that if most Palestinian refugees were to return to what is now Israel (which they assume, on the basis of little or no hard evidence, that most of them would want to do), this would necessarily turn Israel from a state with a Jewish majority into one with an Arab one. It can be argued that such an outcome would indeed be intended by most of them to do just that. Just how Israel could be brought to agree to such a revolutionary outcome is not addressed by partisans of this approach.[46]

Still another group that advocates a one state-solution does so on the basis of a binational approach. This is predicated on the recognition that there are two national communities in Palestine-Israel. It is combined with acceptance of the fact, recognized by many others, that the consolidation of Israel's occupation regime for over thirty-nine years (which constitutes more than two thirds of that country's fifty-eight years of existence), combined with creeping annexation and the metastasis of the settlements, as well as economic imperatives, render impossible the creation of a separate, independent, viable, contiguous Palestinian state. There follows from this realization advocacy of a framework that would take into account these two national realities within the framework of one state.[47]

What must be said about all of these approaches is that they involve—so far, at least—neither very deep nor very detailed thinking about the implications of a one-state solution, whichever variety of such a solution is at issue.[48] Moreover, they face a stone wall of rejection not only in Israel, but also in the United States, where any suggestion that appears to call into question the desirability or the likelihood of the continued existence of Israel in precisely its present form is increasingly being treated as tantamount to anti-Semitism.[49] There are other problems, however. It is worth noting, for example, that beyond the desire of most Israelis to maintain their state as it is, irrespective of what that may do to the Palestinians (and in the long run perhaps to Israel itself), and beyond the unquestioned power of Israel to determine outcomes in the region, the state of Israel as presently constituted has strong roots in international legality. This is a function of its creation as a direct result of UN General Assembly Resolution 181 in 1947,[50] which called specifically for the establishment of a "Jewish State" alongside an "Arab State," and a "Special International Regime for the City of Jerusalem." That resolution, which is the basis of Israel's international legitimacy and standing, explicitly described it as a *Jewish* state.

As I have already pointed out, this formulation was implicitly accepted by the PLO in 1988 when it issued its Declaration of Independence of a Palestinian state on the basis of Resolution 181, and simultaneously recognized Israel. It is true that this resolution specified frontiers that Israel expanded well beyond from the beginning of its existence at the expense of the stillborn Palestinian Arab state. There is presumably nothing that would prevent a change in the nature of this Israeli state should it occur by voluntary choice of its citizens (indeed, profound changes in its nature have been taking place gradually since 1967 as a result of the colonization and effective absorption of much of the occupied West Bank and East Jerusalem into Israel). But Israelis have thus far shown more of a desire for the Palestinians to be out of sight and out of mind than to come to grips with the consequences of the actions of their elected governments insofar as settlements and occupation are concerned. Barring such a voluntary change, this international anchoring of the current nature of Israel as a Jewish state would seem to be yet another obstacle to some forms of a one-state solution.

There are thus major obstacles to considering the logical consequences of the continuation of present trends in the direction of a one-state solution. Yet these trends have perhaps been as forcefully advanced by policies of the Bush administration that undermine the possibility of a two-state solution as by the actions of successive Israeli governments tending in this direction. Ironically, these policies have been combined with statements by President Bush supporting the creation of a Palestinian state. However, the entire conceptual logjam about one state or two may well have been conclusively shattered, and with it the possibility of a Palestinian state ever being created, by the present administration's actions. Notable among them is President Bush's endorsement of the Israeli position on crucial aspects of the conflict between the two peoples in a letter to Prime Minister Ariel Sharon on April 14, 2004, which recognized the permanence of major Israeli settlements in the occupied territories, stressing the irreversibility of "new realities on the ground, including already existing major Israeli population centers." The letter also endorsed the Israeli contention that Palestinian refugees cannot return to Israel proper. In taking these unprecedented positions, the Bush administration has undermined a number of fundamental tenets that have undergirded American Middle East policy for four decades.

One of these is that the core issues between Arabs and Israelis can only be negotiated directly and bilaterally between them. The Bush administration effectively accepted the Israeli argument that "there is no one to talk to on the Palestinian side," failed to initiate negotiations between the two sides, and then negotiated directly with Israel in April 2004 about the crucial questions of settlements and refugees in the absence of representatives of the people most concerned by these questions, the Palestinians themselves. In so doing, it has reversed a position in favor of direct, bilateral negotiations between the parties that the United States originally adopted at the insistence of Israel. Previous to that, under presidents from Harry Truman to Jimmy Carter, the United States had always remained willing to negotiate separately with each of the parties, or multilaterally with several of them. Thus, the secret negotiations with different Arab countries of the 1950s, the Rogers Plan of 1968, the Geneva conference of 1973, Secretary of State Kissinger's shuttle diplomacy, and the American-Soviet Joint Communiqué of 1977,[51] were all devices that permitted the United States to negotiate separately with the different parties, whether regional or international. This also allowed reluctant Arab states to avoid negotiating directly and/or bilaterally with Israel from 1949 through the 1970s.

Thereafter, following the separate Israeli-Egyptian peace treaty of 1979, and at Israeli insistence, it became a touchstone of American policy for the subsequent decades that the United States would refuse to countenance anything but direct bilateral negotiations between Israel and the Arabs. (Kissinger had earlier acceded to Israeli demands that the United States coordinate its position on Middle East peacemaking privately with Israel beforehand, a commitment that has generally been kept over the succeeding three decades.) The American position became that issues had to be settled directly between the two sides, not in side deals between them and the United States, although it was understood that bilateral negotiations between the parties would ideally take place with an American "mediator" present to put a thumb on the scale in favor of Israel when necessary. In April 2004 President Bush discarded this principle by coming to formal agreements with Sharon on key issues relating to refugees and settlements in the absence of representatives of the Palestinians.

A far more important step in terms of whether there will ever be a state of Palestine—and for the standing of the United States in the Middle East and the world—was President Bush's effective repudiation of the principle of the "inadmissibility of the acquisition of territory by war." This phrase, which constitutes one of the core principles embodied in Security Council Resolution 242, has been the bedrock of peacemaking in the Middle East since the 1960s, and as such has been the firm policy of seven American administrations. This principle is grounded in the preamble and the first two articles of the UN Charter, and served as the basis for the campaign to expel Iraqi occupation forces from Kuwait in 1991, as well as other efforts to uphold international law and world order against the rule of the jungle. By cavalierly dismissing this crucial principle, and the related American position that Israeli settlements were an obstacle to peace (a position reiterated only a few years earlier under his father's administration in the American letter of assurance to the Palestinians, quoted above), with a description of the largest of Israel's illegal settlements as "new realities on the ground," George W. Bush has established an exceedingly dangerous precedent.

The president has done much more than that with this 2004 letter. By talking about settlement blocs (without specifying their extent, or which ones he was referring to) as "realities," he has powerfully reinforced the dynamic process of the expansion of Israeli settlements, and by so doing has helped to lay low, perhaps definitively, the increasingly dim prospects of an independent, sovereign, contiguous Palestinian state ever coming into being alongside Israel. Consequently, and paradoxically, George W. Bush has given an enormous impetus to the idea of a one-state solution, even as he was the first American president to make explicit a call for an independent Palestinian state alongside Israel.

This is a momentous change indeed. We must regard skeptically the statements of both President Bush and members of his administration about the United States' commitment to a Palestinian state. At best, this is wishful thinking; at worst, it is something much more sinister, to be understood in terms of something that ingenious Israeli theorists of continued expansion in the West Bank have termed "transport contiguity." This would involve a string of separate Palestinian cantons which would be constricted by the presence all around them of these very "settlement blocs" George W. Bush had just recognized as irreversible realities. "Contiguity" would be assured by linkages between separate isolated Palestinian cantons via tunnels and bridges, and perhaps a high-speed rail link.[52] The net effect of such a policy might be to enable Israel to settle in and annex the choicest sections of the West Bank, while leaving the remaining scraps for the Palestinians to call a "state" should they and others so choose.

It is true that on May 26, 2005, during the first visit to Washington by the new Palestinian president, Mahmoud Abbas, President Bush stated that any changes in the 1949 armistice line, the so-called Green Line, must be the result of negotiations, and would require Palestinian consent. This would seem to contradict the language of his letter of one year earlier to Sharon. However, this letter too called for "agreement between the parties to changes in the 1949 armistice lines," even while describing the settlement blocs as "new realities on the ground." And what the president was in effect reiterating in the April 2004 letter by expressing his support of Israel's retention of its massive "settlement blocs" and of its rejection of the return of any refugees to its territory was a constant of Arab-Israeli negotiations: that the parties were free to negotiate, but that during such negotiations the United States would very likely take Israel's side on the issues, irrespective of its previous commitments.

More important than the rhetoric of the Bush administration about a Palestinian state are a number of enduring and new realities. One of the former is that the putative locus for a truly independent, viable, contiguous Palestinian state is constantly and perhaps irrevocably shrinking, and may indeed have shrunk beyond the possibility of recovery. It is worth keeping in mind, however, that, as the historian Tony Judt has memorably noted, what one politician—American or Israeli—has done, another can undo. One of the new realities is that by removing the last feeble assertion of America's objection in principle to Israel's acquisition of territory by force, and to the building and expansion of illegal settlements, President Bush has given perhaps the last impetus necessary to the bulldozer-like progression of Israeli settlement enterprise across the length and breadth of the occupied West Bank and Arab East Jerusalem.

One can assume that the present Israeli government will make the most of the opportunity provided by these new circumstances. As to what this might entail, it would probably be wise to rely on the words of Sharon himself: he stated before suffering a stroke in January 2006 that his plan for unilateral withdrawals, endorsed by President Bush, would mean that there will be no Palestinian state for the foreseeable future. Sharon's closest advisor, Dov Weisglass, was even more emphatic: the entire idea of a political process with the Palestinians, and with it a Palestinian state, he said, had been put into "formaldehyde" by the Sharon plan, now endorsed by the United States.[53] As Sharon said, just before going to Washington in April 2004 to receive these assurances from President Bush, his plan meant the permanent annexation by Israel not of just one or two settlements, but of several vast settlement blocs, including in particular those that choke off East Jerusalem from its West Bank hinterland, and the Ariel settlement, which splits the northern part of the West Bank in two. The ongoing and ceaseless expansion of these settlement blocs, and their enclosure in the system of great walls, fences, and barriers being rapidly erected by Israel at enormous cost, has now been legitimized by President Bush, and will eventually turn the West Bank permanently into numerous small cantons. Even if the ghost of Orwell rises and walks again, and American and Israeli leaders in future choose to call this patchwork of open-air prison camps a "state," the possibility of a real Palestinian state may well have disappeared with President Bush's April 2004 letter to Sharon.

The future of the Palestinians and of the state of Israel, and the question of whether there will ever be a state of Palestine, will in some measure be defined by these realities, and by how they develop in the near future. In the end, of course, this attempt to impose an American-Israeli devised settlement will backfire: no "agreement" that does not have the freely expressed consent of the Palestinian people will stand, any more than would an agreement made in the absence of representatives of the Israeli people. In the long run, the settlements and the walls that are built to confine the Palestinians can only provoke further Palestinian humiliation, which will lead to further resistance, and perhaps stimulate different political forms and political leadership. The victory of Hamas in the January 2006 PLC elections, and its possible acquiescence in a two-state solution, may be only the beginning of such new forms. The overwhelming negative reaction, the world over, to the processes taking place on the ground in Palestine/Israel will ultimately have an effect. Sooner or later Israelis themselves will realize, as some of their most respected intellectuals already have, that the way to deal with the hostility of the colonized is not to repress it, but to dismantle the structures of colonialism and repression that originally engendered it.[54]

In the meantime, the entire process will involve further damage to the standing of the United States, whose effective support of settlement, colonization, theft, and occupation make it look to all the world like a superpower bully, conniving its powerful local ally to impose its will on the weak and the powerless. Combined with its tragic and epically misguided adventure in Iraq, the Bush administration has brought the standing of the United States in the Middle East lower than ever before in American history. It will soon be hard to recall that the United States was until relatively recently favorably regarded in the region.[55]

What are we left with, as far as the state of Palestine is concerned? Certainly the aspirations of the Palestinians to live as a sovereign people in their own land are likely to be further denied, for a time at least and perhaps lastingly. Their ability to exercise sovereignty in the context of a viable independent Palestinian state may well have been closed off permanently by the success of Sharon's program, materially abetted by the collusion of the Bush administration over six crucial years. Thus if the Palestinian people are to exercise their inalienable national rights, they must take the initiative and devise new forms and conceptions for the future, suitable to the situation in which they find themselves, to their increasing subjugation and denial of rights, to being, in effect, captives of the powerful Israeli nation-state. It is hoped that these forms will be more imaginative, more comprehensive, and more effective than those that have gone before, and that they will produce a more successful leadership.

But unless what politicians have done is undone by other politicians—something that now seems unlikely given President Bush's issuance, in his April 2004 letter, of what has been hyperbolically described as amounting to a new Balfour Declaration—or unless, by some tragic happenstance, ethnic cleansing again takes place in Palestine (which also seems unlikely, in view of the apparent determination of the Palestinians not to allow themselves to be driven yet again from their homes), one thing appears certain. The realities on the ground will drive the Palestinians and the Israelis now living under the unique sovereignty and control of Israel into an entirely new configuration. How long the current configuration will continue (a situation worse, in some senses, than apartheid); what will follow after its evolution, if it does evolve; and what the state of Palestine will be at the end of the process, no one can say. It will certainly not improve if there is a continuing refusal to look honestly at what has happened in this small land over the past century or so, and especially at how repeatedly forcing the Palestinians into an impossible corner, into an iron cage, has brought, and ultimately can bring, no lasting good to anyone.

Notes

Introduction: Writing Middle Eastern History in a Time of Historical Amnesia

1. For a reflection on the implications of devastating failure, see Marc Bloch, *L'Etrange défaite: Témoignage écrit en 1940*, repr. (Paris, Gallimard, 1990).

2. There is no shortage of voices in the blame-the-victim school, which still dominates official Israeli historiography, from the "their leaders told them to leave" canard as an explanation of the expulsion and flight of the Palestinian refugees in 1948—repeated by Likud minister Limor Livnat in an article in *Le Monde* on December 21, 2001 (the Israeli historian Shlomo Sand delivered a devastating reply in the same paper on January 5, 2002), and again in the *Los Angeles Times* on December 28, 2001—to longtime Israeli foreign minister Abba Eban's deathless claim that the Palestinians "never miss an opportunity to miss an opportunity." Whatever kernel of truth this old chestnut may contain, it absolves Israel of any responsibility for the failure to achieve peace. Israeli historians have amply shown that Israel in fact did repeatedly miss, or avoid, opportunities for a peaceful solution, especially during the 1950s. See, for example, Itamar Rabinovich, *The Road Not Taken: Early Arab-Israeli Negotiations* (New York: Oxford University Press, 1991); Avi Shlaim, *Collusion across the Jordan: King Abdullah, the Zionist Movement, and the Partition of Palestine* (New York: Columbia University Press, 1988) and *The Iron Wall: Israel and the Arab World* (New York: Norton, 2001); Ilan Pappé, *The Making of the Arab-Israeli Conflict, 1947–51* (London: Tauris, 1994) and *A History of Modern Palestine: One Land, Two Peoples* (Cambridge, U.K.: Cambridge University Press, 2004); and Benny Morris, *Israel's Border Wars, 1949–1956: Arab Infiltration, Israeli Retaliation, and the Countdown to the Suez War* (Oxford, U.K.: Oxford University Press, 1993).

3. *Introduction to* The Philosophy of History, translated by Leo Rauch (Indianapolis: Hackett, 1988), 35.

4. Rashid Khalidi, *Palestinian Identity: The Construction of Modern National Consciousness* (New York: Columbia University Press, 1997).

5. Boston: Beacon Press, 2004.

6. For early examples of this new scrutiny of Saudi Arabia see "Dismay with Saudi Arabia Fuels Pullout Talk," *New York Times,* January 16, 2002; and "Saudis May Seek U.S. Exit: Military Presence Seen As Political Liability in the Arab World," *Washington Post,* January 18, 2002, A1.

7. During the Israeli invasion of Lebanon, more than seventeen thousand people were killed, the vast majority of them civilians, according to Lebanese official

sources: see Rashid Khalidi, *Under Siege: PLO Decision-Making during the 1982 War* (New York: Columbia University Press, 1986), 200, n. 5.

8. For example, the vitriolic reactions by extreme supporters of Israel to a study by John Mearsheimer and Steve Walt, "The Israel Lobby and U.S. Foreign Policy" (Cambridge, Mass.: Harvard University John F. Kennedy School of Government Faculty Working Papers, RWP06–011, March 2006). A shorter version appeared in the *London Review of Books* 28, no. 6 (March 23, 2006).

9. The man once described by Usama Bin Laden as his "spiritual guide," the Palestinian Islamist theoretician 'Abdullah 'Azzam, was the author of a book titled *al-Waba al-Ahmar* [The Red Plague], describing the PLO as a godless front for communist subversion, a point of view that at the time was congenial to, and supported or subsidized by, the United States, Saudi Arabia, and Israel.

10. Tariq Ali, "Au nom du 'choc des civilisations,' " *Le Monde Diplomatique,* October 2001.

11. At his conspiracy trial, it emerged that 'Abd al-Rahman was allowed into the United States because of his past connections with U.S. intelligence.

12. For details, see Ali Laidi, "L'hypothèse de la piste saoudienne," *Le Monde,* October 5, 2001, 16.

13. See Richard Sale, "Israel Gave Major Aid to Hamas," UPI, February 24, 2001. See also Shaul Mishal and Avraham Sela, *Palestinian Hamas: Vision, Violence and Coexistence* (New York: Columbia University Press, 2000).

14. For an example of how such crucial elements of any rational explanation for recent events are obscured in favor of essentialist, if ostensibly erudite, ones, see Bernard Lewis, "The Revolt of Islam," *The New Yorker,* November 19, 2001, 50–63.

15. Even though this number gives Jews only a bare majority of the total combined population of Israel and the Palestinian territories it had, by 2006, controlled for nearly forty years.

16. Susan Silsby Boyle, *Betrayal of Palestine: The Story of George Antonius* (Boulder, Colo.: Westview, 2001), 13. Boyle's first chapter (1–22) gives a good account of the St. James Palace Conference of February and March 1939 that resulted in the White Paper.

17. This is the main topic of Chapter 2.

18. The reference is to *The Invention of Tradition,* ed. Eric Hobsbawm and Terence Ranger (Cambridge, U.K.: Cambridge University Press, 1992).

19. Israeli officials, for example, escorted Brotherhood agents during an attack on the Palestine Red Crescent headquarters in Gaza, as Dr. Haidar 'Abd al-Shafi (then president of the Gaza Red Crescent Society) described the incident to me (interview, Gaza, August 9, 1999). In another instance the Israeli security services bussed Islamist activists across Israel from the tightly controlled Gaza Strip to the West Bank to break up demonstrations at al-Najah University in Nablus, as described to me by Muhammad Shadid, who at the time was an

al-Najah faculty member and was beaten up in the melee (interview, Beirut, April 24, 1983).

20. See S. Abdullah Schleifer, "'Izz al-Din al-Qassam: Preacher and *Mujahid*," in E. Burke III, ed., *Struggle and Survival in the Modern Middle East* (Berkeley: University of California Press, 1993), and "The Life and Thought of 'Izz-id-Din al-Qassam," *Islamic Quarterly* 22, no. 2 (1979): 61–81.

21. For more on the author's views on this topic, see Rashid Khalidi, "Toward a Clear Palestinian Strategy," *Journal of Palestine Studies* 31, no. 4 (summer 2002): 5–12, and *Resurrecting Empire: Western Footprints and America's Perilous Path in the Middle East* (Boston: Beacon Press, 2004), 142–46. It should be added that Palestinian civilian casualties from the equally morally indefensible use of massive firepower in heavily populated Palestinian areas (some Gaza Strip refugee camps have three times the population density of Manhattan) by the Israeli occupation forces were over four times as high as Israeli civilian casualties between the beginning of the second intifada in September 2000 and what appeared to be its end in early 2005.

22. According to the article by Richard Sale, UPI's "terrorism correspondent," cited in n. 13, the Israeli intelligence services did more than encourage the Palestinian branch of the Muslim Brotherhood and its 1987 offshoot, Hamas. Sale quotes "several current and former U.S. intelligence officials" as stating that Israel "gave direct and indirect financial aid to Hamas over a period of years," with the aim of weakening the PLO.

23. Danny Rubinstein, "Warrier from the West Bank," *Haaretz*, October 16, 2001. See also Husni Adham Jarrar, *al-Shahid 'Abd Allah 'Azzam, rajul da'wa wa madrasat jihad* [The Martyr 'Abdullah 'Azzam, a Preacher and a School of Jihad] (Amman: Dar al-Diya': 1990).

24. Ibid. For more on 'Azzam and Bin Laden, see Gilles Kepel, *Jihad: The Trail of Political Islam* (London: Tauris, 2002), 313–22, and Jonathan Randal, *Osama: The Making of a Terrorist* (New York: Knopf, 2004), 86–97.

25. Private communication with the author by an individual deeply familiar with Saudi Arabia and the Bin Laden family, Washington, D.C., December 12, 2001. See also Randal, *Osama*.

26. For details, see Randal, *Osama*, 68–81.

27. "Terrorism: Theirs and Ours," presentation at the University of Colorado, Boulder, October 12, 1998, published in Iqbal Ahmad, *Terrorism: Theirs and Ours*, foreword by and interview with David Barsamian (New York: Seven Stories Press, 2001), 11–26.

28. New York: Pantheon, 2004.

29. Randal, *Osama*, 90.

30. For British strategic thinking about Palestine before the Balfour Declaration, see Rashid Khalidi, *British Policy towards Syria and Palestine, 1906–1914* (Oxford, U.K.: Ithaca Press, 1980).

31. Shlaim, *Collusion across the Jordan* and *The Iron Wall*; Pappé, *The Making of*

the Arab-Israeli Conflict and A History of Modern Palestine; Tom Segev, 1949:
The First Israelis (New York: Free Press, 1986), and One Palestine, Complete:
Jews and Arabs under the Palestine Mandate (New York: Metropolitan Books,
2000; a new book by Segev on the 1967 war, 1967: Veha-arets shintah et paneha
[1967: And the Land Changed Its Face] (Jerusalem: Keter, 2005), is forthcoming in English from Metropolitan in 2007); Benny Morris, The Birth of the
Palestinian Refugee Problem, 1947–1949 (Cambridge, U.K.: Cambridge University Press, 1987), Righteous Victims: A History of the Zionist-Arab Conflict,
1881–1999 (New York: Knopf, 1999), and Israel's Border Wars. See also Simha
Flapan, The Birth of Israel: Myths and Realities (New York: Pantheon, 1987),
one of the first books to make some of these points, and Gershon Shafir, Land,
Labor and the Origins of the Israeli-Palestinian Conflict, 1882–1914 (Cambridge,
U.K.: Cambridge University Press, 1989).

32. Five is the figure given by Michael J. Cohen, Truman and Israel (Berkeley:
University of California Press, 1990), 223. Terence Prittie and B. Deneen,
The Double Exodus, speak of four armies and contingents promised by three
other states, cited in Flapan, The Birth of Israel, 189.

33. B. Morris, Righteous Victims, 232, says the two battalions of the Lebanese army
(of that army's total of four) deployed in the south of the country "apparently
never crossed the border."

34. A. Shlaim, Collusion across the Jordan.

35. B. Morris, Righteous Victims, 232–33, notes that a force of two infantry battalions, supported by light tanks and artillery, crossed the border on May 16,
1948, retreated four days later, and retreated again after another abortive attack
on June 5. It succeeded in winning a six-by-three-mile toehold across the Jordan five days later. This was the extent of the Syrian invasion.

36. Some of these documents can be consulted by historians; thus Susan Boyle
used the George Antonius papers, some of which are in the Israel State
Archives, in her book Betrayal of Palestine.

37. Morris, in The Birth of the Palestinian Refugee Problem, writes of "the continued unavailability of Arab state papers." However, Salim Yacoub used the
Egyptian archives in writing Containing Arab Nationalism: The Eisenhower
Doctrine and the Middle East (Chapel Hill: University of North Carolina Press,
2004); Madiha al-Madfai used those of Jordan for Jordan, the United States
and the Middle East Peace Process, 1974–1991 (Cambridge, U.K.: Cambridge
University Press, 1992); several studies in Arabic utilized Iraq's Foreign Ministry and other archives; for the Arab League, see Walid Khalidi, "The Arab
Perspective," in Wm. Roger Louis and Robert W. Stookey, eds., The End of
the Palestine Mandate (Austin: University of Texas Press, 1986), 104–36.

38. For example, Sefer toldot ha-Haganah [History of the Haganah] (Tel Aviv:
Am Oved, 1972).

39. The Palestine Research Center's holdings included all or part of the private
papers of a number of Palestinian and Arab figures prominent in the first half

of the twentieth century, such as 'Auni 'Abd al-Hadi, Muhib al-Din al-Khatib, Fawzi al-Qawuqji, and 'Izzat Darwaza; those of the Arab Studies Society include important papers of Musa al-'Alami and of the Arab Information Office that he headed.

40. The archive of the Palestine Research Center was returned to the PLO by Israel as part of a prisoner exchange in 1984, and transferred to Algeria, but its current whereabouts is unknown. The archive of the Arab Studies Society was sealed during each period of Israeli government closure of Orient House, and may have been removed, together with other files, during the most recent Israeli seizure of the premises, ongoing at this time.

41. Morris refrained from interviewing these subjects, claiming that information gained from such interviews was unreliable: *The Birth of the Palestinian Refugee Problem*, 2.

42. The earliest narratives focusing on the Palestinians, from a Palestinian perspective, for all or most of this entire period include the works of Naji 'Allush, *al-Muqawama al-'Arabiyya fi Filastin* [The Arab Resistance in Palestine] (Beirut: Dar al-Tali'a, 1968); 'Abd al-Qadir Yasin, *Kifah al-sha'b al-filastini qabl al-'am 1948* [The Struggle of the Palestinian People before the Year 1948] (Beirut: PLO Research Center, 1975); and 'Abd al-Wahhab al-Kayyali, *The Modern History of Palestine* (London: Croom Helm, 1978); from an Israeli perspective, Yehoshua Porath, *The Emergence of the Palestinian-Arab National Movement, 1918–1929* (London: Cass, 1974), and *The Palestinian Arab National Movement: From Riots to Rebellion, 1929–1939* (London: Cass, 1977); and Ann Mosely Lesch, *Arab Politics in Palestine, 1917–1939: The Frustration of a Nationalist Movement* (Ithaca, N.Y.: Cornell University Press, 1979). See also J. C. Hurewitz, *The Struggle for Palestine* (New York: Norton, 1950; 2nd ed., New York: Schocken, 1976); John Marlowe, *The Seat of Pilate: An Account of the Palestine Mandate* (London: Cresset, 1959); and Christopher Sykes, *Crossroads to Israel, 1917–1948*.

The numerous monographs addressing specific aspects of the larger story of the Palestinians during the Mandate period include (in addition to books cited in n. 31) Ylana Miller, *Government and Society in Rural Palestine 1920–1948* (Austin: University of Texas Press, 1985); Michael Palumbo, *The Palestinian Catastrophe* (London: Faber, 1987); Uri Kupferschmidt, *The Supreme Muslim Council: Islam under the British Mandate for Palestine* (Leiden: Brill, 1987); Philip Mattar, *The Mufti of Jerusalem: Al-Hajj Amin al-Husayni and the Palestinian National Movement* (New York: Columbia University Press, 1988); Muhammad Muslih, *The Origins of Palestinian Nationalism* (New York: Columbia University Press, 1988); Issa Khalaf, *Arab Factionalism and Social Disintegration, 1939–1948* (Albany: State University of New York Press, 1991); Bernard Wasserstein, *The British in Palestine: The Mandatory Government and the Arab-Jewish Conflict, 1917–1929*, 2nd ed. (Oxford, U.K.: Basil Blackwell, 1991); May Seikaly, *Haifa: Transformation of an Arab Society,*

1918–1939 (London: Tauris, 1995); Ted Swedenburg, *Memories of Revolt: The 1936–1939 Rebellion and the Palestinian National Past* (Minneapolis: University of Minnesota Press, 1995); Yitzhak Reiter, *Islamic Endowments in Jerusalem under British Mandate* (London: Cass, 1996). Notable also are works by the eminent scholar Walid Khalidi: *Before Their Diaspora: A Photographic History of the Palestinians, 1876–1948* (Beirut: Institute for Palestine Studies, 1987); (ed.), *All That Remains: The Palestinian Villages Occupied and Depopulated by Israel in 1948* (Washington, D.C.: Institute for Palestine Studies, 1992); *Khamsuna ʿaman ʿala taqsim Filastin (1947–1997)* [Fifty Years since the Partition of Palestine] (Beirut: Dar al-Nahar, 1998), and *Dayr Yasin: al-Jumʿa, 9/4/1948* [Dayr Yasin: Friday, 9/4/1948] (Beirut: Institute for Palestine Studies, 1999). W. Khalidi also wrote a seminal series of articles in the late 1950s and early 1960s analyzing the events of 1948.

43. Three cover the entire Mandate period: Henry Laurens, *La question de Palestine*, vol. 2, *1922–1947: Une mission sacrée de civilisation* (Paris: Fayard, 2002); Segev, *One Palestine, Complete*; and Naomi Shepherd, *Ploughing the Sand: British Rule in Palestine, 1917–1948* (London: John Murray, 1999). Three others cover central aspects of it: Boyle, *Betrayal of Palestine*; Sahar Huneidi, *A Broken Trust: Herbert Samuel, Zionism, and the Palestinians* (London: Tauris, 2001); and Benny Morris, *The Road to Jerusalem: Glubb Pasha, Palestine and the Jews* (London: Tauris, 2002). Other more general recent works, such as Bernard Wasserstein, *Divided Jerusalem: The Struggle for the Holy City*, 2nd ed. (New Haven: Yale University Press, 2002), Morris, *Righteous Victims*, and Shlaim, *The Iron Wall*, include discussions of the Mandate.

44. R. Khalidi, *Palestinian Identity*.

1. Arab Society in Mandatory Palestine

1. The only subdistrict of Palestine that had a Jewish majority was Jaffa, where Tel Aviv is located. Justin McCarthy, *The Population of Palestine: Population Statistics of the Late Ottoman Period and the Mandate* (New York: Columbia University Press, 1990), table, 37, indicates that in 1946 the Arab population of Palestine was 1,339,773, and the Jewish population 602,586. Both had grown larger by 1948. Population by subdistrict is cited in the report of the UN General Assembly committee to consider the United Nations Special Committee on Palestine (UNSCOP) minority report, November 11, 1947, cited in Walid Khalidi, *From Haven to Conquest: Readings in Zionism and the Palestine Problem until 1948*, 2nd printing (Washington, D.C.: Institute for Palestine Studies, 1987), 678, map, 671.

2. W. Khalidi, *From Haven to Conquest*, 680, map, 673, gives UN figures, based on British Mandate statistics. According to these, in 1945 Jews owned 10.6 percent of the privately owned land in Palestine; Arabs owned almost all the rest.

3. The exact number of Palestinian refugees in 1948 is difficult to ascertain, and has long been highly disputed. Contemporary UN estimates put the figure at over 750,000, while Morris, *The Birth of the Palestinian Refugee Problem*, 1, writes of "some 600,000–760,000" refugees. The first figure given by Morris is low; the latter is probably closer to the truth. Morris's book, which drew on the newly opened Israeli archives to dispel some of the most tenacious myths regarding the Palestinian refugees, has become the standard work on this topic. See also Morris's *1948 and After*, rev. ed. (Oxford, U.K.: Oxford University Press, 1994). Norman G. Finkelstein argues convincingly that Morris fails to draw the requisite conclusions from the damning evidence he assembles: see *Image and Reality of the Israel-Palestine Conflict* (London: Verso, 1995), 51–87. Among the first to publish results of research in the Israeli archives regarding the Palestinian refugees that reached conclusions similar to those of Morris were Segev, *1949*, and Flapan, *The Birth of Israel*, published in 1986 and 1987, respectively.

4. For details see Chapter 4.

5. Segev, *1949*, describes Jewish immigration and some of the other rapid changes during the first year of Israel's existence, and the early, and enduring, tensions in the new polity.

6. For a new account of the fall of Tiberias based on Arab and Zionist primary sources, see Abbasi, *Journal of Palestine Studies* 35, no. 4 (forthcoming, summer 2006).

7. This is according to the last British population estimates of 1944.

8. McCarthy, *The Population of Palestine*, table, 163.

9. The most careful work on the topic is W. Khalidi, ed., *All That Remains*, which enumerates 418 such villages, describing in detail what is known about what happened to each. See also Morris, *The Birth of the Palestinian Refugee Problem*, and the extraordinary book by Meron Benvenisti that details the cartographic transformation that followed the demographic one: *Sacred Landscape: The Buried History of the Holy Land since 1948* (Berkeley: University of California Press, 2000).

10. The term appears in the title of the seminal work by Qustantin Zurayq, *Ma'na al-Nakba* [The Meaning of the Catastrophe] (Beirut: Dar al-'Ilm lil-Malayin, 1948). Translated by R. Bayley Winder as *The Meaning of the Disaster* (Beirut: Khayat, 1956). Zurayq was a Princeton-trained historian of Damascene origin who served as a Syrian government minister, acting president of the American University of Beirut, president of the Syrian University, and chairman of the board of trustees of the Institute for Palestine Studies.

11. It was Israel's first prime minister, David Ben-Gurion himself, who gave canonical form to these allegations in a 1961 speech, as is pointed out by Ilan Pappé in *The Making of the Arab-Israeli Conflict*, 88–89.

12. Morris, *The Birth of the Palestinian Refugee Problem*, Segev, *1949*, and Flapan,

The Birth of Israel, all contributed to this refutation, as did Shlaim, *Collusion across the Jordan,* and Pappé, *The Making of the Arab-Israeli Conflict.* See also Palumbo, *The Palestinian Catastrophe.*

13. In many cases, Israeli revisionist works substantiated the much earlier findings of researchers like Walid Khalidi and Erskine Childers. See Walid Khalidi, "Plan *Dalet:* The Zionist Master Plan for the Conquest of Palestine," *Middle East Forum* 37, no. 9 (November 1961): 22–28; "The Fall of Haifa," *Middle East Forum* 35, no. 10 (December 1959): 22–32; "Why Did the Palestinians Leave?" *Middle East Forum* 34, no. 6 (July, 1959): 21–24, 35; and Erskine Childers, "The Other Exodus," *Spectator,* no. 6933 (May 12, 1961): 672–75, and "The Wordless Wish: From Citizens to Refugees," in Ibrahim Abu Lughod, ed., *The Transformation of Palestine* (Evanston, Il.: Northwestern University Press, 1971), 165–202. Khalidi's "Plan *Dalet,*" together with the fascinating 1961 correspondence both it and Childers' work generated, and a number of appendices, is reproduced in *Journal of Palestine Studies* 18, no. 1 (autumn 1988): 4–70.

14. Some six thousand Israelis, about 1 percent of the population, were killed in both phases of what Israelis call their War of Independence. Palestinian casualties during the war are unknown.

15. The best discussion of this topic is in Nur Masalha, *Expulsion of the Palestinians: The Concept of "Transfer" in Zionist Political Thought, 1882–1948* (Beirut: Institute for Palestine Studies, 1992). See also Morris, *The Birth of the Palestinian Refugee Problem,* and Pappé, *The Making of the Arab-Israeli Conflict.*

16. An exception is Tom Segev in his 2000 book, *One Palestine, Complete,* which uses the memoirs of Khalil Sakakini and several other contemporary Palestinian observers of events before 1948.

17. Benny Morris explains that he specifically avoided oral sources in his work because of the greater propensity of interviewees, as compared with contemporary documents, to "misinform, distort, omit or lie," which, given the absence of Palestinian archives discussed in the introduction, necessarily meant a reliance on Israeli and British documentary sources. *The Birth of the Palestinian Refugee Problem,* 2.

18. See notably Henry Laurens, *La question de Palestine,* vol. 1, *1799–1922: L'invention de la Terre sainte* (Paris: Fayard, 1999), and vol. 2, *1922–1947: Une mission sacrée de civilisation* (Paris: Fayard, 2002); and Gudrun Kramer, *Geschichte Palästinas: Von der osmanischen Eroberung bis zur Gründung des Staates Israel* (Munich: Beck, 2002).

19. Morris in particular makes this assertion in *The Birth of the Palestinian Refugee Problem,* 128–31, 286–7.

20. An excellent analysis of this phenomenon, and an examination of several specific cases based on interviews, can be found in the dissertation of Jihan Sfeir-Khayat, "Les premier temps de l'installation des Palestiniens au Liban, 1947–1952" (Institut National des Langues et Civilisations Orientales, Paris, 2005), 47–48.

21. For examples of these Arab views, see, e.g., Ghassan Kanafani, *Thawrat 1936 fi Filastin: Khalfiyyat wa tafasil wa tahlil* [The 1936 Revolt in Palestine: Context, Details and Analysis] (Beirut: Popular Front for the Liberation of Palestine, 1974); A. W. Kayyali, *Palestine: A Modern History* (London: Croom Helm, 1978); Naji 'Allush, *al-Muqawama al-'Arabiyya fi Filastin*.

22. E.g., Naseer Aruri, *Jordan: A Study in Political Development, 1921–1965* (The Hague: Nijhoff, 1972); 'Abdullah al-Tal, *Karithat Filastin: Muthakirrat 'Abdullah al-Tal, qa'id ma'rakat al-Quds* [The Disaster of Palestine: The Memoirs of 'Abdullah al-Tal, Commander in the Battle for Jerusalem] (Cairo: Dar al-Qalam, 1959).

23. 'Abdullah al-Tal, *Karithat Filastin*.

24. Shlaim, *Collusion across the Jordan*.

25. W. Khalidi, in *From Haven to Conquest*, Appendices 8, 9A, and 9B, 858–71, was the first to show that far from having superior forces, the Palestinian irregular forces were inferior in number to the Zionist military formations, and that after May 15 the same was true of the Arab armies in the field in Palestine as compared with the new Israeli army. Khalidi also was one of the first to use Arab primary sources to show the bitterness of the divisions among the Arab states in 1948: W. Khalidi, "The Arab Perspective."

26. The latest and most comprehensive account of this atrocity is W. Khalidi, *Dayr Yasin*.

27. These include first Zurayq, *Ma'na al-Nakba*, and more recently Khalaf, *Arab Factionalism*; Mattar, *The Mufti of Jerusalem*; and R. Khalidi, *Palestinian Identity*.

28. Ministère des Affaires Étrangères, *Correspondence politique et commerciale, Levant* (hereafter MAE), (Palestine, 1930–1940), vol. 69, *Religion musulmane*, [Jacques] d'Aumale to Minister of Foreign Affairs, December 2, 1931.

29. Ibid., d'Aumale to Minister of Foreign Affairs, January 18, 1932.

30. Israeli prime minister Golda Meir made the canonical statement of the "they did not exist" thesis in 1969: *Sunday Times* (London), June 15, 1969, 12. Even ostensibly objective accounts, such as that of Morris in *Righteous Victims*, 253, give the impression that the Palestinians had little political or social cohesion in the period leading up to 1948.

31. The tendency to make such comparisons can be seen, for example, in Hurewitz, *The Struggle for Palestine*, chapters 2–4. Another type of comparison, in this case of the separate Arab and Jewish economies of Palestine, can be found in Jacob Metzer, *The Divided Economy of Mandatory Palestine* (Cambridge: Cambridge University Press, 1998). The statistics kept by the Jewish Agency, some of the best in the region during the mandatory period, rigorously divided the two economies, for obvious reasons, and this division is reproduced in the sources using these statistics, such as the Jewish Agency for Palestine, Economic Research Institute, *Statistical Handbook of Middle Eastern Countries: Palestine, Cyprus, Egypt, Iraq, The Lebanon, Syria, Transjordan,*

Turkey (Jerusalem: Jewish Agency, 1945), and Robert Nathan, Oscar Gass, and Daniel Creamer, *Palestine: Problem and Promise, An Economic Study* (Washington, D.C.: Public Affairs Press, 1946), both reflecting the Zionist perspective, as well as Said Himadeh, ed., *Economic Organization of Palestine* (Beirut: American University of Beirut, 1938), reflecting an Arab perspective. For yet another type of comparison, see W. Khalidi, *From Haven to Conquest*, Appendices 8, 9A, and 9B, 858–71, which compares the military capabilities of the Arab and Jewish sides during different phases of the 1948 fighting.

32. For figures on relative numbers of Palestinian and Zionist forces see W. Khalidi, *From Haven to Conquest*, Appendices 8, 9A, and 9B, and Haim Levenberg, *The Military Preparations of the Arab Community of Palestine, 1945–48* (London: Cass, 1993).

33. See, for example, MAE, Palestine, vol. 69, *Religion musulmane*, Minister of Foreign Affairs to Lucien Saint, Resident General, Rabat, n.d. [November 1929]; MAE, Palestine, Minister to d'Aumale, Consul General, Jerusalem, February 3, 1930. This is part of a lengthy correspondence related to a request from Palestinians of Moroccan origin under French protection to raise money in Morocco in support of the religious endowments (*waqf*) of the Moroccan Quarter in Jerusalem, and in particular the Abu Midyan mosque. The original request for a fund-raising trip to North Africa by a Palestinian delegation of Moroccan origin was refused, as were all similar requests, although d'Aumale eventually convinced the French government to send a small sum for this purpose (however, it took ten months for the money, FFr. 10,000, equal to $400 at the time, to be delivered). The same correspondence mentions in passing that over FFr. 130,000 ($5,200 at the time) was raised among North African Jewish communities and sent to Palestine immediately after the 1929 massacres, with other sums following later, as part of ongoing Zionist fund-raising that took place without obstruction from the French authorities.

34. In 1926 the Jewish population of Palestine as a proportion of the total reached its highest percentage since 1917: 18.4 percent. However, due to very low immigration figures for the next few years, and a large number of emigrants, the proportion thereafter declined to 17.7 percent in 1928, and barely rose again until 1933. See W. Khalidi, *From Haven to Conquest*, Appendix 1, 842–43, and Barbara Smith, *The Roots of Separatism in Palestine: British Economic Policy, 1920–1929* (Syracuse, N.Y.: Syracuse University Press, 1993), Table 3, 65.

35. Cited in Shabtai Teveth, *Ben Gurion and the Palestinian Arabs: From Peace to War* (New York: Oxford University Press, 1985), 166–68.

36. MAE, Palestine, vol. 68, *Sionisme*, Memo by Cannat (director of the Bureau of Political and Commercial Affairs at the Quai d'Orsay) of meeting with von Weisl, June 29, 1935.

37. W. Khalidi, *From Haven to Conquest*, Appendix 1, 842–43, and B. Smith, *The Roots of Separatism in Palestine*, Table 3, 65. The explosive increase in the Jewish population during the 1930s was particularly striking in view of its decline

as a proportion of the total population from 1926 to 1929, from 18.4 percent to 17.7 percent, mentioned in n. 34 above, and was so perceived at the time by both sides in the conflict.

38. This may help to explain the intensive efforts in 1930 and 1931 by Dr. Chaim Weizmann, Dr. Arthur Jacobsen, and other leading Zionists, via the intermediary of politicians like the French Socialist Party leader and future prime minister Léon Blum, to lobby French officials to persuade them to open up Syria and Lebanon to Zionist land purchase and colonization. See extensive correspondence filling most of MAE, Palestine, vol. 68, *Sionisme*, for those two years and sporadically into 1935. Although Weizmann and Jacobsen met with the prime minister, Aristide Briand, the foreign minister, Philippe Berthelot, and many other senior officials, the French were not eager to inflame Syrian nationalist sentiment so soon after the suppression of the 1925–26 nationalist revolt against the French mandatory power, and discreetly declined to go along with this project.

39. According to Metzer, *The Divided Economy of Mandatory Palestine*, 15–16, the Arab share of the economy of Palestine shrank from 81 percent in 1922 to 56 percent in 1931, declining to 43 percent in 1933 and staying in the 42–45 percent range for the rest of the Mandate period. See also Nathan, Gass, and Creamer, *Palestine: Problem and Promise*, Table 1, 148.

40. Note, however, the cautions of Marcel Detienne, *Comparer l'incomparable* (Paris: Seuil, 2000), 29–32, who shows how in the light of a certain smug historical practice, only particular "superior" societies—nations with an "ancient" lineage like England, Spain, or France—can be compared. This is relevant to our case, since Detienne argues that comparisons generally start from a national perspective, with the aim of showing the superiority of one's nation, and from this perspective *les sans-ecrits*—in effect "lesser" peoples— have to be treated in a completely different way. Much Israeli and Western historiography wherein "self" and "other"—specifically the Israeli self and the inferior Arab other—are contrasted, even casually, can be understood perfectly in these terms.

41. Zeev Sternhell, *The Founding Myths of Israel* (Princeton, N.J.: Princeton University Press, 1998), 217.

42. W. Khalidi, *From Haven to Conquest*, Appendix 5, 851–52.

43. Metzer, *The Divided Economy of Mandatory Palestine*, 16, Table 1.3.

44. Ibid., 16–20. See also Roger Owen, "Economic Development in Mandatory Palestine," in George Abed, ed., *The Palestinian Economy: Studies in Development under Prolonged Occupation* (London: Routledge, 1988), 13–15.

45. Owen, "Economic Development," Table 2.6, 26.

46. Metzer, *The Divided Economy of Mandatory Palestine*, 16.

47. Literacy figures are extrapolated from the table in Nathan, Gass and Creamer, *Palestine: Problem and Promise*, 142, and from Jewish Agency for Palestine, *Statistical Handbook of Middle Eastern Countries*, Table 9, 6. Metzer, *The*

Divided Economy of Mandatory Palestine, 54, using different sources, gives the slightly lower figure of 18.6 percent literacy for the Arabs.

48. Metzer, *The Divided Economy of Mandatory Palestine*, 52.

49. A. L. Tibawi, *Arab Education in Mandatory Palestine: A Study of Three Decades of British Administration* (London: Luzac, 1956), tables, 270–71. Again, Metzer, *The Divided Economy of Mandatory Palestine*, 53, gives lower figures, but those of Tibawi seem preferable given his access to the mandatory government's education statistics, and his detailed breakdown of figures.

50. Metzer, *The Divided Economy of Mandatory Palestine*, 53.

51. Ibid., 49.

52. For figures on the expansion of education in Palestine before 1914, see R. Khalidi, *Palestinian Identity*, 46–53.

53. Figures extrapolated from a variety of sources by Metzer, *The Divided Economy of Mandatory Palestine*, 56–57.

54. Ibid., table, 9, showing 26.490 in 1931 and 1946.

55. Kenneth Stein, *The Land Question in Palestine, 1917–1939* (Chapel Hill: University of North Carolina Press, 1984), 211. Stein shows that the Zionist movement's ultimate ability to take control of most of Palestine was largely a function of the establishment of a strategic chain of settlements in the shape of the letter *N* running north along the coast from Tel Aviv to Haifa, from there south-eastward down the Plain of Esdraelon/Marj Ibn 'Amer to Beisan, and northward along the finger of eastern Galilee, shown in map, 210.

56. Jewish Agency, *Statistical Handbook*, Table 4, 3. The figures are based on a 1942 estimate. They are slightly different from those of Metzer in n. 53.

57. The figures for the Jewish population are from ibid., Table 8, 6, and are a Jewish Agency estimate dating from 1943; those for the Arab population are from the 1931 census, cited in Himadeh, ed., *Economic Organization of Palestine*, Table 17, 34. Typically, there is more and better data for the Jewish than for the Arab population of Palestine.

58. Sternhell, *Founding Myths*, 14. See also Anita Shapira, *L'Imaginaire d'Israël: Histoire d'une culture politique* (Paris: Calmann Levy, 2005).

59. Metzer, *The Divided Economy of Mandatory Palestine*, 60–61.

60. R. Khalidi, *Palestinian Identity*.

61. See Zachary Lockman, *Comrades and Enemies: Arab and Jewish Workers in Palestine, 1906–1948* (Berkeley: University of California Press, 1996), and Musa Budeiri, *The Palestine Communist Party 1919–1948: Arab and Jew in the Struggle for Internationalism* (London: Ithaca, 1979).

62. Baruch Kimmerling, *The Invention and Decline of Israeliness: State, Society and the Military* (Berkeley: University of California Press, 2001).

63. The term "notables" was coined by Albert Hourani, in his seminal article "Ottoman Reform and the Politics of the Notables," in W. Polk and R. Chambers, eds., *Beginnings of Modernization in the Middle East* (Chicago: University of Chicago Press, 1968), 41–68.

64. For more on ways in which the yishuv did not live up to its stated ideals in this respect, see Sternhell, *Founding Myths*, 282ff.

65. The only exception was Egypt, whose economy was in some respects highly advanced: see Charles Issawi, "Asymmetrical Development and Transport in Egypt, 1800–1914," in William Polk and Richard Chambers, eds., *The Beginnings of Modernization in the Middle East* (Chicago: University of Chicago Press, 1968). In addition, by the mid-1930s Palestine was dominated by a larger Jewish economy and an increasingly powerful yishuv, which had governmental capabilities nearly on a European level, including the power to collect voluminous data: see the detailed tables of Zionist statistics reproduced in McCarthy, *The Population of Palestine*, 217–35, and the extraordinary compendium produced by the Jewish Agency's Economic Research Institute, *Statistical Handbook*.

66. The dates were 1931, 1927, and 1927, respectively: Nathan, Gass, and Creamer, *Palestine: Problem and Promise*, 142.

67. John Waterbury, *The Egypt of Nasser and Sadat: The Political Economy of Two Regimes* (Princeton, N.J.: Princeton University Press, 1983), Table 3.6, 44.

68. Extrapolated from 1931 census figures in Jewish Agency, *Statistical Handbook*, Table 9, 6.

69. Charles Issawi, *The Fertile Crescent, 1800–1914: A Documentary Economic History* (Oxford, U.K.: Oxford University Press, 1988), 30. Issawi does not specify, but it is clear from the context that these are male rather than overall literacy rates.

70. These figures are derived from tables in A. L. Tibawi, *Arab Education*, 270–71 (those for school-age population and government school enrollment are for 1947–48; the last available figures for private schools are for 1945–46). See Ylana Miller, *Government and Society in Rural Palestine 1920–1948* (Austin: University of Texas Press, 1985), 90–118, for an excellent account of the spread of education in rural areas, generally at the instigation of the rural population, and notwithstanding the obstacles often placed in their way by the British.

71. Miller, *Government and Society in Mandatory Palestine*, 98, citing the Palestine Government Department of Education *Annual Report, 1945–46*.

72. Charles Issawi, *Egypt at Mid-Century: An Economic Survey* (Oxford, U.K.: Oxford University Press, 1954), 67.

73. A. L. Tibawi, *A Modern History of Syria, including Lebanon and Palestine* (London: Macmillan, 1969), 357.

74. For more on literacy and reading in Palestine in general, and the press in particular, see Ami Ayalon, *Reading Palestine: Printing and Literacy, 1900–1948* (Austin: University of Texas Press, 2004).

75. Yusuf Khuri, ed, *al-Sihafa al-'arabiyya fi Filastin, 1876–1948* [The Arabic Press in Palestine, 1876–1948] (Beirut: Institute for Palestine Studies, 1976). These figures include periodicals reopened under different names after being closed by the authorities.

76. Derek Hopwood, *Syria 1945–1986: Politics and Society* (London: Unwin Hyman, 1988), 165, states that only ninety newspapers appeared in all of Syria during this period. The numbers cited in the text are taken from the more precise study of Nadine Méouchy, "La presse de Syrie et du Liban entre les deux guerres (1918–1939)," in *Débats intellectuels au Moyen-Orient dans l'entre-deux-guerres*, eds. Anne-Laure Dupont and Catherine Mayeur-Jaouen, *Revue des mondes musulmans et de la Méditerranée*, nos. 95–96–97–98 (2002): 55–70.

77. Charles Issawi, *The Middle East Economy: Decline and Recovery* (Princeton, N.J.: Markus Weiner, 1995), 137.

78. Méouchy, "La presse," 55.

79. For more details on the Palestinian press see Rashid Khalidi, *Palestinian Identity* and also "Anti-Zionism, Arabism and Palestinian Identity: 'Isa al-'Isa and *Filastin*," in *Political Identity in the Arab East in the 20th Century*, ed. Samir Seikaly (Beirut: American University of Beirut Press, forthcoming).

80. Issawi, *Egypt at Mid-Century*, 83. During the period in question, Egyptian and Palestinian pounds and Iraqi dinars were linked to sterling.

81. The figures in this and the following paragraphs are drawn from Jewish Agency, *Statistical Handbook*, Table 40, 26 (Palestine); Table 37, 94 (Iraq); and Table 27, 111 (Syria and Lebanon).

82. See Awad Barakat, *Le problème budgetaire en Syrie (1920–1939)* (Beirut: Nassar, 1948), Table, 108, which indicates overall per capita government spending of 5 and 5.05 Syrian pounds respectively in Syria and Iraq, as against over 11 in Palestine.

83. Jewish Agency, *Statistical Handbook*, Table 40, 26.

84. Barakat, *Le problème budgetaire*, 108. The per capita figures in Syrian pounds for Syria, Iraq, and Palestine respectively are: 1.86, 1.5, and 2.07.

85. See John Marlowe, *Rebellion in Palestine* (London: Cresset Press, 1946).

86. For an indication of how grievous this harm was, see the casualty figures for the Palestinians during the 1936–39 revolt in W. Khalidi, *From Haven to Conquest*, Appendix 4, 846–49.

87. Ibid., 108. The export figure, including re-exports (in millions of Syrian pounds) for Palestine, Syria, and Iraq were 14.9, 12.1, and 10.7 respectively. The import figures for the same year were even more skewed in favor of Palestine (more than double those of either other country), but most imports to Palestine in this period of intense immigration and capital inflow went to the rapidly growing Jewish economy, so these figures are harder to assess. The most significant export of Palestine was agricultural produce, notably oranges, produced by both the Arab and Jewish sectors, olives, produced mainly by the Arab sector, and cereals, produced mainly by the Jewish sector.

88. See, e.g., the accounts of how the Lebanese regarded the relative prosperity of Palestine in the late 1930s and 1940s, collected by Jihan Sfeir-Khayat in her

dissertation, "Les premier temps de l'installation des Palestiniens au Liban, 1947–1952."

89. See Chapter 4 for details.

2. The Palestinians and the British Mandate

1. This view, which is widespread in traditional Israeli representations of the Mandate period, is best rebutted in Tom Segev's account of the Mandate: *One Palestine, Complete.*

2. The reference here is *not* to Max Weber's idea that modern bureaucracy constitutes an iron cage.

3. More details on this subject can be found in R. Khalidi, *Palestinian Identity.*

4. For an excellent, detailed analysis of the genesis of the terms of the Mandate insofar as both the British domestic debate and international factors are concerned, see Laurens, *La question de Palestine*, vol. 1, *1899–1922: L'invention*, 573–627, especially 624–27.

5. Issued in January 1918, Wilson's Fourteen Points constituted the declarative basis for American participation in a post–World War I settlement, and included provisions relating to self-determination, including that "the interests of the populations concerned" must be considered in the adjustment of colonial claims, and a promise of "autonomous development" for nationalities under Ottoman rule. These encouraged peoples living under colonial rule to believe that they had an ally in the United States and that a new era had dawned. These hopes were generally not realized.

6. Article 4 described the Arab regions that were formerly part of the Ottoman Empire, which included Palestine, as provisionally "independent states" pending the provision of advice by mandatory powers.

7. Beginning with the correspondence of Sharif Husayn of Mecca, leader of the Arab revolt in World War I, and the British high commissioner to Egypt, Sir Henry McMahon, Britain had made a series of promises to support Arab independence, although the area within which that independence was to be exercised, and whether Palestine was included, were matters of contention.

8. MAE, Palestine, 1930–1940, vol. 59, *Affaires politiques*, Consul General, Jaffa, to Foreign Minister Aristide Briand, July 1, 1930, enclosing transcripts of a meeting on May 1, 1930, between the prime minister, Ramsay MacDonald, the colonial secretary, Lord Passfield, and other British officials and a six-person Palestinian delegation, and of another on May 6 between Passfield and the same group. The cover letter notes that the transcript, in English and based on the "shorthand notes of Treasury Reporters," is "strictement secret." It was presumably passed to the French diplomat by a member of the Palestinian delegation.

9. The British government, after all, was unilaterally to introduce sweeping modifications of its understanding of some of the basic terms of the Mandate

only nine years later in 1939, under the pressure of the Arab rebellion, and out of a cold concern for its strategic position in the Arab world as another world war approached.

10. MAE, Palestine, 1930–1940, vol. 59, *Affaires politiques,* minute by Foreign Minister Aristide Briand.

11. This discussion took place at the London meeting of May 1, 1930, in ibid., 226.

12. See Boyle, *Betrayal of Palestine,* 13, for a discussion of the relevant cabinet meeting of February 23, 1939.

13. For more on this topic see Yosef Gorny, *Zionism and the Arabs, 1882–1948: A Study of Ideology* (Oxford, U.K.: Clarendon, 1987), 243–76.

14. As Gorny, ibid., 243, puts it, "Almost all sectors of Zionism wanted a Jewish state in Palestine, whether they declared their intent or preferred to camouflage it." See also Chapter 6, note 10.

15. Memo dated August 11, 1919, cited in J. C. Hurewitz, ed., *The Middle East and North Africa in World Politics,* 2 vols. (New Haven: Yale University Press, 1979), vol. 2, 189.

16. For further details, see Susan Boyle's biography of Antonius, *Betrayal of Palestine.*

17. The only exception was the Crown Colony of Aden, ruled directly by Britain, but not its hinterland, where the British allowed indirect rule by indigenous rulers with British advisors to prevail.

18. The only two Arab states that had no foreign military bases during the interwar period were Yemen and Saudi Arabia, though an American air base was established at Dhahran in Saudi Arabia during World War II.

19. MAE, Palestine, Consul General, Jaffa, to Briand, July 1, 1930, transcript of meeting of May 6, 1930.

20. Ibid., meeting of May 1, 1930, 200.

21. Wasserstein, *The British in Palestine,* 95.

22. Ibid., 96–97.

23. See Ronen Shamir, *In the Colonies of Law: Colonialism, Zionism, and Law in Early Mandate Palestine* (Cambridge, U.K.: Cambridge University Press, 2000), which illustrates the smooth transition from the British Mandate to the Israeli state.

24. See J. Heyworth-Dunne, *An Introduction to the History of Education in Modern Egypt* (London: Murray, 1938), and Hanna Batatu, *The Old Social Classes and the Revolutionary Movements of Iraq: A Study of Iraq's Old Landed and Commercial Classes and of Its Communists, Ba'thists, and Free Officers* (Princeton, N.J.: Princeton University Press).

25. Khalaf, *Politics in Palestine,* 236.

26. Ann Mosely Lesch, *Arab Politics in Palestine, 1917–1939: The Frustration of a Nationalist Movement* (Ithaca, N.Y.: Cornell University Press, 1979), 186–87.

27. MAE, Palestine, Consul General, Jaffa, to Briand, July 1, 1930, transcript of meeting of May 1, 1930, 213.

28. The degree of this support in the economic sphere alone during the first decade of the Mandate can be gauged from Barbara Smith, *The Roots of Separation in Palestine: British Economic Policy, 1920–1929* (Syracuse, N.Y.: Syracuse University Press, 1995).

29. In the Arab world the most notable exceptions here, as in other respects, were the other two cases of European settler-colonialism, Algeria and Libya, where virtually all indigenous structures were destroyed or banned, and the structures of state erected by the colonial power existed almost entirely to benefit the European colonial population. The similarities with the Palestinian situation are most striking.

30. See Jacques Berque, *Egypt: Imperialism and Revolution* (London: Faber, 1972), and, inter alia, Robin Moore, *The Crisis of India Unity, 1917–1940* (Oxford, U.K.: Oxford University Press, 1974).

31. MAE, Palestine, Consul General, Jaffa, to Briand, July 1, 1930, transcripts of meetings of May 1, 1930, 210, and May 6, 1930, 253.

32. Roger Owen, "The Influence of Lord Cromer's Indian Experience on British Policy in Egypt, 1883–1907," in *Middle Eastern Affairs*, St. Antony's Papers 17, ed. Albert Hourani (London: Macmillan, 1965), 109–39, and Roger Owen, *Lord Cromer: Victorian Imperialist, Edwardian Proconsul* (Oxford, U.K.: Oxford University Press, 2004). See also Robert Tignor, "The Indianization of the Egyptian Administration under British Rule," *American Historical Review* 68, no. 3 (April 1963): 636–61.

33. Uri Kupferschmidt has pointed out that several of the most important British officials in Palestine had previous experience in Egypt or Cyprus: *The Supreme Muslim Council: Islam under the British Mandate for Palestine* (Leiden: Brill, 1987), 5, n. 16.

34. In the case of Kuwait and other Gulf dependencies, it was political agents based in India who were responsible for imposition of this system, introduced in Kuwait in 1899 by the viceroy of India, Lord Curzon. In northern Nigeria, the system of indirect rule was established by Lord Lugard on a basis drawn explicitly from the Indian example: D. K. Fieldhouse, *The Colonial Empires: A Comparative Survey from the Eighteenth Century* (London: Weidenfeld & Nicholson, 1966). For one of the most far-fetched examples of this borrowing from other colonial contexts, see Toby Dodge's discussion of how tribal law "codified" by a British officer in India's North-West Frontier in the 1890s was imported into Iraq by British occupation forces from India during World War I, and thereafter made part of Iraqi law, over the objections of many Iraqis: Toby Dodge, *Inventing Iraq: The Failure of Nation-Building and a History Denied* (New York: Columbia University Press, 2003).

35. See the proceedings of "Partition and Memory: Ireland, India and Palestine," a conference held at the Keough Institute for Irish Studies at Notre Dame University on December 8–9, 2001, forthcoming.

36. Radical Palestinian nationalists in the late 1920s and early 1930s were fasci-

nated by the Indian Congress Party's strategy of boycott and self-reliance, as is shown by Weldon Matthews in *Confronting an Empire, Constructing a Nation: Arab Nationalists and Popular Politics in the Palestine Mandate* (New York and London: Tauris, 2006). Similarly, Egyptian nationalists regarded the experiences of Indian and Irish nationalists with deep respect, and there was some cooperation between them, as is shown by Noor-Aiman Khan in a 2006 dissertation, "The Enemy of My Enemy: Indian and Egyptian Nationalism in Contact, 1907–1919" (University of Chicago, Department of Near Eastern Languages and Civilizations).

37. This was one of the objectives of the conference cited in n. 35.

38. See Michael Provence, *The Great Syrian Revolt and the Rise of Arab Nationalism* (Austin: University of Texas Press, 2005); Provence shows how French colonial officials inappropriately insisted on seeing Druze society in Syria as "feudal" and backward as a justification for their "modernizing" colonial efforts to remold it.

39. For a sophisticated analysis of what he calls *le regard colonial* (the colonial gaze) of French officials concerning the Sanusi movement in North Africa in the nineteenth and twentieth centuries, see Jean-Louis Triaud, *La légende noire de la Sanûsiyya: Une confrérie musulmane saharienne sous le regard français (1840–1930)*, 2 vols. (Paris: Editions de la Maison des Sciences de l'Homme, 1995). Triaud examines how French official views and scholarly constructions of this important Islamic brotherhood went hand in hand, and shifted over time in keeping with the state of its relations with the expanding French colonial presence in the Sahara. For a recent study of how scholars have looked comparatively at British and French colonialism, see Véronique Dimier, *Le gouvernement des colonies, regards croisés franco-britanniques* (Brussels: Editions de l'Universie de Bruxelles, 2004). For another recent work on the comparative study of French colonialism, see Claude Liauzu, ed., *Colonisation: Droit d'inventaire* (Paris: Armand Colin, 2004).

40. Ussama Makdisi's excellent book, *The Culture of Sectarianism: Community, History, and Violence in Nineteenth-Century Ottoman Lebanon* (Berkeley: University of California Press, 2000), illustrates this process. For a brilliant literary-historical portrait of Lebanon in this era that evocatively shows how the European powers manipulated local identities, see Amin Maalouf's *Rock of Tanios* (New York: Brazziler, 1994).

41. For details, see Kamal Salibi, *A House of Many Mansions: The History of Lebanon Reconsidered* (Berkeley: University of California Press, 1988), and Engin Akarli, *The Long Peace: Ottoman Lebanon 1861–1920* (Berkeley: University of California Press, 1993).

42. Provence, *The Great Syrian Revolt.*

43. What can be seen in the Irish, Indian, Lebanese, and Palestinian examples, among many others, with respect to the manipulation and construction of religious and ethnic identities in order to facilitate domination by an external

power, may involve universal processes of indirect control, not confined to the British or other classical colonial powers. Thus lessons drawn from traditional colonialism may be applicable to the postcolonial situation of the Cold War, and to the monopolar neoliberal world order that has emerged in its wake. In other words, although the era of classical colonialism is long gone, some means of regarding, and of controlling, former colonies have been inherited by the new postcolonial hegemons, whether these means involve an Orientalist structure, as described by Edward Said, for knowing about, framing, describing, and thereby controlling the "other," or whether they involve more active forms of manipulation of societies, economies, and polities. See Tariq Ali, *The Clash of Fundamentalisms: Crusades, Jihad, and Modernity* (London: Verso, 2002), for descriptions of a number of examples of this sort of manipulation drawn from India, Pakistan, and elsewhere in the world, as well as R. Khalidi, *Resurrecting Empire.*

44. See Ron Inden, *Imagining India* (Oxford: Blackwell, 1991), for a brilliant examination of how the British raj transformed, systematized, and hardened the Indian caste system.

45. The memoirs of Ronald Storrs, *Orientations* (London: Nicholson and Watson, 1937), and Viscount Samuel, *Memoirs* (London: Cresset Press, 1945), are examples. See also A. J. Sherman, *Mandate Days: British Lives in Palestine* (London: Thames and Hudson, 1997). One can find many similar British accounts written about other parts of the empire.

46. For turn-of-the-century photographs of Indian royalty taken during visits to the British court (the photos were found and are now held at the Victoria and Albert Museum), see Russell Harris, *The Lafayette Studio and Princely India* (New Delhi: Roli and Janssen, 2005). Even in some of the great Indian states, the British were capable of creating aristocrats: one of the maharajas of Baroda depicted was "the illiterate son of a village headman" placed on the throne by the raj when "his predecessor was deposed for misconduct" (22). The British used the same tactics in the Gulf principalities, which were controlled from India.

47. George Orwell's first novel, *Burmese Days* (London: Victor Gollancz, 1934), based on his six years as an official in the Indian Imperial Police in Burma, is a scathing indictment of the rigid class, caste, and ethnic hierarchies that permeated the British imperial system, and illustrates how certain categories of colonial natives were allowed and encouraged to perform specific subordinate tasks within that system.

48. For a vivid illustration of this process in the form of a carefully wrought historical novel covering nearly a century, beginning with the 1885 occupation of Burma, in which Britain used largely Indian forces, see Amitav Ghosh, *The Glass Palace* (New York: Random House, 2002).

49. See the essay by Victor Kiernan in *Imperialism and Its Contradictions* (London: Routledge, 1995) for details on how dependent the great colonial powers were

on these forces raised from their colonial populations. As only one example, troops of an Algerian rifle division and a division of Moroccan infantry (*goumiers*) did the lion's share of the fighting, and between them lost more than five thousand men, killed during the savage weeklong battle to liberate the port city of Marseille from the Germans in August 1944.

50. Hourani, "Ottoman Reform and the Politics of the Notables."

51. Kupferschmidt, *The Supreme Muslim Council*, 17. His book gives a good account of the evolution of this institution.

52. These public *awqaf* revenues must be distinguished from those generated by a private, family *waqf*. The latter, termed a *waqf dhurri*, or *waqf ahli*, was an inalienable pious endowment, generally established by a family for a specified purpose, and under control of a superintendent chosen by the donors and approved by the shari'a court. The "Moslem Awqaf" was the term used by the British Mandate administration for public waqf revenues. The administration of public awqaf funds in Palestine was known under Jordan after 1948 and the Palestinian Authority after 1995 as Da'irat al-Awqaf al-'Amma, the Department of Public Awqaf. Inexplicably and confusingly, the Israeli usage for this institution is "the Waqf." For details, see Yitzhak Reiter, *Islamic Endowments in Jerusalem under British Mandate* (London: Cass, 1996). See also Michael Dumper, *Islam and Israel: Muslim Religious Endowments and the Israeli State* (Washington, D.C., and Beirut: Institute for Palestine Studies, 1994).

53. Lord Cromer, *Modern Egypt,* 2 vols. (New York: Macmillan, 1908).

54. Ibid., ii, 127–28.

55. Under the Ottoman millet system, which reached its apex in the nineteenth century, each major religious sect governed its own internal religious and personal status affairs, under a hierarchy that was recognized by the Ottoman government.

56. Thus a French consular official wrote (in MAE, Palestine, 1918–1929, vol. 4, *Affaires politiques,* Acting Consul, Jaffa, to Prime Minister and Foreign Minister Aristide Briand, July 23, 1921) of the Jaffa riots: "En contact permanente avec l'Egypte, les palestiniens ont appris cependent a ne plus redouter les admonestations des autorités britanniques et n'écoutent guère leurs exortations au calme" (In permanent contact with Egypt, the Palestinians have meanwhile learned to not believe the admonitions of the British authorities, and never listen to their exhortations to be calm). See also the memoirs of 'Isa al-'Isa, the most prominent Palestinian journalist of the interwar period, who writes of his lengthy experiences in Egypt. They are transcribed and translated into French in Noha Tadros, "*Min Dhikrayat al-Madi* 'Souvenirs': Autobiographie et Représentation de soi de 'Issa al-'Issa (Journaliste palestinien, 1878–1950)" (doctoral diss., Institut National des Langues et Civilizations Orientales, Paris, 1999).

57. Great Britain, *Parliamentary Command Papers,* Cmd. 5479, "Palestine Royal

Commission Report" (the "Peel report") (London: HMSO, 1937), paras. 80–82. See also Kupferschmidt, *The Supreme Muslim Council.*

58. The new title of Grand Mufti of Palestine, *Mufti Filastin al-akbar,* was a British invention, which most sources agree was based on the Egyptian precedent (e.g., Kupferschmidt, in *The Supreme Muslim Council,* 19, calls it "an innovative British move"; Wasserstein, *The British in Palestine,* 98, n. 55). Importantly, the mufti was also newly styled *Mufti al-Quds wal-diyar al-Filistiniyya* (Mufti of Jerusalem and the Palestine region) rather than the traditional formulation *Mufti al-diyar al-Maqdisiyya* (Mufti of the Jerusalem region).

59. The best study of the mufti's career is Mattar, *The Mufti of Jerusalem.* See also Zvi Elpeleg, *The Grand Mufti: Haj Amin al-Hussaini, Founder of the Palestinian National Movement* (London: Frank Cass, 1993). How the mufti helped the British curb Palestinian radicalism is thoroughly explored by Weldon Matthews in *Confronting an Empire.*

60. This was true in every locality, although at the apex of the Ottoman religious establishment, the Shaykh al-Islam in Istanbul was also the mufti of the capital. See R. C. Repp, *The Mufti of Istanbul: A Study in the Development of the Ottoman Learned Hierarchy* (Oxford, U.K.: Ithaca Press, 1986). For a work that details the greater importance of the qadi in relation to the mufti before the arrival of the British, see Mahmoud Yazbeck, *Haifa in the Late Ottoman Period, 1864–1914: A Muslim Town in Transition* (Leiden: Brill, 1998).

61. For details of how this system worked in Jerusalem during the late Ottoman period, see R. Khalidi, *Palestinian Identity,* 65–69.

62. Eric Hobsbawm and Terence Ranger, eds., *The Invention of Tradition* (Cambridge, U.K.: Cambridge University Press, 1992).

63. See R. Khalidi, *British Policy towards Syria and Palestine,* 353–54, for examples of this Ottoman practice in regard to candidates for parliamentary elections immediately before World War I.

64. Quoted in Zvi Elpeleg, *The Grand Mufti: Haj Amin al-Hussaini, Founder of the Palestinian National Movement* (London: Cass, 1992), 9. A good account of this episode can be found in Wasserstein, *The British in Palestine,* 98–99. See also Y. Porath, "Al-Hajj Amin al-Husseini, Mufti of Jerusalem—His Rise to Power and the Consolidation of His Position," *African and Asian Studies* 8 (1971): 212–56.

65. I had the occasion to meet al-Husayni at a wake in Beirut on September 3, 1968, a few years before his own death in 1974 at the age of well over eighty, and I can attest to the force of his personality.

66. See, inter alia, Afaf Lutfi al-Sayyid Marsot, *Egypt's Liberal Experiment 1922–1936* (Berkeley: University of California Press, 1977); Philip Khoury, *Syria and the French Mandate: The Politics of Arab Nationalism 1920–1945* (Princeton, N.J.: Princeton University Press, 1987); Elizabeth Thompson, *Colonial Citizens: Republican Rights, Paternal Privilege, and Gender in French Syria and Lebanon*

(New York: Columbia University Press, 2000); and Batatu, *The Old Social Classes and the Revolutionary Movements of Iraq.*

67. For a nuanced analysis of the relationships between the mufti and Britain, France, and Germany, see Henry Laurens, "La France le Grand Mufti et la révolte palestinienne," *Revue d'études palestiniennes* 4 (summer 1995): 63–78, and "Le Mufti et la France de la IVe République," *Revue d'études palestiniennes* 81 (fall 2001): 70–87. Both are collected with a short introduction in Laurens, *Orientales II: La IIIe République at l'Islam* (Paris: CNRS Editions, 2004), 301–53. The mufti's years in Germany are the basis for tying the Palestinian national movement to the Nazis, a standard trope in much Israeli historiography on this period. See, e.g., Joseph Schechtman, *The Mufti and the Fuhrer: The Rise and Fall of Haj Amin el-Husseini* (New York: Thomas Yoseloff, 1965).

68. For more details on these secret British subsidies, and other ways the mufti helped the British to calm the situation in Palestine for over a decade, see the illuminating revelations in Matthews, *Confronting an Empire,* chapter 4. For more on the increase in British subsidies to the Supreme Muslim Council in the early 1930s, see Reiter, *Islamic Endowments,* 30–33.

69. For one of innumerable examples of how petty this rivalry could be, see the comments in the leading Palestinian newspaper, *Filastin,* January 30, 1931, 1, "Lajnat al-ihtifal: Hal qamat bil-wajib?" [Did the organizing committee do its duty?], criticizing the organizers of preparations for the funeral ceremony in the Haram al-Sharif in Jerusalem for the Indian Muslim leader Muhammad Ali because they failed to include the Arab Executive, the Jerusalem municipality, or Palestinian Christians. That the mufti was the target of these criticisms is clear both from the elaborate politeness with which "the great work he is undertaking" is mentioned, and from an article a few days earlier ("Qabr wahid yajma' bayna umatayn" [One grave brings together two nations], January 24, 1931, 1) stating that the mufti was responsible for the event.

3. A Failure of Leadership

1. Secondary works that focus on this subject include Porath, *The Emergence of the Palestinian-Arab National Movement,* Lesch, *Arab Politics in Palestine,* and Hurewitz, *The Struggle for Palestine.* See also Manuel Hassassian, *Palestine: Factionalism in the National Movement (1919–1939)* (Jerusalem: Palestinian Academic Society for the Study of International Affairs, 1990), and Khalaf, *Arab Factionalism.*

2. As is described later in the chapter, this was the fate in 1938 of the editor of *Filastin,* 'Isa al-'Isa, who by then had become a harsh critic of the mufti.

3. For earlier periods, political history features in Amnon Cohen, *Palestine in the 18th Century: Patterns of Government and Administration* (Jerusalem: Magnes Press, 1973), and Ahmad Joudeh, *Revolt in Palestine in the Eighteenth Century:*

The Era of Shaykh Zahir al-'Umar (Princeton, N.J.: Kingston, 1987); for socio-economic history see Amnon Cohen, *Economic Life in Ottoman Jerusalem* (Cambridge, U.K.: Cambridge University Press, 1989), Gad Gilbar, ed., *Ottoman Palestine: Studies in Economic and Social History* (Leiden: Brill, 1990), and Amy Singer, *Palestinian Peasants and Ottoman Officials: Rural Administration around Sixteenth-century Jerusalem* (Cambridge, U.K.: Cambridge University Press, 1994).

4. See Rashid Khalidi, "Arab Nationalism: Historical Problems in the Literature," *American Historical Review* 96, no. 5 (December 1991), 1363–73.

5. For social and economic history see Alexander Schölch, *Palestine in Transformation 1856–1882: Studies in Social, Economic and Political Development* (Washington, D.C.: Institute for Palestine Studies, 1993), and Beshara Doumani, *Rediscovering Palestine: Merchants and Peasants in Jabal Nablus, 1700–1900* (Berkeley: University of California Press, 1995). See also Roger Owen, ed., *Studies in the Economic and Social History of Palestine in the 19th and 20th Centuries* (London: Macmillan, 1982), Thomas Philipp, *Acre: The Rise and Fall of a Palestinian City, 1730–1831* (New York: Columbia University Press, 2001), Judith Tucker, *In the House of the Law: Gender and Islamic Law in Ottoman Syria and Palestine* (Berkeley: University of California Press, 1998), Mahmoud Yazbak, *Haifa in the Late Ottoman Period, 1864–1914: A Muslim Town in Transition* (Leiden: Brill, 1998), Pappé, *A History of Modern Palestine*, and Ayalon, *Reading Palestine*.

6. See James Gelvin, *Divided Loyalties: Nationalism and Mass Politics in Syria at the Close of Empire* (Berkeley, University of California Press, 1998), for one example of this critique.

7. Bowman Diary, April 13, 1925, cited in Boyle, *The Betrayal of Palestine*, 127.

8. Segev, *One Palestine, Complete*, 175. Brenner was later killed in the 1921 Jaffa riots.

9. MAE, Palestine, 1930–40, vol. 59, intelligence report on impact in Syria of events in Palestine, enclosed in High Commissioner, Beirut, to Foreign Minister Briand, March 26, 1930.

10. The post had until the end of the eighteenth century been held by members of Musa Kazim's branch of the family: for al-Husayni family genealogy, see 'Adel Manna', *A'lam Filastin fi awakhir al-'ahd al-'uthmani (1800–1918)* [The Notables of Palestine at the End of the Ottoman Period (1800–1918)], 2nd ed. (Beirut: Institute for Palestine Studies, 1995), 109–31.

11. Wasserstein, *The British in Palestine*, 69. For al-Nashashibi's perspective on the dispute, see Nasser Eddin Nashashibi, *Jerusalem's Other Voice: Ragheb Nashashibi and Moderation in Palestinian Politics, 1920–1948* (Exeter, U.K.: Ithaca Press, 1990). For the mufti's perspective, see the account of one of his close collaborators, Emile al-Ghuri, *al-Mu'amara al-kubra* [The Great Conspiracy] (Cairo: Dar al-Nil, 1955).

12. Ottoman exploitation of factionalism was touched on in the previous chapter.

See also R. Khalidi, *Palestinian Identity*, 61, for examples of how the Ottoman authorities exploited these local rivalries for their own ends.

13. British officials such as Storrs came to Palestine from Egypt with ample experience in the divide-and-rule approach. How Storrs operated in Egypt in the period immediately preceding World War I emerges from a careful reading of his engrossing autobiography, *Orientations* (London: Hodder & Stoughton, 1937), 108–9 and 115–23.

14. Reported in a telegram from the Quai d'Orsay to the French High Commissioner in Beirut, MAE, Palestine, 1918–1929, vol. 4, *Dossier général*, March 26, 1921.

15. French Consul General in Jerusalem, d'Aumale, to Foreign Minister Edouard Herriot, November 20, 1932 (MAE, Palestine, 1930–1940, vol. 60, *Affaires politiques*).

16. For evidence of this discrimination, one need only refer to then prime minister Balfour's support of the Alien Exclusion Act of 1902, directed mainly at keeping Jewish victims of Eastern European pogroms from entering Britain, and the refusal of successive British governments to allow the entry into the country of Jewish escapees from Nazi persecution in the 1930s and 1940s.

17. Wasserstein, *The British in Palestine*, 43–57.

18. See for example the virulently anti-Semitic comments of W. J. Farrell, head of the Mandate's Education Department in 1945, cited by Shepherd, *Ploughing Sand*, 178.

19. Israel Shahak, *The Shahak Papers*, no. 31, "Collection on Jabotinsky: His Life and Excerpts from His Writings," 16, cited in Nur Masalha, *Expulsion of the Palestinians: The Concept of "Transfer" in Zionist Political Thought 1882–1948* (Washington, D.C.: Institute for Palestine Studies, 1992), 45.

20. See Neville Mandel, *The Arabs and Zionism before World War I* (Berkeley: University of California Press, 1976), which treats the pre-1914 period. The unpublished autobiography of the prominent Palestinian journalist 'Isa al-'Isa, reproduced in Tadros, "*Min Dhikrayat al-Madi 'Souvenirs.'*" is replete with references to such subsidies by the Zionists. Al-'Isa's daughter recalls being told by her mother that her father was offered a large bribe to silence his newspaper's opposition to a major electricity concession to Jewish engineer Pinhas Rutenberg: Interview, Layla al-'Isa Tadros, Aix en Provence, France, July 25, 2005. For more details on which Palestinian papers were subsidized directly or indirectly by the Zionists in this period see Ya'qub Yehoshu', *Tarikh al-sihafa al-'arabiyya fi Filastin fil-'ahd al-'uthmani 1908–1918* (Jerusalem: Matba 'at al-Ma'arif, 1974), 52–54; and R. Khalidi, *Palestinian Identity*, 58, and 228, n. 77.

21. MAE, Palestine, 1918–1929, vol. 5, *Dossier général*, in a dispatch to the French High Commissioner in Beirut and to the Consul General in Jerusalem, March 13, 1921, the acting consul in Jaffa reported that Ibrahim al-Najjar, publisher of the newspaper *Lisan al-'Arab*, had received support from the Zionists in the form of LP 1,000 for five hundred subscriptions to his paper, though the

French official claimed that the subterfuge fooled no one, and that all knew his organ was subsidized by the Zionists. According to a report by the French High Commissioner in Beirut to Briand (March 26, 1930, MAE, Palestine, 1930–1940, vol. 59, *Affaires politiques*), Zionist agents including Haim Kalvarisky were doing the same thing in Beirut, buying large numbers of subscriptions to *L'Orient,* for example.

22. Thus, Wasserstein, *The British in Palestine,* 94, n. 33, suggests that Musa Kazim al-Husayni was "supported on occasion by Zionist *douceurs* [sweeteners]." His source is Yehoshua Porath, who states in *The Emergence of the Palestinian-Arab National Movement,* 68–69, that payments to al-Husayni were made in 1923, but fails to note that all such payments were apparently abandoned in 1927 and never resumed as a systematic policy: Lesch, *Arab Politics,* 53.

23. Letters from Kalvarisky in the Central Zionist Archives cited in Lesch, *Arab Politics,* 96, n. 33.

24. French Consul General in Jerusalem to Foreign Minister and Prime Minister Aristide Briand, July 1, 1921, MAE, Palestine, 1918–1929, vol. 4, *Dossier général.*

25. Thus Metzer, *The Divided Economy of Mandatory Palestine,* 86, notes that of registered land sales by Arabs from 1929 to 1939, 54 percent were to Jews, but in 1940–46 only 22 percent were, the rest being to Arabs. He ascribes this decline in part to an increase in unregistered sales of land to Jews by Arabs, but fails to consider the greater prosperity of Palestine during the war years, and the rapid growth of the Arab sector of the economy, which increased both the demand for land by Arabs and their capability to purchase it. The point is that in such an active land market, the ultimate destination of a parcel of land sold might not be known by the seller.

26. In this regard, see my review of Stein, *The Land Question in Palestine,* in *Journal of Palestine Studies* 17, no. 1 (autumn 1987): 146–51.

27. Lesch, *Arab Politics,* 53. Morris, *Righteous Victims,* 106, states that most Arab leaders who maintained contacts with Zionist officials "usually did so for bribes." See also Segev, *One Palestine,* 276–83, which includes extensive details of the bribes offered to prominent Arabs by leading Zionist officials like Chaim Kalvarisky and Col. Frederick Kisch. It is worth noting that most of the documents that serve as sources for these allegations come from the period 1922–25 and most are dated 1923. They are primarily located in the Central Zionist Archives, and not surprisingly, it is nearly impossible to obtain confirmation of them from Arab sources, except with respect to charges that appeared in newspapers hostile to the politicians accused.

28. Segev, *One Palestine,* 280. Ze'ev Schiff, "On the Origins of Targeted Assassination," *Haaretz,* June 12, 2006, reports on a 1947–48 Hagana assassination campaign against leading Palestinians, including the order that "each operation should look like an Arab action."

29. Morris, *Righteous Victims,* 106.

30. Ibid.

31. Ibid. For more on Zaslani/Shiloah see Haggai Eshed, *Reuven Shiloah—The Man Behind the Mossad: Secret Diplomacy in the Creation of Israel* (London: Cass, 1997).

32. The 1912 diplomatic exchanges were between British foreign secretary Sir Edward Grey and French foreign minister Henri Poincaré. For the rivalry in Greater Syria, which most concerns us here, see R. Khalidi, *British Policy in Syria and Palestine*, and Jukka Nevakivi, *Britain, France and the Arab Middle East, 1914–1920* (London: Athlone Press, 1969).

33. See, e.g., the scathing comments of a British observer in Damascus in Michael Fry and Itamar Rabinovitch, eds., *Despatches from Damascus: Gilbert Mac-Kereth and British Policy in the Levant, 1933–1939* (Tel Aviv: Dayan Center, 1985).

34. MAE, Palestine, 1918–1929, vol. 4, *Dossier général*, Rais (Acting Consul, Jaffa) to Foreign Minister and Prime Minister Briand, July 23, 1921.

35. MAE, Palestine, 1918–1929, vol. 4, *Dossier général*, Gouraud, High Commissioner, Beirut, to Foreign Minister and Prime Minister Briand, September 8, 1921.

36. All translations from the original French are my own. MAE, Palestine, 1930–1940, vol. 69, *Religion musulmane*, d'Aumale to Foreign Minister and Prime Minister Herriot, November 20, 1932.

37. Ibid., d'Aumale to Briand, December 3, 1931. Of course, Zionist sources suggested that some of those associated with the mufti were also on their payroll: see Porath, *The Emergence of the Palestinian-Arab National Movement*, 68–69ff.

38. MAE, Palestine, 1930–1940, vol. 69, *Religion musulmane*, d'Aumale to Briand, December 22, 1931.

39. For more details, see Martin Kramer, *Islam Assembled: The Advent of the Muslim Congresses* (New York: Columbia University Press, 1986).

40. See Matthews, *Confronting an Empire*, which examines the trajectory of the Istiqlal Party, the first Arab political party to be established in Palestine. Much of the argument that follows is based on Matthews's groundbreaking work as summed up in this book.

41. On late Ottoman Jerusalem, see Wasif Jawhariyya, *al-Quds al-ʿuthmaniyya fil-muthakirrat al-Jawhariyya: al-Kitab al-awwal min muthakirrat al-musiqi Wasif Jawhariyya, 1904–1917* [Ottoman Jerusalem in the Jawhariyya Memoirs: Volume One of the Memoirs of the Musician Wasif Jawhariyya, 1904–1917], eds., Salim Tamari and Issam Nassar (Jerusalem: Institute for Jerusalem Studies, 2003), and Khalil Sakakini, *Yawmiyyat Khalil Sakakini: Al-Kitab al-thani: al-Nahda al-urthuduksiyya, al-harb al-ʿuzma, al-nafi ila Dimashq, 1914–1918* [The Diaries of Khalil Sakakini, vol. 2: The Orthodox Renaissance, the Great War, Exile to Damascus, 1914–1917], ed. Akram Musallam (Jerusalem: Institute for Jerusalem Studies, 2004); Geoffrey Furlonge, *Palestine Is My Country: The Story of Musa Alami* (London: John Murray, 1969), 35–64; and Abigail

Jacobson, "From Empire to Empire: Jerusalem in the Transition between the Ottoman Empire and the British Mandate, 1912–1920" (Ph.D. diss., University of Chicago, 2006).

42. A similar pattern of bottom-up leadership could be seen, at least at the outset, in the intifadas of 1987–91 and 2000–2004. For a comparison of the 1936–39 revolt and the first intifada, see Ken Stein, *The Intifadah and the 1936–1939 Uprising: A Comparison of the Palestinian Arab Communities* (Occasional Paper Series, 1, 1, Atlanta: Carter Center of Emory University, 1989).

43. For more on al-Qassam, see S. Abdullah Schleifer, "The Life and Thought of 'Izz-id-Din al-Qassam," and " 'Izz al-Din al-Qassam: Preacher and *Mujahid.*"

44. The best study of the Istiqlal Party is in Matthews, *Confronting an Empire,* on which much of the following passages are based.

45. Ibid., p. 2.

46. For a discussion of the influence of the Indian Congress Party's noncooperation program, see ibid., chapter 6.

47. Ibid.

48. Eric Hobsbawm, *Bandits* (London: Weidenfeld & Nicholson, 1969).

49. For details see B. Smith, *The Roots of Separatism,* 11–12.

50. K. Stein, *The Land Question,* 88, and Charles Kamen, *Little Common Ground: Arab Agriculture and Jewish Settlement in Palestine, 1920–1948* (Pittsburg: University of Pittsburg Press, 1991), 52–53. See also the Shaw Report: Great Britain, Parliament, Command Paper 3530, *Report of the Commission on the Palestine Disturbances of August 1929* (London: His Majesty's Stationery Office, 1930).

51. Matthews, *Confronting an Empire,* is replete with examples of public bluster and private deal-making on the part of a broad range of Palestinian leaders.

52. For a striking photograph of the prone old man being beaten by British police, see W. Khalidi, *Before Their Diaspora,* 110.

53. Storrs, *Orientations,* 354.

54. In spite of the generally negative portrayal of the mufti and all other traditional pre-1948 leaders by the new post-1948 Palestinian political movements, the latter revered the memory of 'Abd al-Qadir al-Husayni, who was seen as typifying an early instance of the armed resistance to Zionism that they preached, and whose image, often adorned with bandoliers, was common in their early publications.

55. Matthews, *Confronting an Empire,* chapter 6.

56. Ibid.

57. For a vivid eye-witness description of the emotional funeral ceremonies, see Akram Zu'aytir, *al-Haraka al-wataniyya al-filistiniyya 1935–1939: Yawmiyyat Akram Zu'aytir* [The Palestinian National Movement 1935–1939: The Diaries of Akram Zu'aytir] (Beirut, Institute for Palestine Studies, 1980), 30–32.

58. For more details see R. Khalidi, *Palestinian Identity.* See also Haim Gerber, " 'Palestine' and Other Territorial Conceptions in the 17th Century," *International Journal of Middle East Studies* 30, no. 4 (November 1998): 563–72, who

further documents the existence over several centuries of a sense of Palestine as a geographical entity among Arab residents of the country, rooted in the sense of it as a holy land. See also Gerber's article, "Zionism, Orientalism and the Palestinians," *Journal for Palestine Studies* 129 (fall 2003): 23–41.

59. Notably in the introduction to Rashid Khalidi, Lisa Anderson, Muhammad Muslih, and Reeva Simon, eds.. *The Origins of Arab Nationalism* (New York: Columbia University Press, 1991), ix, where I contended that for all its flaws, it was wrong to consider that the press was an unreliable source. It is hard to understand the animus of some against expressions in the press of political and cultural views that reflected and shaped public opinion in the Arab world.

60. This view is accepted by the most careful study of the press thus far, Ayalon, *Reading Palestine,* p. 62

61. Yusuf al-'Isa seems to have carried out most of the editing duties on the newspaper for the first few years, and signed many editorials, although 'Isa al-'Isa's signature can be found on numerous others. After World War I Yusuf remained in Damascus, where he founded and edited the newspaper *Alif Ba.* He occasionally wrote for *Filastin* even after that, and on at least one occasion in 1921 came back to Jaffa and took over the paper for a time, while his cousin was on his honeymoon.

62. Hassan Abu Nimah, a former Jordanian ambassador to the UN, has childhood recollections from the early 1940s of how avidly people in his natal village of Battir, west of Jerusalem, would peruse copies of the newspapers *Filastin* and *al-Difaʻ,* which were passed from hand to hand until copies became soft and supple: interview conducted by 'Ali Abu Nimah, Amman, July 1, 2005. According to other sources, newspapers were read out loud in village gathering places, urban homes, and coffeehouses, enabling those with little or no literacy to follow the news. For a useful discussion of where and how newspapers were read in villages in Palestine during this period, see Ayalon, *Reading Palestine,* 106–7.

63. Of the approximately fifty Zionist agricultural settlements established by 1914, seventeen were located within thirty kilometers of Jaffa, and another thirty were established in central or eastern Galilee or on the coast south of Haifa.

64. R. Khalidi, *Palestinian Identity,* 100–101.

65. Demographic questions in pre-1914 Palestine are bedeviled by the absence of reliable statistics, by divergent estimates produced by sources often unfamiliar with the country, and by the fact that much scholarship is affected by the ongoing political implications of these matters. While McCarthy, *The Population of Palestine,* gives figures on the low side for the Jewish population of Palestine and Jerusalem, works such as Yehoshua Ben Arieh, *Jerusalem in the 19th Century: The Old City* (Jerusalem: Yad Izhak Ben Zvi, 1984), based almost entirely on Western Jewish and other Western sources, give figures that are too high, inflating Ashkenazi numbers and probably undercounting the Sephardi population: Ben Arieh thus describes the latter as a majority of the Jews of

Jerusalem only until 1870: 278. In her dissertation on Jerusalem during the period from 1912 to 1920, "From Empire to Empire," Abigail Jacobson casts doubt on this assertion, and gives a nuanced picture of the different components of the Jewish population of Jerusalem at this time.

66. R. Khalidi, *Palestinian Identity*, 24, based on data in McCarthy, *The Population of Palestine*.

67. Ayalon, *Reading Palestine*, 64, cites figures of seven thousand to ten thousand copies each, daily, by the mid-1940s.

68. For more on the struggle of Arabic-speaking Greek Orthodox in Syria and Palestine to Arabize their church, see A. L. Tibawi, *Russian Cultural Penetration of Syria and Palestine in the Nineteenth Century* (Oxford: Oxford University Press, 1966). See also Derek Hopwood, *The Russian Presence in Syria and Palestine, 1843–1914: Church and Politics in the Near East* (Oxford, U.K.: Clarendon Press, 1969).

69. *Filastin*, no. 241–44, Sept. 29, 1913, 1. The paper was provided free to the *mukhtar*, or headman, of every village within the district of Jaffa.

70. For details, see Chapter 2.

71. The editorial was published as the sole item in a special issue of *Filastin*, dated 7 Nisan 1330/May 1914 (remainder of date erased on extant copy). For details see R. Khalidi, *Palestinian Identity*, 154–56.

72. The speech is reported in 'Ajaj Nuwayhid, *Rijal min Filastin ma bayna bidayat al-qarn hatta 'am 1948* [Men from Palestine between the Beginning of the Century and 1948] (Amman: Filastin al-Muhtalla, 1981), 30.

73. Among studies that examine *Filastin* and 'Isa al-'Isa, the thesis by Noha Tadros, "*Min Dhikrayat al-Madi 'Souvenirs,'*" is perhaps the most thorough. Others include Ayalon, *Reading Palestine*, and R. Khalidi, *Palestinian Identity*.

74. Before the establishment of the Balamand seminary, also located in the Koura region southeast of Tripoli, the school at Kiftin was one of the preeminent Orthodox educational institutions in all of Greater Syria: private communication with author, Beirut, December 16, 1997. The school was then under the direction of the Orthodox bishop of Tripoli, Gregorius Haddad, later patriarch of Damascus: this information is from p. 16 of a seventy-six-page autobiographical memoir in 'Isa al-'Isa's own hand, covering the period from 1904 until 1941, and titled "Min Dhikrayat al-Madi" [Memories of the Past], which his son, Raja al-'Isa, kindly allowed me to utilize. Raja al-'Isa noted that "the memoirs of my father . . . were written as remembered from memory in his late years in Beirut," letter to author, Nov. 25, 1997. For a perceptive analysis and French translation of this important document, as well as much else on the life of al-'Isa, see Tadros, "*Min Dhikrayat al-Madi 'Souvenirs.'*"

75. Ya'qub 'Awadat, *Min A'lam al-Fikr wal-Adab fi Filastin* [Leading Literary and Intellectual Figures in Palestine], 2nd ed. (Jerusalem: Dar al-Isra', 1992), 477–78.

76. Details can be found in "Min Dhikrayat al-Madi," 3–5.

77. R. Khalidi, *Palestinian Identity*, 154–56, and R. Khalidi, *British Policy towards Syria and Palestine, 1906–1914* (London: Ithaca, 1980), 356–57.

78. Although 'Isa al-'Isa suffered hardship during his exile of nearly three years in remote Anatolian villages, some of the qualities that made him such a respected journalist served him in good stead with his Turkish neighbors. Among them was his wide knowledge of the Arabic language and of Islam, including his ability to recite verses of the Qur'an and hadiths of the Prophet, which he had learned at the AUB: 'Isa al-'Isa, "Min Dhikrayat al-Madi," 34.

79. Ibid., 44–45.

80. This is vividly described in ibid., 44.

81. For more on this period, see Muhammad Muslih, *The Origins of Palestinian Nationalism* (New York: Columbia University Press, 1988), 115–54; R. Khalidi, *Palestinian Identity*, 145–76; and Malcolm B. Russell, *The First Modern Arab State: Syria under Faysal, 1918–1920* (Minneapolis: Biblioteca Islamica, 1985).

82. 'Isa al-'Isa, "Min Dhikrayat al-Madi," 48.

83. 'Isa al-'Isa's photo appears among those of other senior government officials in a volume commemorating Syrian independence, Sa'id al-Tali', ed., *Dhikra Istiqlal Suriyya* [A Memento of Syrian Independence] (Cairo: Taha Ibrahim and Yusuf Barladi, 1920), which describes him as "Secretary of the Royal Court."

84. His cousin Yusuf, who had founded the paper *Alif Ba* in Damascus in 1920, remained there to edit it, although he frequently wrote articles for *Filastin* after that.

85. He implied that the delay in reopening the newspaper was caused by the determined opposition of the Zionist movement to him: 'Isa al-'Isa, "Min Dhikrayat al-Madi," 57.

86. Ibid., 11.

87. Ibid., 47.

88. Interview with 'Isa al-'Isa's daughter, Layla al-'Isa Tadros, Cairo, December 20, 1996.

89. Soon after the fall of Jaffa, the newspaper was moved to Jerusalem. After al-'Isa's death in 1950 *Filastin* continued publication until March 1967, when it was taken over by the Jordanian government and moved to Amman, where it was merged with *al-Dustur* and disappeared as an independent title.

90. Tadros, "*Min Dhikrayat al-Madi 'Souvenirs,'*" 310, n. 111.

91. 'Isa al-'Isa, "Min Dhikrayat al-Madi," 9. See also Bayan Nuwayhid al-Hout, *al-Qiyadat wal-mu'assasat al-siyasiyya fi Filastin, 1917–1948* [Political Leaderships and Institutions in Palestine, 1917–1948] (Beirut: Institute for Palestine Studies, 1981), 861.

92. Al-'Isa was speaking at the Arab Orthodox club in Jerusalem: 'Ajaj Nuwayhid, *Rijal min Filastin*, 30.

93. Details can be found in Hopwood, *The Russian Presence in Syria and Palestine*.

94. The patriarchate of Jerusalem is still controlled by the Order of the Holy Sep-

ulcher, which is predominantly ethnically Greek, a situation that continues to cause bitter resentment among many of the Arab Orthodox faithful in Palestine and Jordan.

95. The question of land sales to Israeli settlers and to other Israeli bodies by members of the Greek hierarchy remains a subject of intense dissension in the Orthodox Church in Palestine to this day, and in 2005 led to a popular movement to unseat the patriarch, who was removed after the intervention of the Orthodox ecumenical patriarch of Istanbul and other senior Church leaders.

96. Important though they were, the significance of Arab Christians in the rise of the Arab movement was probably overemphasized by George Antonius in his pioneering work, *The Arab Awakening* (London: Hamish Hamilton, 1938). For a corrective, see A. L. Tibawi, *A Modern History of Syria* (London: Macmillan, 1969). Population figures for 1944 are from Albert Hourani, *Minorities in the Arab World* (Oxford: Oxford University Press, 1947), 52.

97. Several verses, political, elegiac, and social, are quoted in 'Awadat, *Min A'lam al-Fikr*, 477–78. Others are translated in Tadros, "*Min Dhikrayat al-Madi* 'Souvenirs,'" 316–20.

98. 'Awadat, *Min A'lam al-Fikr*, 478. My translation. This was probably intended as a particular reference to the diminutive stature of King 'Abdullah of Transjordan.

99. For details, see Porath, *The Emergence of the Palestinian-Arab National Movement*, 71–75.

100. 'Isa al-'Isa, "Min Dhikrayat al-Madi," 36.

101. Ibid., 64–65 and 68–69.

102. *Rose al-Yusuf*, Nov. 29, 1948. The pseudonym was "Father of the two eyes," a play on words (in both Arabic and English, as it happens) on the initials of his name. The Arabic wording of the verse is: "Bayna al-jalalati wal-samaha, da'at biladi, la mahala." According to al-'Isa's daughter, whom he was visiting in Egypt at the time, within days after publication of the poem, her father received a telegram from the mufti, in which al-Husayni indicated that he knew that al-'Isa had written the poem "Lam yakhfa' 'alayi ruhuka ya 'Isa" (You cannot hide your soul from me, oh 'Isa): interview with Layla al-'Isa Tadros, Aix-en-Provence, France, August 6, 2005.

103. 'Isa al-'Isa, "Min Dhikrayat al-Madi," 9.

104. R. Khalidi, *Palestinian Identity*, chapter 6, 119–44, conveys the results of the survey.

105. al-'Isa claims that the abrupt change in tone of the Egyptian press had a sinister cause: he relates a conversation that a friend overheard during which Nisim Malul informed an interlocutor that *al-Muqattam* had stopped publication of articles on Zionism in return for his offer to take out five hundred new subscriptions: 'Isa al-'Isa, "Min Dhikrayat al-Madi," 10–11. In "An Open Letter to His Excellency the High Commissioner from the Editor and Proprietor of 'La Palestine' Newspaper" [in English], *Filastin*, April 7, 1922, 1, al-'Isa claimed

that the British authorities had closed down his paper seventeen times. According to an article in *Mira't al-Gharb*, by the 1930s *Filastin* had been the target of twenty-seven similar actions: cited in Tadros, *"Min Dhikrayat al-Madi 'Souvenirs,'"* Annex 2.

106. During the prewar period, *Filastin* published an important series on agricultural conditions, in the form of letters from a fallah. This series, entitled "Rasa'il fallah" [Letters of a Fallah], began in October 1911 and continued for several months. Over a period from 1921 until 1931, *Filastin* published at least eighteen leading articles devoted solely to agricultural matters.

107. "Al-Fallah al-watani al-Filastini wa fawzihi fil-ma'rad al-zira'i" [The Palestinian National Peasant and His Victory at the Agricultural Fair] *Filastin*, October 7, 1927, 1.

108. *Filastin*, November 25, 1927, 1.

109. See R. Khalidi, *Palestinian Identity*, 89–117.

110. "Al-Bay' bil-jumla" and "Hizb al-samasra wa hizb al-hukuma," *Filastin*, September 5, 1924 and July 24, 1925.

111. "Ghuraba' fi biladina: Ghaflatuna wa yaqthatuhum," *Filastin*, March 5, 1929, 1.

4. The Revolt, 1948, and Afterward

1. Report by General Robert Haining, August 30, 1938, cited in Lesch, *Arab Politics*, 223.

2. Morris, *Righteous Victims*, 159.

3. The seventy-five-year-old Shaykh Farhan al-Sa'di was hanged by the British on charges that a bullet was found in his possession. He was in fact one of the first and most important leaders of the revolt, and had been a lieutenant of Shaykh 'Iz al-Din al-Qassam in November 1935, escaping the British police ambush in which al-Qassam had been killed: Zu'aytir, *Yawmiyyat*.

4. W. Khalidi, *From Haven to Conquest*, Appendix 4, 846–49.

5. This calculation is based on the figures in McCarthy, *The Population of Palestine*, Table A4–5, 104, which indicates that less than 40 percent of the male Muslim population (and a slightly larger proportion of the male Christian population) was between the ages of twenty and sixty in 1940.

6. See photos of fifteen leading commanders of the 1936–39 revolt, ten of whom were killed in combat, in Zu'aytir, *Yawmiyyat*, pp. following 660.

7. This is clear from the figures in W. Khalidi, *From Haven to Conquest*, Appendix 3, 845, which indicate that the British confiscated over 13,200 firearms from Arabs from 1936 until 1945. During the same period, confiscations from Jews totaled 521, at a time when the British were encouraging Jewish military formations to participate in the repression of the revolt alongside British forces, and giving them arms and training.

8. While the Egyptian Muslim Brotherhood publicized its involvement in sending volunteers to Palestine, other parties such as Misr al-Fatat sent volunteers

as well: interview with Muhammad Hasanayn Haykal, Cairo, December 27, 2005. A Zionist intelligence report, produced for the French government by a certain "M. Jarblum," describes the recruitment of 150 Syrian volunteers, mainly from the Hauran region, to be sent to Palestine: MAE, Palestine, 1930–40, vol. 61, memo enclosed in Foreign Minister Delbos to High Commissioner Martel, Beirut, February, 16, 1938. The Hama regional museum, located in that city's 'Azm palace, had a section exhibiting portraits of scores of Syrian volunteers from the region who had died fighting in Palestine in 1937–39 and in 1948.

9. The mufti offered his services to the British and the French against Germany and Italy as late as August 1939: MAE, Palestine, 1930–40, vol. 61, High Commissioner Puaux, Beirut, to Foreign Minister Bonnet, August 5, 1939.

10. Evidence of this mistrust on the part of the militants is extensive. See Zu'aytir, *Yawmiyyat,* and the newly published memoirs of Rashid al-Hajj Ibrahim, *al-Difa' 'an Haifa wa qadiyat Filastin: Mudhakirrat Rashid al-Hajj Ibrahim, 1891–1953* [The Defense of Haifa and the Palestine Question: The Memoirs of Rashid al-Hajj Ibrahim, 1891–1953], ed. and with an introduction by W. Khalidi (Beirut: Institute of Palestine Studies, 2005). See also Fawzi al-Qawuqji's memoirs, ed. Khayriyya Qasmiyya, *Filastin fi mudhakirrat al-Qawuqji, 1936–1948* [Palestine in the Qawuqji Memoirs, 1936–1948] (Beirut: PLO Research Center, 1975).

11. Prof. Walid Khalidi recounts seeing the mufti meeting with 'Abd al-Qadir al-Husayni and other Palestinian military leaders in Beirut during the 1940s: interview, Cambridge, Mass., November 8, 2003.

12. An example of the degree of surveillance of the mufti by the nascent intelligence service of the Zionist movement is a report on the mufti's activities in Lebanon delivered to the French government by Nahum Goldmann, representative of the Jewish Agency in Geneva: MAE, Palestine, 1930–40, vol. 61, October 14, 1938.

13. MAE, Palestine, 1930–40, vol. 61, High Commissioner Puaux, Beirut, to Foreign Minister Bonnet, August 5, 1939.

14. To gauge the extent of that harm, see Schechtman, *The Mufti and the Fuhrer,* which well represents the way the mufti was generally portrayed after he fled to Germany in 1941.

15. MAE, Palestine, 1930–40, vol. 61, telegram from Foreign Ministry to High Commissioner, Beirut, January 2, 1939.

16. MAE, Palestine, 1930–40, vol. 61, High Commissioner Puaux, Beirut, to Foreign Minister Bonnet, March 29, 1939.

17. Although the secondary sources differ on this question, Bayan al-Hut, in *Qiyadat,* 397, offers what seems to be a conclusive interpretation, showing from contemporary sources that a majority of the Arab Higher Committee favored acceptance of the White Paper.

18. Communiqué of April 10, 1939, cited in Porath, *The Emergence of the Palestinian-Arab National Movement,* 291.

19. The French were astonished when the British requested that the surveillance on the mufti's activities in Lebanon be relaxed, after repeated British demands that it be tightened. On inquiring about this at the Foreign Office, French diplomats were told that the British government wanted "tous les éléments même les plus extremes" (all elements, even the most extreme) represented at the London conference, including "quelques personnalités reflétant les idées du Mufti" (some personalities who reflect the ideas of the mufti), but that the ban on him personally was still in place: MAE, Palestine, 1930–40, vol. 61, telegram, Foreign Ministry to High Commissioner, Beirut, January 10, 1939. This did not prevent indirect British contacts with the mufti at various stages. Even after World War II, during which the mufti had worked openly with the Nazis, recently released Colonial Office documents (CO 537/2643) show that British officials maintained clandestine contacts with him in Cairo and Lebanon. The commander of British forces in Palestine, Sir Alan Cunningham, in late 1947 recommended more formal contacts with the mufti, but was rebuffed by London: Robert Fisk, "Flirting with the Enemy," *Independent*, February 20, 1999.

20. Perhaps the best existing treatment of the dilemmas that faced the Palestinians in this regard is the chapter titled "Proposals for a Legislative Council," in Lesch, *Arab Politics in Palestine*, 179–97. See also Porath, *The Emergence of the Palestinian-Arab National Movement*, 123ff.

21. Ironically, among those few was King 'Abd al-'Aziz al-Sa'ud of Saudi Arabia, who in 1933 signed an oil-exploration agreement with a consortium of American companies, rejecting a competing British offer, and who in 1944 was the first independent Arab ruler to meet with an American president (Amir Faysal, son of Sharif Husayn of Mecca, had met President Wilson in Paris in 1919, but he was not then recognized by the Western powers as an independent sovereign), conferring with President Roosevelt aboard an American cruiser in Egypt: see R. Khalidi, *Resurrecting Empire*, 106–11, 125.

22. Transjordan obtained its (nominal) independence from Britain in 1946, and Amir 'Abdullah crowned himself king in May of that year.

23. British foreign secretary Ernest Bevin said as much to Musa al-'Alami, although al-'Alami's biographer is not convinced that the foreign secretary necessarily believed what he was saying: Furlonge, *Palestine Is My Country*, 135.

24. In the words of Avi Shlaim, *Collusion across the Jordan*, 139, "It is hardly an exaggeration to say that he [British Foreign Minister Bevin] colluded directly with the Transjordanians and indirectly with the Jews to abort the birth of a Palestinian Arab state."

25. Ibid., 110ff.

26. For an excellent survey of the early years of this relationship see Michael Suleiman, ed., *U.S. Policy on Palestine from Wilson to Clinton* (Normal, Il.: Association of Arab-American University Graduates, 1995).

27. 'Abdullah also had ambitions to expand his rule northward into Syria and even into the Iraqi domain of his Hashemite relatives. See Mary Wilson, *King*

Abdullah, Britain and the Making of Jordan (Cambridge, U.K.: Cambridge University Press, 1985), 155–215, and Shlaim, Collusion across the Jordan.

28. For a fascinating account of this effort, see Walid Khalidi, "On Albert Hourani, the Arab Office, and the Anglo-American Committee of Inquiry of 1946," Journal of Palestine Studies 35, no. 1 (autumn 2005): 60–79. Hourani's testimony to the commission is included in the same issue. See also al-'Alami's biography, Furlonge, Palestine Is My Country, 130–51.

29. Its commander, the Syrian Fawzi al-Qawuqji, left memoirs, which must be used with some care: Qawuqji, Filastin fi mudhakirrat al-Qawuqji. See also Levenberg, The Military Preparations, and W. Khalidi, Haven to Conquest, Appendices 7, 9A, and 9B.

30. See ibid. for detailed figures on the ALA and other Arab irregular forces.

31. For details, see Introduction, n. 33.

32. As with so much else about the 1948 war, the work of Walid Khalidi is indispensable, in this case his seminal article "Plan Dalet."

33. For fall of Haifa, see Rashid al-Hajj Ibrahim's newly published memoirs, al-Difa' 'an Haifa, and Walid Khalidi, "The Fall of Haifa," Middle East Forum 35, no. 10 (Dec. 1959), 22–32.

34. Walid Khalidi, Dayr Yasin, aljum'a, 9 nisan 1948 [Dayr Yasin, 9 April 1948] (Beirut: Institute for Palestine Studies, 1999).

35. See Muhammad al-Az'ar, Hukumat 'umum Filastin fi dhikraha al-khamsin [The All Palestine Government: On Its Fiftieth Anniversary] (Cairo: Dar al-Shuruq, 1998), for more on this body.

36. The only exception was after Israel's February 1955 Gaza raid embarrassed the Egyptian government, which had not previously made confronting Israel a priority, and led to Egypt briefly encouraging Palestinian raids into Israel. After the Suez war of 1956, the Egyptian authorities clamped down again.

5. Fateh, the PLO, and the PA: The Palestinian Para-State

An earlier version of sections of this chapter appeared in the London Review of Books under the title "After 'Arafat" 27, no. 3 (Feb. 3, 2005): 16–18.

1. These "noms de guerre," in these cases meaning "father of Iyyad" and "father of Jihad," were often based on real names: thus Salah Khalaf had a son named Iyyad, and Khalil al-Wazir a son named Jihad. 'Arafat was known as Abu 'Ammar. For biographical details, see Abu Iyyad, with Eric Rouleau, My Home, My Land: A Narrative of the Palestinian Struggle (New York: Times Books, 1981), and Alan Hart, Arafat: Terrorist or Peacemaker? (London: Sidgwick & Jackson, 1984).

2. Perhaps the definitive work on the Palestinian refugee population in Lebanon is Julie Peteet, Landscape of Hope and Despair: Palestinian Refugee Camps

(Philadelphia: University of Pennsylvania Press, 2005). See also Rosemary Sayigh, *Palestinians: From Peasants to Revolutionaries* (London: Zed, 1979), and *Too Many Enemies: The Palestinian Experience in Lebanon* (London: Zed, 1994), and Mohamed Kamel Dorai, *Les réfugiés palestiniens du Liban: Une géographie de l'exile* (Paris: CNRS Editions, 2006).

3. Regarding the civil war in Jordan, see John Cooley, *Green March, Black September: The Story of the Palestinian Arabs* (London: Cass, 1973), Yazid Sayigh, *Armed Struggle and the Search for State: The Palestinian National Movement, 1949–1993* (Oxford, U.K.: Clarendon Press, 1997), 243–81; regarding the PLO in Lebanon, see Walid Khalidi, *Conflict and Violence in Lebanon: Confrontation in the Middle East* (Cambridge, Mass.: Harvard Center for International Affairs, 1979), and Rex Brynen, *Sanctuary and Survival: The PLO in Lebanon* (Boulder, Colo.: Westview, 1990).

4. In this criminal attack on the cruise-ship *Achille Lauro*, a handicapped, elderly, Jewish American, Leon Klinghoffer, was hurled to a watery death in his wheelchair: see Sayigh, *Armed Struggle and the Search for State*, 586.

5. For details, see ibid., 640–41.

6. This description of 'Arafat is based on the impressions of a number of people who saw him over a lengthy period of time, which coincided with my own observations.

7. Most respected studies of Palestinian politics, the modern Palestinian national movement, and the PLO have this explicit or implicit premise. Among them are Helena Cobban, *The Palestinian Liberation Organization* (Cambridge, U.K.: Cambridge University Press, 1984); Alain Gresh, *The PLO: The Struggle Within: Towards an Independent State* (London: Zed, 1985); Nadine Picaudou, *Le movement national palestinien: Genèse et structures* (Paris: Harmattan, 1989); Glenn Robinson, *Building a Palestinian State: The Incomplete Revolution* (Bloomington: Indiana University Press, 1997); Laurie Brand, *Palestinians in the Arab World: Institution Building and the Search for State* (New York: Columbia University Press, 1988); Sayigh, *Armed Struggle and the Search for State*; and Shaul Mishal, *The PLO under 'Arafat: Between Gun and Olive Branch* (New Haven, Conn.: Yale University Press, 1986).

8. E.g., Barry Rubin, *Revolution until Victory: The Politics and History of the PLO* (Boston: Harvard University Press, 1994), and Raphael Israeli, ed., *PLO in Lebanon: Selected Documents* (London: Weidenfeld & Nicholson, 1983). One does not find such hostility in the work of respected Israeli experts on Palestinian politics and society such as Baruch Kimmerling and Joel Migdal, *Palestinians: The Making of a People* (New York: Free Press, 1993); Avraham Sela and Moshe Maoz, eds., *PLO and Israel: From Armed Conflict to Political Solution* (New York: St. Martin's, 1997); Mishal, *The PLO under 'Arafat*; and Shaul Mishal and Avraham Sela, *Palestinian Hamas: Vision, Violence and Coexistence* (New York: Columbia University Press, 2000).

9. Eminent Palestinian critics of the PLO and the PA include Dr. Haydar 'Abd al-

Shafi and Edward Said. See an interview with 'Abd al-Shafi, "Looking Back, Looking Forward," *Journal of Palestine Studies* 125 (autumn 2002): 28–35; and Said's writings on the subject, which are collected in *Peace and Its Discontents: Essays on Palestine in the Middle East Peace Process* (New York: Vintage, 1996); *The End of the Peace Process: Oslo and After* (New York: Pantheon, 2000); and the posthumously published *From Oslo to Iraq and the Road Map* (New York: Pantheon, 2004). See also Rashid Khalidi, "Blind Curves and Detours on the Road to Self-Rule," *New York Times*, September 14, 1993, A25.

10. Israel evacuated all its troops and its six thousand settlers from the Gaza Strip in August 2005, but has maintained effective control by air, land, and sea by preventing the rebuilding of Gaza's airport or the building of a port, and through insisting that passage to Israel and all egress and exit of goods and services go through crossing points run by the Israeli security services. Palestinians can now travel to Egypt by the Rafah crossing, which is monitored by the Israeli security services. Since its evacuation, Israel has maintained air surveillance over the Gaza Strip, and has launched air attacks and artillery strikes at will. Most experts, including Israeli legal specialists, therefore agree that the Gaza Strip is in some essential ways still in practice occupied territory.

11. For a presentation of this argument, see Raja Khalidi, "Reshaping Palestinian Economic Policy Discourse: Putting the Development Horse before the Governance Cart," *Journal of Palestine Studies* 34, no. 3 (spring 2005): 77–87, which reviews the important book edited by Mushtaq Husain Khan, George Giacaman, and Inge Amundsen, *State Formation in Palestine: Viability and Governance during a Social Transformation* (London: Routledge Curzon, 2004).

12. The term "irreversibility" has long been used by one of the most respected of these analysts, former Jerusalem deputy mayor Meron Benvenisti, to denote the tipping point (which he argues was reached many years ago), after which it becomes impossible to reverse Israel's colonization process in the West Bank and constitute an independent Palestinian state, a topic discussed further in Chapter 6. For works that lay out Benvenisti's main theses, see n. 41 in that chapter.

13. For the history of the PLO, in addition to works cited in n. 7, see Walid Kazziha, *Revolutionary Transformation in the Arab World: Habash and His Comrades from Nationalism to Marxism* (London: Charles Knight, 1975); R. Augustus Norton and M. Greenberg, eds., *The International Relations of the Palestine Liberation Organization* (Carbondale: Southern Illinois University Press, 1989); Julie Peteet, *Gender in Crisis: Women and the Palestinian Resistance Movement* (New York: Columbia University Press, 1991); William Quandt, Fuad Jabber, and Ann Lesch, *The Politics of Palestinian Nationalism* (Berkeley: University of California Press, 1973); 'Isa al-Shu'aybi, *al-Kiyaniyya al-filistiniyya: al-Wa'i al-dhati wal-tatawwur al-mu'assasati 1947–1977* [Palestinian "Entity-ness": Self-consciousness and Institutional Development] (Beirut: PLO Research Center, 1979); and Rashid Khalidi, *Under Siege: PLO*

Decision-making during the 1982 War (New York: Columbia University Press, 1985).

14. Polling of Palestinians in the West Bank and Gaza Strip since the 1990s consistently bears this out. Among the respected institutions engaged in polling is the Jerusalem Media and Communications Center, which has been engaged in this activity since 1993. Skepticism about the sincerity of the Palestinians' adoption of a two-state solution, widespread among Israelis until the late 1980s, was thereafter confined to the Israeli right, until the second intifada of 2000 led the Israeli mainstream to doubt it again. Similar attitudes in rightwing American public discourse and among major institutions of the American Jewish community have been less well-informed and more extreme than in Israel.

15. Among those arguing the former was Edward Said, in the works cited in n. 9. The latter argument is made for example in Sayigh, *Armed Struggle and the Search for State.*

16. For further discussion of the Palestinian secular democratic state proposal, see Chapter 6.

17. This was ironical, as the United States had already voted in the General Assembly in favor of such a state by supporting the 1947 partition resolution, which called for the establishment of an Arab state alongside a Jewish one.

18. One of the few to do so was the late Edward Said, in a series of coruscating analytical articles later collected in the three volumes cited in n. 9.

19. I was one of several advisors to this delegation during its twenty months of existence. For Palestinian participant accounts see: Haydar 'Abd al-Shafi, "Looking Back, Looking Forward"; Hanan Ashrawi, *This Side of Peace: A Personal Account* (New York: Simon & Schuster, 1995); Camille Mansour, "The Palestinian-Israel Peace Negotiations: An Overview and Assessment," *Journal of Palestine Studies* 87 (spring 1993), 5–31; Mamduh Nawfal, *al-Inqilab: Asrar al-masar al-filastini-al-isra'ili, Madrid-Washington* [The Upheaval: Secrets of the Palestinian-Israeli Track, Madrid-Washington] (Amman: Dar al-Shuruq, 1996); and Raja Shehadeh, "Negotiating Self-Government Arrangements," *Journal of Palestine Studies* 21, no. 4 (summer 1992): 22–31.

20. The individual who had long before been charged by the PLO leadership with leading a team to prepare position papers for eventual negotiations with Israel arrived in Madrid just as members of the delegation were checking out of their hotel the day after conclusion of the conference. It later transpired that these papers were largely unusable in any case: personal information of the author.

21. For an account of the Oslo negotiations by the two PLO leaders who were in charge of them, see Mahmud Abbas (Abu Mazin), *Through Secret Channels: The Road to Oslo, Senior PLO Leader Abu Mazen's Revealing Story of the Negotiations with Israel* (Reading, U.K.: Garnet, 1995); and Ahmad Quray' [Abu al-'Ala], *al-Riwaya al-filistiniyya al-kamila lil-mufawadat: Min Oslo ila kharitat*

al-tariq. 1 *Mufawadat Oslo, 1993* [The Complete Palestinian Account of the Negotiations: From Oslo to the Road Map. 1, The Oslo Negotiations, 1993] (Beirut: Institute for Palestine Studies, 2005).

22. Hilde Henriksen Waage, "Norway's Role in the Middle Eastern Peace Talks: Between a Strong State and a Weak Belligerent," *Journal of Palestine Studies* 136 (summer 2005): 6–24.

23. For participant accounts, see Akram Hanieh, "The Camp David Papers," special document, *Journal of Palestine Studies* 118 (winter 2001): 79–97; Dennis Ross, *The Missing Peace: The Inside Story of the Fight for Middle East Peace* (New York: Farrar, Straus and Giroux, 2004); Uri Savir, *The Process: 1,100 Days That Changed the Middle East* (New York: Random House, 1998), and Shlomo Ben Ami, *Scars of War, Wounds of Peace: The Israeli-Arab Tragedy* (New York: Oxford University Press, 2006). See also Clayton Swisher, *The Truth about Camp David: The Untold Story about the Collapse of the Middle East Peace Process* (New York: Nation Books, 2004), and Hussein Agha and Robert Malley, "Camp David: The Tragedy of Errors," *New York Review of Books* 48 (August 13, 2001), and the review of Ben Ami's book by Joel Beinin, "When Doves Cry," *Nation* 282 (April 17, 2006): 15, 31–39.

24. Waage, "Norway's Role."

25. Leaders who died or were disabled included Khalid al-Hassan, Nimr Salih (Abu Salih), and George Habash. Nine of these sixteen individuals were members of the Fateh Central Committee, the most important leadership body in the PLO since the late 1960s.

26. *Sunday Times* (London), June 15, 1969, 12.

27. This standing was anchored in the terms of Article 4 of the Mandate for Palestine, as was noted in Chapter 2. See Henri Laurens, *Orientales II: La IIIe République et l'Islam* (Paris: CNRS Editions, 2004), 301ff, for how the Zionist movement was able to use its international diplomatic status in dealing with the French government.

28. As Shlomo Gazit, former head of Israeli military intelligence and a close advisor to Israeli prime minister Rabin put it at the time, " 'Arafat has a choice: he can be a Lahd or a super-Lahd." The derogatory reference was to General Antoine Lahd, commander of the Israeli-controlled "South Lebanese Army," which collaborated with Israeli forces in the occupation of Southern Lebanon until 2000: response to a question, Amherst College, March 4, 1994.

29. While UNRWA provided Palestinians in Lebanon with elementary education, and some health care and other forms of social support, the PLO until 1982 provided kindergartens, hospitals, air raid shelters, scholarships for secondary and university education, some welfare and social support, as well as extensive employment opportunities. See Rashid Khalidi, "The Palestinians in Lebanon: The Social Repercussions of the Israeli Invasion," *Middle East Journal* 38, no. 2 (spring 1984): 255–66, and Brynen, *Sanctuary and Survival*.

30. See R. Khalidi, *Under Siege,* chapter 1.

31. For details, see R. Khalidi, *Under Siege*, and "The Palestinians in Lebanon," and Brynen, *Sanctuary and Survival*.

32. Mamdouh Nofal, "Yasser Arafat, the Political Player: A Mixed Legacy," *Journal of Palestine Studies* 35, no. 2 (winter 2006), 23–37.

33. Strikingly, the Israeli foreign minister, Tzipi Livni, has stressed the distinction between terrorist attacks on unarmed civilians and Palestinian resistance against the Israeli military. "Somebody who is fighting against Israeli soldiers is an enemy and we will fight back, but I believe that this is not under the definition of terrorism, if the target is a soldier," Livni said in an interview with ABC-TV that was broadcast by Israeli radio: "Palestinians Who Target Soldiers not Terrorists, Israel FM," AFP, April 11, 2006. Her father, Eitan Livni, was chief of operations of the Irgun, which repeatedly attacked British officials and soldiers in the 1940s (as well as civilian targets like public markets).

34. Seventeen members of these groups, and others, died under torture in PA prisons during this period, according to reports by Palestinian human rights groups, which were harassed by the PA for reporting such violations.

35. Nofal, "Yasser Arafat," 35–36.

6. Stateless in Palestine

This chapter is in part based on a lecture originally delivered at a conference, The Uncertain State of Palestine, at the University of Minnesota in Minneapolis on April 23, 2004.

1. See R. Khalidi, *Palestinian Identity*, for further details.

2. For nearly a century, perhaps nothing in Palestine and Israel has been more contentious than demography. Thus, although most respected Israeli and Palestinian demographers and statistical compilations are in agreement on this general trend, it has been challenged by some who argue, with clear political overtones, that the Palestinian population is in fact smaller than has been believed.

3. In particular, this is what perhaps the greatest modern historian of the Jewish people, Salo Baron, memorably called the "lachrymose conception of Jewish history": Salo Baron, *History and Jewish Historians* (Philadelphia: Jewish Publications Society, 1964), 64.

4. According to an authority on demography in Ottoman Palestine, Justin McCarthy, in *The Population of Palestine*, 12, as late as the 1880s only a small proportion of Palestine's Jewish residents were Europeans who were not Ottoman citizens. Even as late as 1914, he suggests (23), a majority of Palestine's Jewish residents were Ottoman citizens.

5. Jacobsen, "From Empire to Empire," examines the transformation of identities among communities in Palestine during World War I.

6. The Covenant described Syria and Palestine as areas "whose existence as inde-

pendent nations can be provisionally recognized." Cited in J. C. Hurewitz, *The Middle East and North Africa in World Politics: A Documentary Record*, vol. 2 (New Haven, Conn.: Yale University Press, 1979), 179.

7. For an early statement of this case, see Antonius, *The Arab Awakening*.

8. Among these mandates, only Iraq had obtained even nominal independence when the League of Nations went out of existence with the eruption of World War II.

9. For the full text of the program adopted at the Biltmore Conference of American Zionists attended by Chaim Weizmann and David Ben-Gurion in New York on May 9–11, 1942, see W. Khalidi, *From Haven to Conquest*, 495–97.

10. Yehuda Reinharz, *Chaim Weizmann: The Making of a Statesman* (Oxford, U.K.: Oxford University Press, 1993), 356–57, describes a meeting at Balfour's house in 1922 at which Balfour, Winston Churchill, and Lloyd George told Weizmann that "by the [Balfour] Declaration they always meant an eventual Jewish state." Lloyd George added that Britain must not allow representative government in Palestine.

11. Nur Masalha, *Expulsion of the Palestinians*, 29. Ben-Gurion agreed privately. He wrote in an internal memo titled "Lines for Zionist Policy" in 1941: "It is impossible to imagine general evacuation [of the Arab population] without compulsion, and brutal compulsion," cited in ibid., 128.

12. Anita Shapira, *Land and Power: The Zionist Resort to Force, 1881–1948* (Oxford, U.K.: Oxford University Press, 1992).

13. W. Khalidi, *From Haven to Conquest*, Appendix 1, 843, and 680.

14. The term "politicide" was coined by the Israeli sociologist Baruch Kimmerling, who used it to describe the policies of Ariel Sharon, which he saw as an extension of earlier trends, going back to 1948: *Politicide: Ariel Sharon's War against the Palestinians* (London and New York: Verso, 2002).

15. The concept derived in part from the transfers of Greeks to Greece and Turks to Turkey in the wake of the Turkish-Greek war that followed World War I.

16. For more on this issue, see Benny Morris, *Birth of the Palestinian Refugee Problem*, and Nur Masalha, *Expulsion of the Palestinians: The Concept of "Transfer."* There is a vast polemical debate on the topic of intentionality and prior planning for the expulsions that largely misses the point.

17. This made possible the creation of a state with a large Jewish majority in an area of 78 percent of Palestine (instead of the 55 percent specified by the 1947 UN General Assembly partition resolution) that previously had had a large Arab majority.

18. Text of Article 6 of the Palestinian National Charter, cited in Faysal Hawrani, *al-Fikr al-siyasi al-filastini, 1964–1974: Dirasa lil-mawathiq al-ra'isiyya li-munazzamat al-tahrir al-filastiniyya* [Palestinian Political Thought, 1964–1974: A Study of the Principle Documents of the PLO] (Beirut: PLO Research Center, 1980), 236.

19. For details see Furlonge, *Palestine Is My Country,* 127, and Khalaf, *Politics in Palestine,* 77.

20. For a devastating deconstruction of these myths, see Simha Flapan, *The Birth of Israel.*

21. See Segev, *1949: The First Israelis,* which nicely captures the new nature of the Israeli polity after the great influx of immigrants.

22. These processes are best described by Ian Lustick, *Arabs in the Jewish State: Israel's Control of a National Minority* (Austin: University of Texas Press, 1980); Elia Zureik, *The Palestinians in Israel: A Study in Internal Colonialism* (London: Routledge Kegan Paul, 1979); and Sabri Jiryis, *The Arabs in Israel* (New York: Monthly Review Press, 1976).

23. On Mizrahis in Israel, see Shlomo Swirski, *Israel: The Oriental Majority* (London: Zed, 1989), and Gershon Shafir and Yoav Peled, *Being Israeli: The Dynamics of Multiple Citizenship* (Cambridge, U.K.: Cambridge University Press, 2002), 74–95.

24. One of the most comprehensive contemporary statements of the democratic state idea can be found in Muhammad Rashid (pseudonym for Nabil Sha'th), *Towards a Democratic State in Palestine* (Beirut: PLO Research Center, 1970). For a thoughtful and well-informed discussion of the internal Palestinian debate on this matter, see Gresh, *The PLO: The Struggle Within,* 9–57.

25. Segev, *1949: The First Israelis,* 95ff.

26. George Tomeh, ed., *United Nations Resolutions on Palestine and the Arab-Israeli Conflict,* I, *1947–1974* (Washington, D.C.: Institute for Palestine Studies, 1975), 143.

27. For details on how the PNC and other PLO leadership bodies functioned, see Cobban, *The Palestinian Liberation Organization.*

28. For an account of the process whereby this shift took place, see Hawrani, *al-Fikr al-siyasi al-filastini,* 183–218.

29. Former Israeli chief of staff Mordechai Gur said during the signing ceremony for the 1993 Oslo Accords that had Israel taken advantage of PLO overtures, an agreement with the Palestinians would have been possible fifteen years earlier: Tom Segev, "Looking Back in Anger," *Haaretz,* January 30, 2006.

30. "Invitation to Peace Conference" from the United States and the Soviet Union, dated October 18, 1991. The text of the letter of invitation and the U.S. letters of assurances to the various parties can be found in "Special Document File: The Madrid Peace Conference," *Journal of Palestine Studies* 21, no. 2 (winter 1992): 117ff.

31. On the origins of the settlements, see Gershom Gorenberg, *The Accidental Empire: Israel and the Birth of the Settlements, 1967–1977* (New York: Holt, 2006).

32. The letter of invitation, also dated October 18, 1991, was sent to all participants. Separate letters of assurance with the same date were sent to each of the parties, and shared with all of them.

33. "Special Document File: The Madrid Peace Conference," *Journal of Palestine Studies* 21, no. 2 (winter 1992): 117ff.

34. See interview with 'Abd al-Shafi: "Looking Back, Looking Forward," *Journal of Palestine Studies* 32, no. 1 (autumn 2002): 28–35.

35. About which see Clayton E. Swisher, *The Truth about Camp David: The Untold Story about the Collapse of the Middle East Peace Process* (New York: Nation Books, 2004), which is superior to the self-serving work of one of the central participants on the American side from 1991 until 2000, Dennis Ross, *The Missing Peace: The Inside Story of the Fight for Middle East Peace* (New York: Farrar, Straus and Giroux, 2004).

36. Among the most reliable and consistent polling of Palestinian opinion in the West Bank, Gaza Strip, and East Jerusalem has been that of the Jerusalem Media and Communications Center, whose website (www.jmcc.org/) provides easy access to all their polls dating back to 1993. Arafat's high in this JMCC polling was 46.4 percent in Poll No. 23 in November 1997; his low was 21 percent in Poll No. 48 in April 2003. The trend is unmistakably and precipitately downward after the mid-1990s.

37. These developments were amply reported in Israel's press, particularly in that country's newspaper of record, *Haaretz,* by its correspondents in the occupied territories, Amira Hass and Danny Rubinstein, and by Gideon Levy, Akiva Eldar, and others, as well as in *Yediot Aharanot* by Alex Fishman, and in *Maariv* by Ben Caspit.

38. I am indebted to a recent lecture by Amira Hass for this insight.

39. This new situation is summarized by Amira Hass ("The Roads Not Taken," *Haaretz,* March 24, 2006) as follows:

> The regime of restriction on movement imposed by Israel on the Palestinians has crumbled the West Bank into dozens of closed or partially closed enclaves isolated from each other despite their geographical proximity. Permanent and mobile checkpoints, along with physical barriers of various kinds, fencing off of main roads, limitations on Palestinian traffic on east-west and north-south arteries, have cut off direct transportational links between areas of the West Bank.
>
> Thus, a new geographic, social and economic reality has emerged in the West Bank. Hundreds of exits from Palestinian communities to main and regional roads are blocked. Traffic among the enclaves is directed to secondary roads and a small number of main roads passing through Israel Defense Force–controlled bottle-necks. Entry to the Jordan Valley, Palestinian East Jerusalem and to enclaves between the separation fence and the Green Line is barred to all Palestinians except those registered as residents of those areas. To enter such areas, special authorization to "non-residents" must be obtained, which is rarely given.

40. Statistics from UNCTAD "Report on UNCTAD's Assistance to the Palestinian People," TD/B/52/2, July 21, 2005, Table 1, 6.

41. The data collected by the project was presented in a series of works by Benvenisti including (with Shlomo Khayat) *The West Bank and Gaza Atlas* (Jerusalem: West Bank Data Base Project, 1988); *1987 Report: Demographic, Economic, Legal, Social and Political Developments in the West Bank* (Boulder, Colo.: Westview Press, 1987); *1986 Report: Demographic, Economic, Legal, Social and Political Developments in the West Bank* (Boulder, Colo.: Westview Press, 1986).

42. See Edward Said's *From Oslo to Iraq and the Road Map*, with a foreword by Tony Judt, as well as the latter's article, "Israel: The Alternative," *New York Review of Books* 50, no. 16 (October 23, 2003).

43. Victoria Tilley, *The One State Solution: A Breakthrough for Peace in the Israeli-Palestinian Deadlock* (Ann Arbor: University of Michigan Press, 2005).

44. The parallels with South Africa are only superficially accurate. The disparity in numbers between nonwhites and whites there was much greater than that between Arabs and Jews in Palestine (at least since the earliest decades of the twentieth century). Moreover, the South African liberation movement always had relatively secure rear areas from which to wage its struggle, and strong allies, unlike the Palestinians. Also unlike the Palestinian national movement, which has repeatedly changed its focus over more than eighty-five years, the South African liberation movement never wavered from its goal of a single democratic state with equal rights for all. South Africa always claimed sovereignty over its entire territory, and over the entire people, even as it tried to turn some areas into "self-governing" Bantustans: Israeli governments have shown no desire for sovereignty over Palestinian populations, even as they have coveted their land. Most importantly, although less based on a formal, explicit, legal framework of separation than was apartheid, the flexible, dynamic, ad hoc regime that Israel has erected in the occupied territories over nearly four decades, and especially since 1991, is more controlling, and more flexible, than anything undertaken under the apartheid regime. Leaving aside superficial similarities between the South African pass system and Israel's permit system, there are thus only limited parallels between the defunct apartheid system and the comprehensive and sophisticated matrix of control that Israel has created in the occupied West Bank, Gaza Strip, and East Jerusalem.

45. This right is enshrined in UN General Assembly Resolution 194 of December 11, 1948, which states in part that "refugees wishing to return to their homes and live at peace with their neighbors should be permitted to do so at the earliest practicable date, and that compensation should be paid for the property of those choosing not to return." Full text in Tomeh, ed., *United Nations Resolutions*, I, *1947–1974*, 15–17.

46. One outspoken advocate of such a view is Salman Abu Sitta, author of *Palestinian Right to Return: Sacred, Legal and Possible* (London: Palestinian Return Centre, 1999), and *Atlas of Palestine, 1948* (London: Palestine Land Society, 2004).

47. This, as well as moral considerations, seems to be the basis for the views of the late Edward Said, and of Tony Judt.

48. Among the exceptions are the book by Tilley, cited in n. 43, and some of the writings of Said and Judt, cited in n. 42, above.

49. See the essays in Beshara Doumani, ed., *Academic Freedom after September 11* (New York: Zone Books, 2006), especially those by Judith Butler, Joel Beinin, and Doumani himself.

50. The text of the resolution can be found in Tomeh, ed, *United Nations Resolutions*, I, *1947–1974*, 4–14.

51. For details of the secret negotiations see Itamar Rabinovich, *The Road Not Taken*, and Shlaim, *The Iron Wall*, 95–142. The Rogers Plan was put forward by U.S. secretary of state William Rogers. His successor, Dr. Henry Kissinger, organized a brief peace conference meeting in Geneva in 1973, after which he shuttled through the region, negotiating disengagement accords between Israel and Syria and Egypt. The Carter administration tried to return to multilateral diplomacy with the 1977 joint communiqué.

52. Such a rail link was proposed by researchers for the Rand Corporation, in Doug Suisman, Steven Simon, Glenn Robinson, C. Ross Anthony, and Michael Schoenbaum, *The Arc: A Formal Structure for a Palestinian State* (Santa Monica, Calif.: Rand, 2005).

53. In an interview with Ari Shavit in *Haaretz* magazine, October, 8, 2004, Weisglass stated: "The disengagement is actually formaldehyde. It supplies the amount of formaldehyde that's necessary so that there will not be a political process with the Palestinians." Later, Shavit asked: "From your point of view, then, your major achievement is to have frozen the political process legitimately?" Weisglass's response was: "That is exactly what happened. You know, the term 'political process' is a bundle of concepts and commitments. The political process is the establishment of a Palestinian state with all the security risks that entails. The political process is the evacuation of settlements, it's the return of refugees, it's the partition of Jerusalem. And all that has now been frozen."

54. Among those whose statements and writing indicate this realization are Amos Oz, David Grossman, Tom Segev, and Gideon Levy.

55. For more on this now-forgotten period, see Khalidi, *Resurrecting Empire*, 30–35.

For a complete bibliography, as well as additional information, please visit www.beacon.org/ironcage.

Acknowledgments

As with any book that has been long in gestation, this one has caused me to incur many debts. I should have kept better track of them over the ten years while this book was a work in progress, as I fear that I may have forgotten some of those from whose advice or help I have benefited.

Several institutions provided support for the research for and writing of this book. It was initially conceived and I wrote parts of it at the University of Chicago, one of the world's greatest research universities. I am grateful to the university for support in a variety of forms, including funding from the Division of Social Sciences and a sabbatical in 2001–2002, during which much of the work on it was completed. The Maison Mediterranéenne des Sciences de l'Homme in Aix-en-Provence and its director, Dr. Robert Ilbert, and his colleagues and staff provided me with a hospitable and friendly intellectual environment for this sabbatical. Columbia University has provided me with generous research support for this book over the past three years.

I am grateful also to the institutions that invited me to present portions of this book in lectures and conferences between 1997 and 2005, including the American University of Beirut; the University of Chicago; Bogazici University; the St. Antony's College Middle East Centre, Oxford University; Erlangen University; the University of Utah, Salt Lake City; the Keough Institute for Irish Studies, Notre Dame University; the Maison Mediterranéenne des Sciences de l'Homme in Aix-en-Provence; Bir Zeit University, Ramallah, Palestine; the University of Minnesota; and the Princeton University History Department. In numerous cases I received valuable feedback from participants and attendees at these conferences and lectures.

I received assistance with research and in the form of valuable research materials or leads from numerous individuals, including Dr. Haidar 'Abd al-Shafi, 'Ali Abu Nimah, Raed Badr, Musa Budeiri, Muhammad Hasanayn Haykal, Laila al-'Isa, Raja al-'Isa, Walid Khalidi, Noor Aiman Khan, Mona Nsouli, William Raley, Noha Tadros, Ramzi Tadros, and the staffs of the archives of the Ministère des Affaires Etrangères, Paris, and the libraries of the University of Chicago, the Institute for Palestine Studies, the Maison Mediterranéenne des Sciences de l'Homme, and Columbia University.

A number of people have read parts of this book in different forms at different times, or have discussed its main arguments with me, or have provided me with valuable ideas or information. They include Rena Barakat, Musa Budeiri, Jim Chandler, Sylvie Denoix, Selim Diringil, Thierry Fabre, Israel Gershoni, Lamya Khalidi, Muhammad Ali Khalidi, Raja Khalidi, Ahmad Khalifa, Henry Laurens, Issam Nassar, Roger Owen, Jean-Claude Pascual, Nadine Picaudou, Eugene Rogan, Avi Shlaim, Salim Tamari, and Fawwaz Trabulsi. I have learned much from the research and writing of doctoral students, current and former, whose theses I have had the pleasure to supervise or read, including Lori Allen, Rena Barakat, Yuval Ben Bassat, Louis Fishman, the late Tania Forte, Sarah Gualtieri, Abigail Jacobsen, Noor Aiman Khan, Loren Lybarger, Weldon Matthews, Maha Nassar, Tamara Neumann, and Jihan Sfeir-Khayat.

I undoubtedly learned the most about the period before 1948 from Walid Khalidi, whose important writings are essential reading for any student of Palestinian history and are liberally cited throughout this work. Although all of these individuals helped to improve the book, none of them necessarily agrees with or is responsible for the views expressed herein, nor are they responsible for any errors or omissions that it may contain.

I am grateful to everyone at Beacon Press who worked on this book. Pam MacColl, Tom Hallock, Lisa Sacks, and P. J. Tierney made the difficult process of turning drafts into a finished book as painless as possible. Helene Atwan helped me to develop the initial themes of the book and persuaded me to carry the story more fully up to the present. Once again, beyond gracefully editing the finished product, she spent much time in phone conversations and in emails refining my ideas, restraining my sometimes excessive ardor, and smoothing my tangled prose. She has made this book far better than it otherwise would have been.

Many people have supported and sustained me over the years I was working on this project, including colleagues and coworkers who put up with my prolonged absences and my frequent distraction as I worked on this book. I owe special thanks in this regard to Vera Beard, Jackie Bhabha, Susan Gzesh, Linda Butler, and Astrid Benedek, as well as my colleagues in the History and Near East Languages and Civilizations Departments at the University of Chicago and the Department of History at Columbia University.

Others have supported me in other ways, including innumerable friends whom I have bored discussing the topic of the book, and most importantly my family, who has had to tolerate my absorption with this project for a prolonged period. My wife, Mona, deserves particular appreciation for her good humor and constructive criticism as my obsession with this seemingly endless travail, and its painful themes, occupied many an evening, many a weekend, and many a vacation. The subject of this book is something that both of us, and most Palestinians, have had to live with for much of our lives. It appears that our children will have to do so as well for quite some time. I dedicate it to their generation, in the hope that they will see more clearly and act more effectively than did ours or those generations of the people of Palestine whose successes, failures, and suffering I describe in this book.

Index